THE NEW ENVIRONMENTALISM?

Urban Anthropology

Series Editors: Italo Pardo and Giuliana Prato,
University of Kent, UK

Urban Anthropology is the first series of its kind to be established by a major academic publisher. Ethnographically global, the series includes original, empirically based works of high analytical and theoretical calibre. All volumes published in the series are peer-reviewed.

The editors encourage submission of sole authored and edited manuscripts that address key issues that have comparative value in the current international academic and political debates. These issues include, but are by no means limited to: the methodological challenges posed by urban field research; the role of kinship, family and social relations; the gap between citizenship and governance; the legitimacy of policy and the law; the relationships between the legal, the semi-legal and the illegal in the economic and political fields; the role of conflicting moralities across the social, cultural and political spectra; the problems raised by internal and international migration; the informal sector of the economy and its complex relationships with the formal sector and the law; the impact of the process of globalization on the local level and the significance of local dynamics in the global context; urban development, sustainability and global restructuring; conflict and competition within and between cities.

Other titles in the series

Citizenship and the Legitimacy of Governance
Anthropology in the Mediterranean Region
Edited by Italo Pardo and Giuliana B. Prato
ISBN 978 0 7546 7401 6

Multiculturalism's Double-Bind
Creating Inclusivity, Cosmopolitanism and Difference
John Nagle
ISBN 978 0 7546 7607 2

Beyond Multiculturalism
Views from Anthropology
Edited by Giuliana B. Prato
ISBN 978 0 7546 7173 2

The New Environmentalism?
Civil Society and Corruption in the Enlarged EU

DAVIDE TORSELLO
University of Bergamo, Italy

Routledge
Taylor & Francis Group

LONDON AND NEW YORK

First published 2012 by Ashgate Publishing

2 Park Square, Milton Park, Abingdon, Oxon OX14 4RN
711 Third Avenue, New York, NY 10017, USA

Routledge is an imprint of the Taylor & Francis Group, an informa business

First issued in paperback 2016

British Library Cataloguing in Publication Data
Torsello, Davide.
　　The new environmentalism? : civil society and corruption in the enlarged EU. –
　　(Urban anthropology)
　　1. Environmentalism – European Union countries. 2. Environmental protection –
　　European Union countries – Citizen participation. 3. Civil society – European
　　Union countries. 4. Political culture – European Union countries. 5. Transportation
　　– Planning – Corrupt practices – European Union countries – Case studies.
　　6. Transportation engineering – Corrupt practises – European Union
　　countries – Case studies.
　　I. Title II. Series
　　306.2'094–dc22

Library of Congress Cataloging-in-Publication Data
Torsello, Davide.
　　The new environmentalism? : civil society and corruption in the enlarged EU / by
　　Davide Torsello.
　　　　p. cm. – (Urban anthropology)
　　Includes bibliographical references and index.
　　ISBN 978–1–4094–2364–5 (hardback : alk. paper)
　　1. Social movements – Europe. 2. Environmentalism – Europe.
　　3. Corruption – European Union countries. 4. Political participation – European Union
　　countries.
　　I. Title.
　　HM881.T676 2011
　　333.72094–dc23　　　　　　　　　　　　　　　　　　　　　　　　　　　　2011031611

ISBN 978-1-4094-2364-5 (hbk)
ISBN 978-1-138-26123-5 (pbk)

Contents

Contents

Acknowledgements

The idea of this book came after I decided to explore the impact of EU transport development projects mainly in Central Eastern Europe. Although in the beginning I was mainly concerned with understanding the meaning that local people attributed to the Enlargement process, as my research proceeded I had to discover that a number of complex socio-political forces were at play. Initially, I did not have any intention to deal with corruption, since I was still convinced that an ethnographic study could not satisfactorily, and ethically, deal with this phenomenon increasingly present in the headlines of news. Later on, I changed my perspective. Corruption was becoming inherently part of the discourses on the Enlargement process, its narratives, more or less punctual and descriptive, or at times only evocative, had been used almost regularly by those civic movements seeking to oppose to poorly planned or environmentally blind projects. The remarkably common point of these projects was that they faced similar paths, from the implementation to the discussion and planning of the transport development, to environmentalists' actions, the disclosure of non-transparent and even scarcely legal practices, struggles between different political actors, changing forms of communication between truly environmental movements and local citizens, long legal and bureaucratic battles, and difficult resolutions. One might argue that the EU enlargement project is responsible for linearity in these case studies, as one might argue that civil society in these cases cannot do without the notion of corruption, or a strong political alignment.

In spite of the timeliness of the three notions dealt with in this book, it has not been, from the very beginning, an easy endeavour to analyse their interrelation. Being a social anthropologist who had mostly done fieldwork research in rural communities, the choice to deal with a topic that required a 'mainly urban' and many-sited ethnography was not easy. The complexity of this task expresses well my twofold objective in this volume. The first is to provide a contribution in the field of urban anthropology; the second is to stress the importance of engaging with the neighbouring social science disciplines. Transdisciplinarity can, particularly in areas such as environmentalism and corruption, become analytically very fruitful, whereas ethnographic investigations can provide innovative empirical solutions to general theoretical debates.

My first and most important thank is to Italo Pardo and Giuliana Prato, who since the beginning have given me enthusiastic support to this book. Without their help and consultation this book project would not have been accomplished. Among the many scholars who, directly or indirectly, have contributed to strengthen my ideas on the multidisciplinary thrust of this work I am thankful to Bo Rothstein and Andreas Bågenhom, who have proved genuinely supportive interest in this book.

Jane and Peter Schneider helped to improve the theoretical and methodological reflections on civil society. Moreover, I owe much of the writing of this book to a generous research fellowship by the Aleksanteri Institute, University of Helsinki, that offered me a stimulating intellectual setting for discussing the contents of the book, and also a peaceful and charming work environment. I owe my thanks to Petr Firbas, who substantially improved the chapter on the Czech case and continues to update me on present debates, and to all environmental groups' members, journalists, local officers or intellectuals who kindly agreed to dedicate their times and share their knowledge with me. I find it difficult to name them all, but it is doubtless that I owe the results of this research to their cooperation, patience and kind availability. A very final thanks is to the whole Department of Scienze dei Linguaggi, University of Bergamo, that provided funding for this research in the last six years.

Introduction

This book is about new forms of civic participation in the environmental sector examined from a comparative ethnographic perspective. In the last four decades environmentalism, the study of social and political dynamics of civic movements that develop under the common aim of promoting an ecological discourse, has become a crucial and extremely timely research theme. Like any field in the social sciences, it has been subject to geo-political transformations that have altered the boundaries of continents, as well as the borders of states and the regions within them. What environmentalism meant in the early 1970s, when an unfortunately relentless process of environmental degradation began to be widely debated, is hardly comparable to what it means today, after the recent Fukushima nuclear disaster that forced Japan to its knees. From different theoretical perspectives, economists, political scientists, sociologists, geographers and anthropologists have analysed the changing patterns of environmental movements in the world starting from 'Western' settings. As for all these disciplines, the threshold of 1989 was particularly significant for environmentalism. Debates and discourses over differences between 'West' and ' East', 'capitalist' or 'neo-liberal' and 'post-colonial' or 'post-communist' gained momentum in the 1990s, but rapidly lost significance as soon as a number of scholars shifted their focus to the global nature of present environmental movements.

Civil society is the second notion to find extensive analytical treatment in this book. Civil society, as an important component of environmentalism, has a much longer intellectual and philosophical tradition, and is thus extremely difficult to approach empirically. Over the years a number of anthropologists have declared themselves sceptical of the use and applicability of this notion to non-Western socio-cultural contexts, but nonetheless they have all used the term. As an inherent part of the dual nature of environmentalism, that is the relationship of human beings with the natural environment, and the practices, ideas and ideologies that aim to promote the safeguard of the environment, civil society is in this book one of the two hands of a new form of environmentalism. Although I agree with anthropologists and sociologists who argue against the indiscriminate use of 'civil society' in settings such as Eastern Europe, where until some decades ago there was no such thing as a distinct, clear-cut separation between state and civil society, as the classical western political philosophy envisioned, I am still convinced about the need to use this notion. For one thing, civil society is the label that all the environmental movements that I investigate below (in Slovakia, Hungary, Czech Republic and Italy) attribute to themselves and to their operations. Civil society is both an *emic* and an *etic* notion, and as such it is hard to deny its applied value, even though anthropology is rightly wary of easy generalizations.

The main goal of this book is to provide a new characterization of social and political movements, characterized as 'civil society', that departs from environmentalist concerns and objectives. All the case studies analysed in the book have the same origin in common, i.e. structural development projects funded (more or less partially) by the EU and within far-reaching EU policies; these movements all have to address arenas of political interaction that are wider than local and national settings. In their daily operations, when they need to seek funds or legal advice, draw up projects or gain public legitimacy, they are classified and termed as civil society movements. This is a fundamental fact that the analyst cannot deny. In the same way that it is undeniable that the different national traditions of civil society in Eastern and Western Europe still play an important role in the ways in which environmentalism is perceived, promulgated and practised today. The case studies will reveal that practices that are both successful and unsuccessful in promoting the defence of natural resources and of human well-being in general depend very much on these traditions, though this does not have a causal explanation. This is why this book does not take a culturalistic stance when comparing the case studies. On the contrary, it aims to question some common assumptions that have informed much of mainstream literature on civil society in Europe. One assumption is that, for historical and 'cultural' reasons, Eastern civil society movements are weaker than those in Western Europe. I argue that if the term weaker applies to the number of movements and successful protests, then the assertion may be right. But if the term refers more critically to a variety of forms, public discourses, strategic views, and to the links that these organizations have with wider, transnational entities, then the assertion is wrong. This book does not aim to provide another demonstration of this last point as it has already been provided by other works. It aims to demonstrate that through attention to one particular aspect of environmental activism, namely its political dynamics, it is possible to detect important continuities and discontinuities in time and similarities and dissimilarities in space to understand the true nature of present environmentalism.

The second aspect of environmentalism described in this book arises from its involvement in the political sphere, and focuses on corruption. Corruption is a powerful concept nowadays, even more so than civil society; cognitively it implies negative and immoral practices whereas civil society is by definition its opposite. Corruption has a similar history to environmentalism, in that it was 'discovered' by the social sciences only recently. The booming field of social science studies of corruption is another of the features of the post-1989 global transformation. However, corruption is much less clearly delineated and has a more indefinite operational scope than environmentalism. Few scholars today agree on a single analytical (and not operational) definition of corruption, and even fewer agree that one theoretical approach to the origins, causes and consequences of corruption dominates over the others. After providing rich empirical bases on which political scientists and economists, the most accurate developers of theoretical models of the notion, were able to draw in the years that followed, anthropology has since remained silent on corruption. After revealing some of the phenomena which are the essence of corruption, namely clientelism, informal economic practices, gifts and reciprocity, anthropologists (with the famous exception of James Scott) abandoned the field until the 1990s. Peculiar as it may appear, whereas civil society has become an uncomfortable notion since the end of state socialism, corruption has (slowly) become a well-debated topic among anthropologists and sociologists, a number of whom actually work in Eastern Europe.

Under the legitimate constraints of ethnographic fieldwork, anthropological studies of corruption found it difficult to deal with individual practices and choice-making processes. Thus anthropology has been able to focus on ways in which corruption becomes a discursive practice, which has been widely neglected as an area of interest until recently by the other disciplines. This book contributes to this approach by pursuing two main aims. The first is to analyze the impact that public local discourses on corruption, which emerge in the planning and implementation of the structural development projects under exam, have on processes of power configurations, legitimacy and institutional trust building. The second is to shed light on how corruption is used in environmentalist practices and ideas. Corruption becomes the second hand of environmentalism because it is part of the daily narratives that media, civic organizations and interest groups themselves construct in the course of a complex interplay of political and economic forces. However, like civil society, corruption is both an *emic* and *etic* notion that relates to forms of local communication as well as to actual disclosures of political misconduct. The book does not aim to detect the different forms of corruption in a comparative perspective. Nor does it provide ethnographic insights into the ways corruption works to undermine or strengthen the public role of sets of institutions from local governments to the state, since these two fields need to be addressed in a different, more dedicated manner which does not fall within the scope of the case studies. The ethnographic material on which this book is based, collected in the period from 2006 to 2010, provides an approach that looks at ways in which corruption provides a meaningful scheme through which environmental movements make sense of the political reality in which they operate. The main argument of the book is that through corruption, and a constant re-definition of the scope and action fields of civil society, environmentalism transcends the dichotomic perspective (ecological-technological, eastern-western, local-global) and acquires a new meaning. This meaning is constructed both as outcome of the EU enlargement process and of institutional transformation from above, and of strategic decision-making from below.

Methodology

The book is based on five case studies, which have been obtained through ethnographic fieldwork. I started my ethnographic investigations in Slovakia, by following the case of the Považska Byztrica highway during different sessions in the period from February 2007 to September 2008, with subsequent updating (Chapter 4). I conducted scheduled interviews with the main actors involved in the transport development project, local politicians and technicians working on the environmental assessment impact reports. The second part of my fieldwork session included interviews with environmental activists, observation as a participant at meetings, public events and during the communication of the strategies of the environmental groups. I also gained access to national and local media (newspapers and television) reports and articles covering the stages of the protest.

My second case study, the Brno-Vienna highway connection, was undertaken in 2008 (Chapter 5). I arranged interviews with local activist groups, as well as politicians. Although I was less successful in obtaining direct access to local media reports and to interviews with regional politicians, the precious help of some of the environmental group members compensated for this. In this case study, the network of trans-local and local civic organizations proved to be particularly dense, rendering a local investigation in the urban centre and communities affected by the project insufficient. I therefore sought to meet consultants and members of larger environmental umbrella organizations based in Vienna and Brussels. The wealth of research reports and policy papers available facilitated my investigation in this case.

The third case study in chronological order was the Susa Valley railway development project, undertaken in 2009–2010 (Chapter 6). This is the case study for which there was the greatest amount of data available to the public on the internet. I was able to follow retrospectively some of the most relevant moments of the protest, the longest among those presented in the book, through electronic video files made available by activists and in some cases also present on the web. Extensive media coverage allowed me to contrast these data with first-hand material.

The fourth case study, the Budapest M0 ring-road, was the object of ethnographic investigation in the year 2010 (Chapter 7). I conducted a number of interviews with local activists and collected data from local governments and regional offices. Also, the number of scholarly studies on this case is higher than for any of the others presented in this book. This allowed me to pursue an approach that examines the structural development project from a long-term perspective of transformation.

The fifth case study, concerning the treatment of illegal waste, was undertaken in 2010–2011 (Chapter 8). I conducted research mainly in Hungary, the country for which there is the most data, and the one in which I had easiest access to data thanks to my proficiency in the language. However, this proved to be the most problematic of the case studies in terms of availability of and access to data. The cases of illegal waste disposal, although exposed by local and national media, are often reluctantly disclosed to researchers. This is a field in which ethnographic and qualitative research is still in an embryonic form, and the severe methodological limitations (access was granted mainly through environmental associations, archival material, policy and press reports) make it difficult to establish concrete research plans.

Finally, I had hoped to complete my ethnographic investigation through a number of selected interviews with personnel operating at the European Commission, Directorate of Transport. In particular, the TEN-T operational section has an extremely well organized archive of reports and policy publications. I participated in one international meeting, in Genoa, in which the Directorate presented one Corridor project, and I was able to conduct some short interviews afterwards. However, my plans to further develop these interviews, in the light of my research results on some cases belonging to the TEN-T scheme, could not be implemented since I have been regrettably unable to obtain subsequent appointments with members of the Directorate.

Chapter 1

Environmentalism

There is little agreement over when the term environmentalism was first used in social science. The difficulty in tracing a common root of environmental thought, at least in Western European intellectual history, is due to the basic dualism inherent in the notion of environmentalism. Environmentalism signifies on the one hand the complex and variegated body of ideas and ideologies about the environment. These have been represented, through time, in an array of shifting positions that examine the relationship of man with ecological resources. On the other hand, environmentalism also refers to those social movements which have evolved, in the course of history, with the common goal of condemning environmental damage and hence making political claims centred upon the protection of nature and its resources. These movements are in essence political and hence support not only a generalized view of mankind living in harmony with nature, but also a number of strategies that seek to enhance civil participation in decision-making and planning processes in the use of environmental resources.

This dual character means that the history of the way environmentalism is dealt with in the social sciences is complex and is characterized by a number of factors. First, the key contributions of each of the disciplines have focused on different aspects of both the human use of the environment and the social movements set up around environmental discourses and ideologies. Economics, sociology, geography, political science and anthropology have opened up multiple fields of investigations, but their research methodologies do not necessarily coincide with or complement one another. For instance, the contribution made by environmental economics, by far the largest among the social science disciplines, is not always followed up or found to be helpful in the sociological and anthropological approaches that are more interested in qualitative and ground level analyses. Conversely, anthropology has developed a number of approaches which, departing from the study of non-western societies, have in the long run enriched political science and even economic approaches to the notion, for instance, of 'indigenous knowledge' (see Brush 1993; Sillitoe 1998; Lauer and Aswani 2009). Secondly, the language of environmentalism is highly fragmented and often inconsistent between the disciplines. This is due to the different intellectual and theoretical traditions, on the one hand, and to the research methodologies on the other. In this context, anthropological and sociological approaches have tended to overlap in some particular fields, namely the study of environmentalist movements and the use of cultural theory to investigate how humans use ecological resources (Douglas and Wildavsky 1983; Milton 1996).

Thirdly, the study of environmental movements has been the object of diversified theoretical approaches in the various disciplines. There is generally a common starting point from which these approaches develop: the origin of movements envisioning a greater participation of the general public in the protection of the environment. How these movements develop common views and strategies and manage to raise awareness is dealt with differently. Again, theoretical differences between the social science disciplines become manifest in their approaches to the study of political strategies, of the nature of the movements themselves and their contextualization in wider ideas of modernization, post-modernity or risk-society, in their use of local knowledge and culturally constructed ideas of ecology.

I believe that what renders the study of this second aspect of environmentalism a complex interdisciplinary project is the tension between the universalism and relativism of this notion. One thing is to identify movements arising from a universal call to safeguard nature as patterns of civil society, or civic movements coming from below. Another thing, however, is to investigate how these movements make use of the environmental discourse to interact with larger institutions (from the state to the market, corporations and transnational organizations), to gain power through this interaction, or simply to legitimize their own standpoint at a public level. This final aspect, which has been, in my view, somewhat overlooked by the social sciences, is the main thrust of this book. One possible reason for this is that the nature of environmentalism in conditions of global change is such that it makes it difficult to thoroughly investigate the power structures and constellations that emerge in the negotiation between social movements and larger institutions.

Milton (1996) argues that environmentalism is best understood as a trans-cultural discourse, which, because of its 'particular understanding of the planet as "one"', has consolidated its ideas as a global phenomenon (1996: 171). On the other hand, Mol recognizes that 'quite diverse – and interdependent- social mechanisms connect globalization to environmental disruption and reform, of which the net effect will vary and change depending on place, time and the type of environmental problem' (Mol 2000: 142). Thus, the view that environmentalism, as a social movement, is influenced by global conditions, bringing about either common or locally diversified strategies of protest or political action seem to point to two different interpretations. However, I will argue that these two positions are not mutually exclusive if one pays attention not only to the global conditions in which these movements originate, but also to the local ways in which they make use of these conditions to attain power and legitimacy. In other words, by shifting attention from the founding of environmentalist movements and their typologies to the discourses and the power strategies they use when interacting with larger institutions, it is possible to conciliate the basic dichotomy between the global and local nature of environmentalism.

Therefore, the main argument of this book is that environmentalism, intended as social movements arising both to promote the protection of the environment and to politicize the citizens' claims to this protection, has become a project of political interaction which makes use of local and global resources to achieve legitimacy. The common element of the environmental movements introduced in the case studies is that they are all to be found in conditions of transnational institutional change, namely they are products of the fluxes of EU policies in the enlarged European Community. As such, these movements have to deal with global concerns, because political planning does not take place any longer within the boundaries of the single states. What has proved to be the main challenge of the environmental projects is that they have to cope with increasingly conflicting realms of political action, from local up to EU level. This has produced a number of languages, semantics and coping strategies that are not easily analysed on the basis of the traditional state-civil society partitioning. These movements move both within and outside the state, they take advantage of or are undermined by their existences in conditions of globalization, they adopt strategies which at times privilege the local arena of environmentalist action, at times transcend it. This is where corruption comes into play. Corruption is used, along with and instead of ecological discourses, to give meaning to illegal or semi-legal practices which cannot always be located in time and space in the way 'old' environmentalist movements used to be. Corruption is a powerful discourse, which is deeply embedded, in the ground-level social realities where these movements are set up and where they operate. However, corruption is about practices and ideas that are conceived beyond the local, regional, state arenas. Corruption allegations, in the view presented by this book, are used to create breakthroughs among these arenas that can be used strategically (although not always successfully) to allow the real political nature of new environmentalism to find its place in ideas, ideologies and practices. New environmentalism is one concrete solution to the paradox brought about by the global dimension of its political engagement and the local nature of its movements.

The development of environmentalist theory

The first part of environmentalist theory is concerned with the study of the relationship between mankind and nature in terms of subsistence, production and technological progress. As indicated above, this relationship has been studied in different manners by the social sciences, and it is beyond the scope of this volume to produce a comprehensive review of this literature (see Mehta and Ouellet 1995; Barrow 2006). I will here mainly refer to some common points and terminologies used to describe the different theoretical positions.

O'Riordan (1981), in one of the earliest works on environmentalism, introduces the difference between the eco-centric and the techno-centric model. The eco-centric model develops from the assumption that a natural order prevails in the man-nature relationship, and that all things should move according to a natural law. In this perspective, human actions should seek a constant balance with the environment, seeking not to alter the delicate ecological equilibrium. The techno-centric model, instead, looks at the deliberately interventional quality of the human-ecological relationship. The environment is the subject of man's utilitarian quest for progress, well-being and technical development. Human needs and priorities follow an underlying, constant rationality, in their quest for efficiency and for control over technical means and progress. In other words, in this second model the human being does not seek compromise or equilibrium with the environment as a final goal, but he pools from it resources for the public good. According to O'Riordan these two schools of thought stemmed respectively from the romantic transcendentalist thinkers and from positivistic approaches to the role of science and technology in ecological terms (1981: 5–6). Within each model a number of different approaches developed historically focusing on different moral standpoints towards the environment. Among them the main distinction lies between the so-called bio-ethical and self-reliance approaches.

The bio-ethical approach, which constituted the underpinning rhetoric of the early environmental movements in the 1970s, sought to protect the integrity of the natural ecosystem as a biotic right. Human beings, in this perspective, should take a definite ethical standpoint *vis-à-vis* nature, even by developing a body of legal regulations of biotic rights. Seen in this light, environmental politics is part of a different sphere, one in which negotiation or bargaining is a difficult endeavour, due to the intransigent character of activists and environmentalists. One of the notions related to this approach is that of 'limit', seen as nonnegotiable barriers which set the ecological boundaries defining human action (O'Riordan 1996: 7).

The self-reliance approach takes an overtly political standing towards the devastating effects of industrialization and mass capitalism. Its aim is to propose local models of environmental protection (or responsibility) in which human safety and progress can be achieved through regional, small-scale patterns of economic development where agriculture and small enterprises play major roles. In this approach democratic participation in environmental movements is potentially sought at neighbourhood and 'community' levels, and values such as communal sense of belonging where the sharing of meaning attributed to ecology is emphasized.

Both approaches, however, have a common pessimistic view of human interaction with the natural environment. Man acts 'violently' in his attempt to fulfil his goals and satisfy his needs; hence participation in ecological movements has intrinsic political goals. On the other hand, so-called techno-centric models depart from a comparatively optimistic standpoint, in which growing technological and economic specialization and amelioration bring about (almost 'naturally') a better control of ecological resources. This position is constructed upon the strategic use of two notions: objectivity and specialization. Objectivity refers to the allegedly unchallengeable role of (exact) science which is committed and determined to advocate a proper balance in the use of environmental resources. O'Riordan (1996) and others (Pepper 1996; Nelissen et al. 1997; Smith 1999) reflect critically on this notion which may be instrumentally manipulated to justify environmental mismanagement and misconduct. The idea of specialization is also an integral and pristine part of the technocratic model; its implications, however, are not only ethical, but also more concretely economic and political. Growing specialization and sophistication in the management of environmental resources has called for the consolidation of a class of specialized, technical personnel. Over the last few decades, these specialists have become professional elites to which policy makers and planners have to turn to in order to comply with the national and transnational procedures of environmental law. The EU legislation is, for instance, very strict on these issues: each of its structural projects undertaken in any country applying for EU funds has to follow the procedures dictated by the EIA (Environmental Assessment Impact, see below in the case studies). Hence, specialists and specialized firms producing these assessments are often in a position to actually dictate the rules of the game, both with local governments and even at a national level of economic planning. It goes without saying that these specialists may become liable to corruption practices, or they may be directly involved in those interest groups and personalities who benefit from the projects.

The basic distinction between the eco-centric and techno-centric models is presented by other scholars through different terminologies. Norton (1991) introduces the distinction between 'conservationists' and 'preservationists': the former refers to the idea of protecting nature for human use; the latter recognizes a moral obligation towards nature, which needs to be protected from human use. Cotgrove (1976) has made a distinction between those environmentalists who propose policies which do not challenge the dominant economic value system (conservative) and those who propose alternative value systems in which the environment is in the forefront (radical). Dobson (1990) has further stressed the standpoint of environmentalists, distinguishing between 'environmentalism', as a more conservative mode, and 'ecologism' as its radical counterpart. In his view, environmentalism assumes the existence of a centre, an ecosystem with which individuals interact. Ecologism, conversely, tends not to recognize one single centre because the individual is not seen as being in a relationship of direct control over the ecosystem; he is inserted in a wider ecological environment on which he depends for his own subsistence.

The complexity of these theorizations has led some authors to criticize the gap between the theories and practices of environmentalism (Lowe and Rüdig 1986; Bell 2004). The general theoretical understanding of the man-nature relationship is an important feature of the social science tradition of environmentalist research; however, taken alone, it does not clarify why, at certain points in time and in some particular places, social movements with an environmentalist agenda assume more or less clear political positions. Before looking at this perspective I think it is necessary to shed some further light onto the development of environmentalist theories in the last two decades in the social sciences and in particular on the role of anthropology in those debates.

Environmentalism in the social sciences

Among the social scientific disciplines, economics has by far produced the most complex and variegated body of theorization. Environmental economics has exerted a strong influence in debates on the use of ecological resources for two main reasons. One, as Milton underlined, is because economists have been the only social scientists to which governments and policy makers have listened with regards to environmental issues (Milton 1996: 71). The second point is that over the last two decades, the environment has steadily surged to occupy a top position among the most profitable sectors of economic investment. This has led some authors to suggest that nature has been enlisted as the third most productive force in the world after capital and labour (Buttel 2000a: 30).[1] Thus, in an evolving and growing world market of environmental industries it is easily understood how environmental economics plays a leading role in the social sciences.

The economics approach is not particularly relevant to the content of this book; what is more important is to look at the contributions from anthropology, sociology and political science. These disciplines developed a theoretical interest in the social and political aspects of environmentalism relatively late in history, starting from the mid-1970s. Although some accounts trace the relevance of the environment back to classical sociological theory of Marx and Weber tradition, current-day sociological concern with environmental debates started in North American contexts, as a reaction to circumstances and cases of environmental crisis and degradation (Dunlap and Catton 1979; Schnaiberg 1980; Murphy 1997). On the one hand, these approaches emphasized a pessimistic standpoint towards the effects of industrialization and market capitalism on the natural environment. On the other hand, environmental sociology was deeply rooted in the analysis of the emergence of social movements, which were often viewed with sympathy and at times with a lack of impartiality by the scholars who studied them (Spargaaren 2000).

Later analyses, carried out both by US and European scholars, began to make use of different paradigms that had in the meantime been employed to describe and analyse other complex social phenomena. This is the case of social constructivism, ecological modernization, risk-theory and postmodern theories. Each of these theoretical approaches has been applied to environmentalism, framing it in debates on modernity, post-modernity, risk-taking and cultural constructivism (see Spaargaren 2000; Mol 2000 for a comprehensive review). In these approaches the relationship between social action and environmental concerns was analysed mainly in line with mainstream theoretical paradigms of modernization, capitalism and

---

1   According to a 2007 estimate, the global environmental business was in that year worth 758 billion USD, of which roughly 600 billion USD generated by the US, Western Europe and Japan. In Western Europe and in Japan this sector amounts to over 20% of overall exports (http://web.ita.doc.gov/ete/eteinfo.nsf/068f3801d047f26e85256 883006ffa54/4878b7e2fc08ac6d85256883006c452c/$FILE/Full%20Environmental%20 Industries%20Assessment%202010.pdf, accessed 1–4–2011).

global capitalism, changing cultural and social institutions, postmodern conditions and globalization. Environmentalism was rarely given a space of its own as an independent field of theorization, but it was treated as one of the forces subjugated to more general processes of institutional, economic and social change. This is demonstrated, for instance, by one widespread idea that the risks and hazards of modernization prejudice the quality of life and bring about ecological crises which reveal the weakness of the state in regulating market capitalism (Buttel 2000: 29). Or, in the modernization paradigm, the assumption that in conditions of state-society controlled market capitalism, contemporary capitalist enterprises are able to adapt to ecological constraints. This process of adaptation would be achieved, at least in OECD countries, without any general loss of productivity and without hampering progress on scientific and technological levels.

These approaches have been criticized from a number of perspectives (Escobar 1991; Ribeiro 1994; Crush 1995; Dryzek 1997; York and Rosa 2003). One of them, somewhat common in anthropological accounts, condemns the Eurocentric nature of these theories and questions the applicability of such models to countries where colonial, post-colonial and neo-colonial powers have often forced the emergence of environmental discourses to the sphere of intervention of non-localized transnational green movements. Another critique is that these approaches tend to equate technological and economic risks with ecological risks, without considering the weakness of this perspective. Ecological resources, as recent world events and previsions have alarmingly proved, are not unlimited and hence cannot be treated as pools of common resources, as the famous Tragedy of the Commons argument has suggested.[2] The time spans for regenerating technological and economic resources are not at all comparable with those for ecological ones; this alone explains why the optimistic stance of ecological modernization theories is untenable. Furthermore, the risks are not distributed equally among social groups and actors. This suggests that the risk approach may fail to tackle the complexity of social orders, particularly in cases when profound institutional transformation is an everyday reality, like in post-socialist Eastern Europe.

More recent contributions in sociology and political science focus on the nature, scope and strategies of the environmental movements, which became widespread in the 1980s and early 1990s (Hasegawa 2004; van der Heijden 2006; Dunlap and McCright 2008; Kousis et al. 2008; Salleh 2010). Some of these studies have openly challenged the modernization, anti-modernization and post-modernity theories and have advocated a more solid concern with the role of the state and the welfare state in supporting or opposing these movements, with the impact of political discussions and ideology on the nature of green movements, the impact of the emergent ecological rationality as opposed to the dominant

---

2 The Tragedy of the Commons argument has been widely followed in economists' approaches to the study of the management of environmental resources, in particular in relation to the shift from the idea of 'surplus' to that of 'limited good'. See for instance Hardin 1968; Berkes 1989; Ostrom 1990; Swanson 1996.

neoliberal economic rationality, the major changes in the actual organization and implementation of environmental policies at national levels and the rule-altering effects of these policies on political networks and groups. Some of these approaches will be introduced in a section below because they are strictly related to the content of this book.

The contribution of anthropology

Anthropology has only relatively recently engaged with the second nature of environmentalism, in ways similar to those in which this field is dealt with by the other social science disciplines. There are two main reasons for this delay. The first is that anthropology, by focusing on the nature-culture relationship, has developed an extremely rich and sophisticated theoretical literature on the ecological adaptation of human populations. Secondly, due to the historical development of the discipline, it was only with the dissolution of the colonial domains and following epistemic changes in anthropological approaches from the late 1960s that new formulations and approaches in the field were developed.

In the first case, from the work of Julian Steward onwards, ecological anthropology has dealt extensively with the environment as a battlefield of survival, in which human cultural and social features and institutions have taken shape in the course of time. Because anthropologists originally performed fieldwork research mostly in non-western societies, the environment was one of the most prominent fields in which social forms, structures, and cultural responses were investigated. These responses have been initially studied through perspectives that focused on a deterministic concern for natural pressure forces, which not only influenced cultural responses, but eventually led to universal biological explanations in some cases (see for instance Brown 1991). At the other end of the spectrum, relativism was enforced by the idea that cultures were 'adjusted by the unique features of their local environments' (Meggers 1954: 801). This led anthropologists to oppose the deterministic view in favour of a relativist explanation that sought to distinguish between the forms and strategies of ecological adaptation. After the 1970s the situation changed rapidly. On the one hand the positions of cultural materialism, influenced by Marxist thought, became less attractive due to their determinism and synchronic approach that left little space to true dialectical analyses of the influence of colonialism and capitalism on so-called indigenous people. On the other hand, a new interest developed in what Kottak (1999) defined the 'new ecological approach', imbued with a theoretical and empirical interest in political awareness and policy concerns. This shift profoundly affected the way in which the ecological field was conceived and studied and the difference between ecological and environmental anthropology became manifest.[3] Therefore the first

---

3   For textbooks and reviews that summarise the results of ecological anthropology see Bennet 1975; Hardesty 1977; Morán 1990; Orlove 1980.

came to define the interaction between a human population and the ecosystem in which its society is organized in a narrower sense, whereas the second referred more broadly to social movements operating to promote environmental protection (Townsend 2000: 12–13).

It was at this point, no earlier than the late 1970s, that anthropology started engaging with the second nature of environmentalism, as a natural consequence of the ethnographers' encounters with social, grass-roots movements, NGOs and other forms of organization that put nature at the top of their agendas. Environmentalism was often an alien discourse to the localities where classical anthropological fieldwork had taken place. However, in the post-colonial history of these localities, environmental concerns came to the forefront as an outcome of the influence of two main forces. On the one hand, there was increased international visibility of the social and cultural disruption of several populations, as well as of environmental depredation brought about by an indiscriminate rush to exploit raw and precious materials in the so-called 'developing countries'. On the other hand, international attention to the conditions of populations and their environment produced 'excessively romanticised' pictures of these cultures, which perpetuated colonial images of people living more closely to or respectfully of nature than in the 'Western' world (Brosius 1999: 280). The intellectual debate on whether anthropological studies of indigenous knowledge could be applied to the field of ecology at times became rather heated and provoked many diatribes and ruptures among those in favour of a more applied perspective and those who envisaged that anthropological contributions would remain mainly theoretical (Headland 1997).

Thus, the outcome of these conflicting forces was positive for fruitful scientific debate, but negative in that it represented a further example of fragmentation in the anthropological perspective. True, environmental concern crossed boundaries and increasingly became the spark which generated international cooperation networks and global campaigns. However, some of these campaigns actually had (and still have) the effect of perpetuating stereotyped knowledge of these populations in the Western world, and in the worst-case scenario, of imposing views and methods of environmentalism which did not originate in these regions but were mere exported copies of what had been done in Western regions (Escobar 1999). At this point anthropology was compelled to address these issues, since wherever in the world an anthropologist was engaged in fieldwork there was some kind of environmentalist association or movement.

However, as highlighted by Escobar (1999), the caesura between ecological and environmental anthropology marked an 'odd' development in the discipline's theoretical history. The lack of continuity between these two 'traditions' is what has put anthropology in an unfavourable position vis-à-vis the theoretical traditions of sociology, political science and geography. If it is true that few anthropologists have been able to prove in their work that such continuity was ever indeed possible, one must admit that this tendency for theoretical discontinuity is one that marks the discipline in general. Once political-economic and structuralist approaches were criticized by postmodernist, interpretative and reflexive approaches, it became increasingly difficult to establish analytical perspectives in which the old and the new approaches to studying the relationship between human beings and the environment could be easily brought together (Alvard 1993).

A relevant contribution to the study of environmentalism from anthropology has come from the volume edited by Kay Milton (1993). Milton sets the agenda for dealing with a number of aspects related to environmental movements, in both industrialized and non-industrial societies, some of which are part of this book. Milton advocates the role of anthropology in tackling environmentalism following two perspectives: the social and the political. Concerning the first, emphasis is put on investigating those forms of social commitment that emerge out of the 'implementation of culturally defined responsibilities' (Milton 1993: 2). Anthropology, along with the other social sciences, can help to refine the building process of environmental advocacy, which in several instances and mainly in the case of non-industrialized societies, has fostered direct intervention and activism by anthropologists themselves (Cowell 1990).

Concerning the second perspective, the more relevant one to this volume, environmentalism can be objectified as a discourse, drawing on Foucauldian theory, of trans-cultural nature. As a discourse, environmentalism defines, on the one hand, the field of communication between different sets of agents and different responsibilities. On the other hand, discursive practices are part of the struggles through which different claims are established and clash in the various efforts to gain control of resources (McCay 1993). In the same volume, Prato (1993) and Peace (1993) make points about the disputes through which agents in the local communities under investigation assert their environmental rights in opposition to commercial and economic interests. Prato, in particular, drawing from ethnographic material collected in Apulia, southern Italy, demonstrates how the difficult alignment of ecological claims with the socio-political needs of local communities weakened the public role of the environmental discourses. Not only did issues of public representation and morality remain unsolved in the construction of the environmental movement, but the attempts by a number of these newly emerging movements to seek allegiances among those same political exponents which they claimed to oppose in the beginning of the protest, were self-defeating strategies (Prato 1993: 182)

The Gerlach and Douglas-Wildavsky models

Two of the most continuative theoretical contributions in environmental anthropology that bridge those so far discussed in the other social science discipline are those developed by Luther Gerlach (1980, 1987, 1991) and Mary Douglas and Aaron Wildavsky (1983). Gerlach, an anthropologist based in Minnesota, was the first among his colleagues to develop a theoretical approach using the notion of risk to study the impact of climate change. In a number of writings (see Brandt 2007 for a critical review) he approached climate change policy through his extensive knowledge of social movements related to environmental protection both in the US and Europe. He observed that social movements are segmented and possess a number of organizational components, each endowed with its own identity, related to its place of origin. They are also polycentric, presenting different foci around which they are organized, and which are affiliated to form horizontal networks. Gerlach refers to these features with the acronym SPIN (segmented, polycentric, integrated networks). The main strengths of these movements is that they have a degree of innate independence which allows them to raise funds through different activities, and that they can easily switch strategies according to the specific demands of the movement.

Another significant point in his model is that environmental movements develop their own distinct languages through which their strategies and mutual interaction can be examined. This is true in particular for ideology, which 'works by motivating participants, legitimating the movements and what participants do and integrating the segments. [..] On the one level, each segment develops its own ideology. On the other level, there are ideas general and ambiguous enough to run across all segments' (quoted in Palmer 2007: 23).

Gerlach, Palmer and Stringer (2000) observed that by considering the language used in the political negotiations, the scholar can follow the changes of the ecology movements' organizational roles. The emergent structure of cooperation and opposition between polycentric (environmental movements) and centralized organizations becomes 'part of the organizational structure of the ecosystem' (Palmer 2007: 27). The only way to meaningfully investigate this form of interpenetration, according to Palmer, is through the study of the language and the discursive practices used in the negotiation process. This point will be developed further in this volume, but with attention not only to the negotiation process, but also to the communication strategies that each movement (or environmental organization) adopts.

The language of these strategies is, as Gorlach observed, polyfunctional and polysemic. This happens because of the SPIN feature, but also because of the different interlocutors with which movements have to interact in the course of their political action. I believe that the contents, meanings (both revealed and unrevealed), and tones of this language are what provides strength to some movements as opposed to others. Not only are technical words and jargon (which are abound in the case studies described in this volume) natural barriers to the environmentalists' way of communicating with the general public (Brandt 2007), but also the attentive and deliberate switching of themes, semantics, levels of discourse and styles are more or less successfully employed by activists to seek legitimacy. In this sense environmentalism is, as Gerlach advocated, to be studied with attention to both the practices and the discursive strategies, which explain the differences between the movements, particularly in the case of interaction between their global and local forms, as in the case studies in this book. It is true that what Brandt defines 'primary discourse', as 'the arguments that carry the greatest political power in decision-making' (Brandt 2007: 39) is constituted by what the environmental activists assess to be 'facts', i.e. qualitative knowledge. However, I am not convinced that qualitative knowledge, as Brandt argues, made up by 'explanation of facts and issues' is to be opposed to quantitative knowledge, represented through numbers in the discursive strategies of environmental activism.[4] In the case studies I present below the two types of knowledge are not separate entities, they become in conjunction a significant part of the discursive strategies through which activists seek to involve citizens and to appeal to a more general public. These two forms of knowledge are both facts and explanations about facts, as the interpretation of corruption scandals and practices condemned by the local media is actually left to the public. Often it is through numbers and quantitative accounts that environmental organizations succeed in spurring public attention, thus demonstrating that explanations of facts alone are insufficient when complex political dynamics are involved.

Douglas and Wildavsky have a different approach to the investigation of environmentalist responses to perceived risk and danger. One of the basic assumptions of their work is that each society faces a type of risk and it is the kind of debate that develops when facing these risks that influences the structure of social organizations. Thus, for them the only way to investigate this critical relationship with risk is from a cultural perspective which 'can integrate moral judgements about how to live with empirical judgements about what the world is like' (1983: 10). The main thrust of their book is to demonstrate that each society possesses (and forms) its own empirical assessment of risk in the case of environmentalism. Therefore, risks are socially selected since they are biased by the social assumptions made about them (1983: 14).

Risk selection becomes, then, a cultural effort defined by the very essence (or 'particular identities') of each culture, although all share some common structural conditions. These conditions are illustrated by the authors through the famous grid and group framework, which Mary Douglas introduced in her earlier work (1970). The grid-group perspective is applied as a form of cultural analysis to compare the different interest groups involved in the process of environmental concern and mobilization. The 'grid' factor represents the regulation of social activity, the 'group' the degree of cohesiveness. Thus, four positions come into play. The first, high grid and high group, produces a hierarchical form; this is when people's actions are controlled by authorities, and allegiances, tendency towards cooperation, are considered important. The second, high grid and low group, is when people do not pursue a collective interest, and a fatalist approach to social change dominates. The third, low grid high group, is characterized by egalitarian, or 'sectarian' forms of society where people pursue collective interests but are less committed to regulation. The fourth, individualism, i.e. low grid low group, is the

---

4   One of the criticisms raised against environmental anthropology has been its scarce attention to quantitative facts, as well as to building models which attempt to dialogue with biological approaches; for a review of the issue see Charnley and Durham 2010.

most similar to 'market-orientation' where people are free-runners in the pursuit of their goals and in the organizational structures.

Some later studies by ecologists (Thompson and Tayler 1986; James et al. 1987) have used Douglas' grid-group theory and the cultural implications she developed with Wildavsky to map ecological responses. Thus, in accordance with the so-called 'surprise theory', they distinguished between hierarchists (high grid-high group) who believe that nature is robust only to a certain extent, egalitarians (low grid-high group) who believe it is fragile, fatalists (high grid-low group) who see nature as capricious and hence difficult to control, and entrepreneurs (low grid-low group) who see nature as robust and hence controllable and utilizable for market purposes (Milton 1996: 92). These positions, matched by analyses by the local movements that produce assessments of environmental risk, are conceived as multiple variables which need to be accounted for when building predictive models. Thus, the main merit of Douglas and Wildavsky's model is that it re-established the role of cultural theory within the environmentalism project. Culture has been brought back in response to the positivistic standpoints of modernity theory to give empirical emphasis to the different local responses to the perception of environmental damage (Thompson et al. 1990).

A number of anthropologists have been critical of Douglas-Wildavsky's model. There are some basic contradictions which seem to be difficult to resolve in anthropological thought. One is the idea that forms of social organization determine cultural responses. This approach seems, along with several structuralist works in ecological anthropology, to downplay the role of social change in relation to people's choices to act or perceive differently (Milton 1996: 97). Douglas-Wildavsky's approach seems to accept the assumption that culture determines reality, since knowledge is a cultural and not a social construct. This assumption is difficult to accept for those anthropologists focusing on the production of meanings and identities through discursive practices. This trend is indeed manifest in the great variability in recent interests of environmental anthropology. These range from the examination of practices of resistance, to the relationship between representation, knowledge making, subject making, and domination in postcolonial theory, forms of articulation between 'the local' and globalizing processes, discussions about indigenous peoples and indigenous rights movements, the centrality of networks linking techno-science with socio-natural practices, the nexus between governmentality, economic production and nature, the nature of contestation and its socio-cultural implications (Wilk and Haenn 2005; Morán 2006; Dove and Carpenter 2007; Kopnina 2011).

Although environmental anthropology has already established itself as a sub-discipline of its own with a wide number of academic courses named in this manner (particularly in the US), its distinction from the rest of anthropological debates in politics, economics and even legal issues is rather questionable. Concern about environmental issues and problems is one of the most sensitive topics in globalization theories and has, in the last two decades, achieved a forefront position even in the study of political and social movements. In what follows I would like to sketch some of the most relevant positions in these fields that are related to the issues of this volume.

Environmentalism as a political movement

Since the late 1980s, in the aftermath of the Cold War, environmentalism has definitively become entrenched in a number of activist movements. This development was not new, what constituted novelty was a widespread perception of the risks of environmental disasters (such as the Bhopal and Chernobyl cases), and a major international concern with environmental protection culminating in the Kyoto Protocol in 1997.

Marsh (1981) suggests that activists fall into four categories: conformists who believe in the decisional power of political parties, reformists who support legitimate means of opposition, activists who adopt unconventional and conventional forms of protest, protesters who participate mainly in unconventional forms of protest. Some of the values shared by these movements have been defined as 'post-materialist values' (Inglehart 1977) and include rejecting consumerism and alienation from capitalism, avoiding bureaucracy in favour of participation, freedom of speech, communal purpose. This approach, common in political science and sociology, tends to see movements as groups which use environmentalism as a mechanism to induce political change. According to Mitchell (1984) environmental movements can be conceived as political only when their projects match those of the welfare and consumer organizations, thus they have to adopt clear standpoints within the public arena.

Diani and Donati (1999) define political organizations as shaped by their responses to two functional requirements: resource mobilization and political efficiency. To meet the first requirement they have to mobilize human, time and capital resources. Political efficiency refers to the bargaining power that these movements are able to acquire in their confrontation with institutional politics (1999: 15). Concerning resource mobilization, one basic option choice with which all political movements are faced is between the mobilization of time or of money. The first aims to establish a long-term set of strategies, requiring common ideologies that build a number of interest groups and persons related through semi-emotional ties. The second is a short-term oriented strategy which, according to the nature of the donor and the specific context of the movement, can inspire wide public participation or not.

The difficult methodological question about the nature of environmental movements is whether they are to be conceived as movements born from, and aimed at, an optimally wide public participation or as institutionalized political movements acting with clearly defined strategies in the short and long run. This issue is rather thorny and difficult to solve, since environmental movements, amongst several others, have demonstrated a capacity to adapt to changing circumstances and work in symbiosis with other, more openly political, movements (see the case of the NO-TAV protest, Chapter 6). Therefore, even assuming, as Diani and Donati do, that since the 1980s confrontational strategies have gradually abandoned open forms of expression (demonstrations, boycotts, petitions and so on) in favour of more targeted 'pressure' strategies on political decision-makers (Diani and Donati 1999: 17), I am not convinced that one can underestimate the local strategies through which these movements seek to achieve public legitimacy[5]. Local politics, as shown in the case studies below, does not offer sufficient negotiation and pressure space to these movements, as they tend to expand well beyond local and even national boundaries in order to diversify their strategies. However, because these movements tend to organize their activities around single, locally focused issues, their ties to local communities cannot be easily circumvented. One approach, developed in this book, to deal with the political agenda of these movements is to relate them to local and foreign imported ideas of civil society. By looking at the links between different forms of civil society, their relations to institutions and policy schemes, the ways in which they interact at local, national and transnational level and the ways in which legitimacy is sought through formal and informal strategies, I will elaborate an approach to environmentalism as a political movement that integrates both a top-down and a bottom-up approach.

One region that renders the complexity of these analytical efforts is Eastern Europe. Eastern European environmental movements are still inadequately studied. Recent empirical sociological and anthropological literature has suggested three major points for analysis. First, the political nature of environmental movements in Eastern Europe is difficult to define. Although it is undeniable that environmentalism has in itself a political standpoint in these movements, their projects' communication and implementation strategies often assume more technical and ideological rather than political stances. This leads to a major difference between Eastern and Western European movements: the difficult alignment with political parties. In Eastern Europe the green parties are fledgling, highly fragmented creations. They were initially generated more out of the importing ideas and organizational techniques from Western Europe than out of endogenous tendencies. The fact is that in the 1990s in most post-socialist countries the politicization of movements was openly avoided or kept hidden under the surface. For most of the civic environmental organizations operating at a local level with which I deal in this book, one of the initial strategies was to win people's faith and trust by denying political orientation. This brings about the necessity to look at Western and Eastern discourses, practices and knowledge building in environmental discourses through different lenses.

The second point is that environmentalism has a marked 'global' connotation in Eastern Europe due to a number of structural conditions, which differ from those operating in Western regions. One of these is the lack of generalized donor activity within the countries (see Chapter 2) which is related, according to some

---

5   Some examples in the political science of works in this direction are for instance Novotny 2000; Dryzek et al. 2003; McCright and Dunlap 2008.

scholars, to cultural practices, and to others to a generalized lack of private resources spendable in environmental protection, as well as to the traditionally strong role of the state in supporting civil society under the previous regime. This is not a matter of simplistically suggesting that environmental movements are less effective in Eastern Europe since they depend too much on external donations and project funds (see Howard 2003). The nature of environmental activism in several post-socialist regions has been such that spontaneously formed movements have sought connection with wider networks to counterbalance the difficult access to funds as well as to specialized and technical knowledge generated by changing and new legislation, especially since EU accession. Transnational networks and links to other European environmental movements have facilitated the pursuit of the two strategies indicated above: resource mobilization, and political efficiency. Political efforts have been made more openly at transnational and national levels before being re-addressed and re-directed at a local level.

The third point is that communication strategies used by movements in these regions are mixed, follow an intermingling of formal and informal strategies and are not necessarily guided by environmental issues alone. This constitutes one of the focuses of this volume, where corruption and political implications become at times similar, and even more important than environmental concerns. I would not argue that Douglas and Wildavsky were right in theorizing the critical role of culture in defining social responses to events of risk. There is no such thing as a post-socialist culture, as the copious anthropological literature on the transformation has demonstrated (Hann 2002). Rather, as Gerlach has suggested, the strategies and language of protest may change because the heterogeneous character of these movements concede internal dynamism. I prefer to state that the diversification of the discursive strategies, practices and ideologies transmitted to the general public by these movements is influenced by the two points mentioned above (detachment from political parties and the global character of movements) and by the shifting arenas in which protests take place. In this sense, there is still some space to define ways in which the historical development of civil society in Eastern Europe and the institutional transformation following post-socialism and EU enlargement processes affect environmentalist practices and discourses.

Global and local environmentalism

One of the fields that has produced a rich literature on environmentalism regards the intersection, juxtaposition or opposition (depending on the perspectives) of local and global practices. This issue has sometimes been overexposed in the social sciences, so as to create a jargonized view of the contemporary features of political activism in the environmental sector. The reason why I find it useful to introduce, finally, some insights into the binary use of the terms local-global, which are not in real opposition, is because this debate is particularly relevant for the case studies.

As far back as 1981, O'Riordan recalled those 'writers with an interest in the Third World [who] believe passionately in the amalgamation of national states into a new world order [...] they all believe that global unity is the inevitable end state of human progress' (O'Riordan 1981: 303). His critique of these positions, which appear to depart from a common Eurocentric assumption that in human history 'social evolution' is sought through ties of wide cooperation, is that they do not consider that 'issues of sovereignty and self-determination remain[ed] unsolved'.

Moreover, he quotes Toffler who, in 1975 wrote: 'What is happening ...is the breakdown of industrial civilization on the planet and the first fragmentary appearance of a wholly new and dramatically different social order. A superindustrial civilization that will be technological, but no longer industrial' (quoted in O'Riordan 1981: 304). This gloomy forecast is, to the author, attributable to the case where 'man is confronted with the very real possibility of annihilation from a clearly defined enemy'. Hence he asks rhetorically whether the same can be affirmed 'when the "enemy" is at once ephemeral and all embracing, when the threat falls more heavily on the weak than on the strong, when even the strong begins to feel threatened and the response is far more difficult to forecast' (*ibidem*).

One might feel distressed by the applicability of these words to the present, three decades after they were written. Or one might admit that he and other scholars, writing in the darkest years of the Cold War, were actually able to predict how global capitalism would establish its grip on national boundaries. Certainly not even the most enlightened and prophetical of the scholars at that time was able to outline the issues which are on the present agenda: the shrinking of national versus transnational boundaries and the expansion of political decision-making processes, uncontrollable transnational flows of capital, workforce and human beings, the strengthening and artificial construction of local identities and discourses of localism, the steadily worsening climatic conditions, the fore-fronting of environmental issues both in industrial production and in social protest movements, large environmental disasters and the questioning of the nuclear energy solution. All these issues, which endure to present day, are associated with the dominance of neoliberal global capitalism. However, here the main questions are: to what extent do global conditions favour the dynamic unravelling of environmental discourses and practices at a local level? Is the classic and overused distinction between global and local of any help in describing present environmentalism? What is the role of the state, in conditions of global governance, in setting and negotiating the boundaries with environmental movements?

Social scientists have sought different pathways to answer these questions. Economists and political scientists have looked at the new opportunities offered by global transformation for the environmentalist organizations. One conclusion is that there is a global institutionalization of environmentalism (Frank et al. 2000), thanks to the transnational capital flow and funding bodies that do not (or cannot) move locally and nationally. This has produced some important outcomes which are indicated in a growing global isomorphism (the spreading of similar environmental policies and legislations), the creation of complex bodies of pro-environmental laws and framework for action which will have a relevant impact on the market and on economic value (Schofer and Granados 2006). These developments are, according to some sociologists, accompanied by an increasingly positive role of environmentalism in reducing the risks and damage of industrial production throughout the world. Mol (2000) refers this to the explicit need for large, global enterprises to request the implementation of common environmental regulations and legislation all over the globe as a way to cut costs. In his view, the least polluting and environmentally noxious companies are multinationals, which have every reason to share global agreements on environmental protection, as part of the ESG factors that characterize corporate social responsibility[6]. This rather optimistic view, partially reminiscent of modernity theory in environmentalism, has found a number of supporters among environmental sociologists. Instead, anthropology has been sceptical about the positive involvement of corporations to solve or at least contrast environmental hazards, particularly when development projects or access to natural resources in less wealthy countries are the main justification for intervention (Bennett 1993; Milton 1996; Crumley et al. 2001; Haenn and Wilk 2006).

Under global transformation, increased diversification of local production, de-territorialization of industries, emphasis on the transport of goods and materials, intensification of the division of labour and productive tasks, loss of local biodiversity accompanying development projects worldwide, the proliferation and sophistication of machineries, as well as the lower costs of passenger air-transport will continue to raise the risks and dangers of environmental collapse. In addition, the different national forms of environmental damage control and risk assessment, the gaps in legislative measures between leading and developing economies, the difficult fiscal control in a number of both leading and developing economies, the enormous discrepancy in workforce costs among world regions and the diminishing power of states to negotiate multinational interests all contribute to rendering the global threats forecast by early scholars far from being mere eschatological visions.

Within this panorama of transformation, environmental movements are increasingly caught in the quasi-paradoxical condition of being set up as transnational movements and having to operate locally, or vice versa, of originating locally and having to spread their activities translocally. As such, they need to operate within shifting political contexts, from regional to national and transnational arenas, according to the recent patterns of institutional transformation in their countries of origin. In this book the case studies presented all reveal the tension arising from this perspective. It is increasingly difficult to assess whether a genuinely global movement can have the prerogative of being more successful than one set up locally. Both situations are possible. I think it is more significant to consider

---

6   The ESG factors (Environmental, Social and Governance) constitute a set of non-financial performance indicators used in capital market and by investors to assess corporate behaviour in different fields of sustainability.

which political and discursive strategies are sought in order to achieve particular goals. This is the main methodological line of this book. I am not concerned with the human relationship (ideological and heuristic) with the environment, which is what most of the classic works in ecological anthropology address. I am also not concerned with assessing how culture or societal organizations can influence the way in which the risk of environmental damage is perceived. The local-global binomial category, whether we agree with it or not, explains alone why such an endeavour is today anachronistic. I am finally not concerned with the role of the state in setting, desperately according to some, domineeringly according to others, the limits and forms of environmental movements. This issue is, as I will demonstrate when dealing with the 'revived' notion of civil society, not relevant to the case of Eastern Europe (the case of Italy is different, Chapter 7). My main concern is the diversification of the organizational, discursive and political strategies of a number of environmental movements that arose in Eastern European countries during the years of the EU enlargement. In the regions I have studied, environmentalism is a product of the European Union enlargement and of its common policies and structural development projects. However, the characteristics and language of environmental movements are not themselves a product of this process. I am interested in investigating the dynamics through which this process comes into conflict with local, ground-level strategies, as well as the ideas and images which arise from this conflict. I adopt the approach that proposes, mainly in anthropology, that one of the most productive ways in which social science can engage with environmentalism is by looking at the ways in which the global-local binomial is attributed meaning by those who face the force and threat of transnational development projects.

Chapter 2

Civil Society: Ambiguities and Opportunities

The aim of this chapter is twofold. First, I will trace the most relevant features of the theoretical tradition, which accompanies the development of the notion of civil society in Western Europe, and its employment in conditions of political transformation in Eastern Europe. Second, I will sketch out some of the prevalent trends in the anthropological critique of civil society as an empirical field of investigation. In this second aim, I will develop an approach that looks at the operational use of the notion and to its practical fields of application in the contexts of EU eastward enlargement.

The idea of civil society is one of the oldest and most contested in Western political and sociological thought. Anthropology has been, among the social sciences, the discipline that has moved the boldest critiques of the concept, following a number of methodological perspectives which account for the different area specializations of the scholars. Civil society is ideally defined as a 'category that describes and envisages a complex of dynamic ensemble of legally protected non-governmental institutions that tend to be non-violent, self-organizing, self-reflexive and permanently in tensions with each other and with the state which "frames", constricts and enables their activities' (Keane 1998: 6). The complexity of the definition closely reflects the wide spectrum of (social and political) activities that it encompasses, as well as the difficulty in classifying the domains and arenas of these activities. Hence the first of the critiques moved by social anthropology to the application and even usefulness of the notion of civil society: it is hard to define to what it concretely applies.

The second critique refers to the origins of the notion, which is located in particular times (from the development of classical Greek and Latin philosophy onwards, to the Enlightenment period, the late 18th Century and the consolidation of Marxian and Marxist thought), and in a particular place, Western Europe. The extremely rich philosophical body of literature on civil society in Western Europe alone suggests that anthropology could only play a marginal role to the development of a notion which, by many of its original definitions, is abstracted from non-western societies. The very idea of 'civility', as suggested by Jack Goody, is extremely suspicious when it is not applied 'to technical archaeology' (Goody 2001: 152).

The third critique, raised by Hann and Dunn (1996) and Comaroff and Comaroff (1999), relates to the use of this notion in the social sciences, and in applied research, which can easily foster ethnocentrism. This would be manifest for instance in the discourse about the so-called 'revival of civil society' (as indicated below) in regional settings such as Eastern European and Latin American countries. This position is, according to some anthropologists, tinged with exoticism, because such a revival implies that civil society becomes, as Goody proposes a 'weapon of the weak' (Goody 2001: 153), exported and later put aside by the 'progressive West'.

In spite of the several ambiguities related to the historical development of the notion of civil society and even more to its methodological testing in the study of contemporary social phenomena, there are some opportunities that its use encloses. First, by applying the notion to a number of social, political and anti-political movements which in Western as in Eastern Europe have pursued similar and dissimilar goals, forms of protest, expressions of desires and anxieties, it is possible to create a common basis of empirical investigation and comparative analysis. The main objective of this book is to shed light onto processes through which shared awareness, a common language and public legitimacy can be sought and achieved by the environmental protest movements. This language, taking forms not always clear to the general public, has been developed through the adoption of the notion of civil society, of Western European origin. In Eastern Europe, for the dissident organizations that, especially in Hungary, Czechoslovakia and Poland, contributed to legitimize the dismantling of state socialism, the notion of civil society in its non-Marxist definition, have created the intellectual framework within which to voice the necessity of reforms and to establish the tracks for subsequent political strategies.

Second, Eastern European intellectuals who were by the Western academic and activists labelled as 'dissident thinkers' have proved prophetic towards the global opportunities of the civil society paradigm. This 'global' outlook, along with its pluralistic and self-reflective natures, has allowed them to consolidate extraterritorial and supra-national dynamics of resistance, protest and negotiation. In the early 1980s Konrád György in Hungary and Vacláv Havel in Czechoslovakia had already advocated the opportunities offered respectively by 'globalization' and by 'global technological civilization' (quoted in Kaldor 2003: 587). As the case studies in this book openly suggest, one of the most significant opportunities provided by civil society after the fall of the Berlin Wall is its engaging with global transformations, such as the EU enlargement and the creation of a communitarian *acquis*, to gain strength and legitimacy at the local level.

Third, the undefined character of the notion can be used, for analytical purposes, as a strength by closely following the instrumental use that actors make of this idea. Tracking down the classical position of Western philosophical thought that emphasizes its function as a shock-absorber of state or central power over individuals, it is possible to conceive of the opportunities that this notion provides to its several fields of operationalization. Hence whether it is law, social contract, social networks, social movements, informal activities, decision-making processes from below and so forth, it makes sense to include all these actions, ideas and ideologies under a common umbrella as long as they work jointly for a common goal. The ultimate objective of this operation of emic-holism is to individuate ways and strategies through which social actors interpret the role of the state under conditions of neoliberal capitalism and global governance. Within the EU enlargement project this approach does not constitute a novelty, what is new is that in the countries which have faced post-socialism alternative forms of political power can be built and eventually compete with the state (and local governments) to influence decision-making processes. Hence the state is not the enemy to defy, as in the 1980s' intellectual cries for the possibility of global civilization, or to avoid, as in the 1990s' calls for anti-political civic organizations. The global and pluralistic civil society, with its language and linkages, becomes the place where the state is demystified as the central locus of authority, emulated in its communication strategies and eventually reinterpreted as an entity with which negotiation can or cannot be sought. This is the main novelty of the opportunities caused by the new civil society, in Eastern, but also in Western Europe, where the state is not (as Gramsci argued) a secondary organization, but a constant point of reference which does not contain any longer civil society, but rather helps it to adjust its forms and strategies.

The chapter is divided into four sections. In the first section I introduce some of the most relevant historical and theoretical foundations of the notion of civil society. The aim of this section is not to provide yet another history of the notion (see for instance Cohen and Arato 1994; Hall 1995; Keane 1998; Hall and Trentmann 2005), but to sketch out the most recurrent conditions under which, according to western philosophical and political thought civil society emerges and consolidates. The second section deals with the contemporary debate over the usefulness of the notion and of its revival. This section creates a link between the notion and issues of globalization as well as between the notion and the role of the state in the post-Cold War period. In the third section I review some of the anthropological critiques to civil society, with particular reference to the case of Eastern Europe. The final section deals with the analysis of empirical case studies in Eastern Europe, their results and the implications that these provide to the ongoing debate over the concept. The aim of this chapter is to introduce the notion of civil society and to engage in a critical analysis of its applicability to the case studies as well as to define the fields in which the cases under exam will be framed at both methodological and analytical levels.

On the nature of civil society

Civil society is described by Keane as an 'ideal-typical'[1] (in the Weberian sense) category, which can find different ways of definition in political phenomena ranging from the decline of the welfare state, neoliberal democracy and the emergence of social movements (Keane 1998: 7). As an ideal-typical category there is hardly such a thing as a concrete and unique definition of civil society,

---

1   In Weberian thought, the ideal type category of phenomenon is meant to refer to characteristics and elements of common to most phenomena. The word 'ideal' does not refer to a state of reputed perfection, rather to the world of ideas (Gedankenbilder) which arrange these phenomena in way sto reduce chaos and social disorder.

and this is clear from the different historical and intellectual origins of the notion. Rather than tracing back these origins in a developmental fashion, I would like to identify the most salient aspects that characterize the nature of civil society as an analytical category in western thought.

Civil society is commonly understood as the intermediate level between the state and the individual, or between the established central authority and the most basic social unit, the family or kinship. However, civil society is not immanent in society, but it is established through communality of interests, needs and goals of a group that harmonize or collide with those of another part of the society. This leads to the first problematic aspect of the notion, the relationship between politics and society. The original use of the notion, dating back to Ciceronian and Aristotelian philosophical tradition, was in relation with the body of laws which govern the state and society as an extension. Cicero, in *De Republica*, describes the 'bond' which in civil society (*societas civilis*) can bring together the state with equality of status, but not of money and talent, which is law (quoted in Black 2001: 33). Aristotle, in his *Politics*, develops what is believed to be the first historical idea of political society. He assumes that individuals pursue what they consider good, and enters into partnerships with others they believe to hold similar conceptions of the good in order to pursue that end. The political society (*koinônía he politikê*) is what allows for this public good to be channelled, within the state (Politics, 1252a). Aristotle implies that a man is by nature a political being, who needs to enter in partnership first through the marital union, then in different forms of association. He underlines that 'a man who is so self-sufficient that he has no need to do so, is no part of a state, so he must be either a lower animal or a god' (1253a). This final point, the equation of the non-political man with an animal is similarly developed by Latin and early Middle Age thinkers who drew on the classic dichotomy between civil and barbarian, human or beast-like, social or natural (Black 2001).

The pre-modern origin of civil society contains three indications on the nature of the notion which will be developed further in history: the opposition between a natural (uncivil) and a social (civil) status, the pre-eminent position of law or social contract as foundation of civil society and the association between civil society and political society in relation with the state. Each of these features developed in the different philosophical positions from the Enlightenment thinkers onwards. Leaving aside the first feature, the normative aspect entailed in the notion of civil society has made space for the development of the social contract theory (also derived from Socrates) in the works of Thomas Hobbes, John Locke and Jacques Rousseau.

Hobbes argued that political authority and obligation are based on individual self-interests of members of society who are understood to be equal to one another. In the *Leviathan*, he stresses that in the State of Nature, which is purely hypothetical, men are naturally and exclusively self-interested, they are approximately equal, there are limited resources, and yet there is no force leading men to cooperate. Because men are rational beings, they can seek their way out of such a state and create a civil society. Being reasonable, and recognizing the rationality of this basic precept of reason, men can be expected to construct a social contract. This is constituted by two distinguished contracts: first they must decide on collectively renouncing to the rights they have on one another, second they have to establish an authority invested with the task of enforcing the contract.

Unlike Hobbes, Locke believed in the moral essence of the State of Nature, which, being given by God, assures that humans will not necessarily be at war against each other. What may cause war is indeed a step out of this natural condition, when private property is established. At this point the civil government based on contract, or law, is necessary to prevent or resolve war.

Rousseau developed two ideas of social contract. The first, similarly to Locke, derived from the need to regulate differences of private property and avoid conflict. However, this contract is for Rousseau unjust in nature, since it protects and perpetuates the privileges of the private owners. The second type, normative social contract, is introduced to guarantee that all individuals, free by nature and equal in rights, renounce their rights in the interest of the collective and establish a common source of government ruled by law.

The third feature, the relationship between civil society and political power, emerges more distinctively from the contributions of, among others, Ferguson, Hegel, de Tocqueville, Marx, Gramsci and Foucault. The Aristotelian idea of 'political society' is developed in different ways by these thinkers and adds significantly to the problem of defining the interrelation between civil society and state structures. Some, like Ferguson, believed that civil society is inherently political (as Aristotle did), because man cannot be extrapolated out of society and hence cannot exist outside political interaction. Hegel, who is considered the most influential thinker for the modern development of the notion, defines civil society as the intermediate realm between the family and the state, in which individuals, through membership in various institutions, become public persons. Civil society, bringing together different individuals with their egoistic demands and achievements, is a continuous battlefield, which is by him distinguished from political society, the state. The state is, in the Hegelian political conception, the third moment of the Ethical Life, providing the final synthesis to the other two: the family and civil society. The rationality of the state, which embodies the universal will (or the social contract), is what makes possible the harmonization of individual interests, since it is only through its membership that individuals obtain objectivity, real individuality and an ethical life.

Alexis de Tocqueville, in two of his influential writings (*Democracy in America, The Old Regime and the Revolution*), developed the two notions of political and civil society. In his view, since many people see the state as a danger to their freedom, and they acknowledge at the same time that individuals can counterbalance the state, they start to form free social and political associations. The former are created to promote common private interests, the latter to promote collective powers in the political participation of individuals to the public life. The paradox emerging from his vision is that the state should recognize the competence of these associations, but in the meantime has the task of leading their administration for purposes of public order. This form of state intervention needs a 'social basis', which is constituted by a combination of 'material life conditions and immaterial factors (patterns of thought, behaviour and moral values) that generates mores: different notions, various opinions, and ideas that shape mental habits' (Woldring 1998: 370–71).

Marx followed the Hegelian conception of separation between civil society and the state, positioning the former in bourgeois society. Its emergence would have marked the end of the feudal political systems, with power in the hands of the new class, the bourgeoisie. If socio-economic distinctions constituted the *differentia specifica* of the newly emerging civil society, it was on this distinction that class conflict (between the bourgeoisie and the proletariat) was grounded. By bringing about the separation of the productive and exchange spheres from the public sphere of the state, civil society, with its immanent struggles, causes the independent evolution of the state as an institution separate from economic society. Thus the evolution of civil society is a process framed in history, and it is within civil society (and not the state as Hegel maintained) that historical development takes place (Hoare and Smith 1989).

Antonio Gramsci followed Marx in the basic standpoint that sees civil society as a set of economic relationships (a system of needs). He believed that it is in civil society that the interpretation of history finds shape. The state is to him usually 'intended as the political society (or as coercive apparatus to conform the masses according to the type of production and the economy of a given moment)'. He contrasts this view with the idea that the state is 'an equilibrium of political and civil society (or the hegemony of a social group over the whole national society exerted through the so-called private organizations, such as the church, the syndicates, schools, etc.)' (Gramsci 1968: 481, my translation). The grip of the property-owning class is most vulnerable within the cultural institutions of civil society, which functions to popularize and reproduce among the subordinate classes and groups the dominant bourgeois sense of reality or hegemony. Civil society worked as a 'fortress' to protect the outer ditch of state power and shield the ruling class from the shock waves of economic crises. The empowerment of the subordinated classes depends vitally on the prior capturing of civil society (Keane 1998: 12).

Foucault's approach to civil society refused the Hegelian analytical distinction with the state on the groundings that power cannot be isolated, since it informs every kind of social and political action. The state is to him the consolidation of processes of statization (*etatisation*) of forces immanent in power relations. Civil society is a society based on discipline, as the state is, and the kind of education it provides to its individuals is one of normalization (Hardt 1995). Foucault opposes fiercely the idea of a common form of morality (derived from the Enlightenment tradition) which for Habermas was at the core of the development of civil society (see Flyvbjerg 1998). Such a morality would endanger the existence of civil society, because the existence of universals as such 'has never been demonstrated in social sciences and philosophy' (Foucault 1984: 247 quoted in Flyvbjerg

1998). The law, he continues, the institutions and the state have never provided guarantees of freedom and equality, nor can such a freedom be achieved through abstract systems. The problem is not to achieve new rules which can empower civil society, but to provide 'the rules of law, the techniques of management and the ethics which allow these games of power to be played with a minimum of domination' (quoted in Flyvbjerg 1998: 223).

Two main implications can be drawn, from the classical western theoretical works on civil society. The first is that civil society ideally occupies the space in which the reconciliation of private and public interests is sought, in the form of voluntarily coordinated associations. These associations are governed by law, or other forms of social order, which allow the collective harmonization of goals. The second point is that civil society is in a dialectical relationship with other forms of political control, be them the state or global forces (as below). This relationship is far from being given, or inherent in a kind of ethical society, as Hegel argued, but it belongs to a determinate time and space. As a product of history, civil society is in constant transformation in the hegemonic rapport it has with the state and political society. However, in order not to overstate the abstract and universal functions and natures of civil society, it is necessary to recognize the plurality of forms it can assume, mediated during the continuous struggle for power, as Foucault and Gramsci assumed. This approach is one which can still make the analytical use of the notion a meaningful effort, in spite of the several critiques that, following dissatisfaction with the Marxist approaches, and Foucaultian pessimism, has tended to consider the notion withering, or even dead in the late 1960s (Hardt 1995; Setianto 2007).

The 'revival' of civil society: the demise of state socialism

The recent 'revival' of the notion, or its 're-remembering' as Comaroff and Comaroff argue (1999: 5), is seen as taking place in three intellectual environments. The first is under the influence of the Japanese Marxist school which, following the work of Uchida Yochihiko and Hirata Kiyoaki, made a clear use of cultural explanations to investigate the then weak civil society in Japan (Matsuda 2004).

The second is the context of Latin American republics, where in the 1970–1980s the use of civil society became instrumental to the populist positions of local political movements. Here, the notion was often revitalized in its full Marxist terminology, even when the mass political and social mobilization it was meant to imply was no more than a dictatorial strategy to gain control over large shares of voters (Castro Leiva and Pagden 2001; Roberts 2007).

The third environment is Eastern Europe in the wake of the anti-socialist movement of the 1980s. Here, unlike in the previous two cases, civil society was adopted as a meaningful notion in reaction and not in accordance to the Marxist intellectual tradition.

In Eastern Europe, following the violent ends of the 1956 events in Hungary, the Prague spring in 1968 and the beginning of the Solidarnosc movement in Poland in the 1980s, civil society was felt as a fruitful theoretical framework for establishing discourses of cooperation with Western European intellectuals and activists. The problem stemmed out of the difficult dialogue between the two sides, the West concerned about global (and more sensitive to its regions) issues such as nuclear disarmament, peace and environmental damage and the Eastern counterpart striving to gain freedom from the totalitarian regimes. In this panorama of mutual incomprehension it has been argued that civil society provided a common language to bridge this semantic and political orientation gap (Tismăneanu 1990; Kaldor 1990). A number of publications in English in the early 1990s praised with eloquence the civic activism of the main figures of the Central Eastern European dissidentism, often attributing to them the revival of the notion of civil society. They were intellectuals like Konrád György, Adam Michnick, Jacek Kuron, Václav Havel. Some of them had explicitly made use of the notion in a number of their works.

Civil society, in the use that intellectual dissidents made of the term meant basically three things: the aspired notion of individual liberty and inviolability of private life, a moral and normative form of political practice and a direct critique of totalitarian state power (Plamenova Ivancheva 2007). Following these epistemological positions, some recent arguments have envisioned three different approaches to civil society, exemplified as: to ignore the state, to engage the state from outside or to engage within the state (Renwick 2006).

The first approach developed two notions, particularly in the writings of Konrád and Havel: anti-politics and parallel polis. In Politics and Conscience (1988) Havel wrote:

> I favor anti-politics, that is, politics not as the technology of power and manipulation, of cybernetic rule over humans or as the art of the utilitarian, but politics as one of the ways of seeking and achieving meaningful lives, of protecting them and serving them (quoted in Renwick 2006: 289).

This proposition is derived from his famous idea of 'life in truth', developed in *The Power of Powerless* (1978). Here Havel sketched his own view of civil society (although he did not mention the word itself) in the idea of life in truth:

> The singular, explosive, incalculable political power of living within the truth resides in the fact that living openly within the truth has an ally, invisible to be sure, but omnipresent: this hidden sphere..This is where the potential for communication exists. But this place is hidden and therefore, from the perspective of power, very dangerous (1978: 148).

Konrád, on the other hand, used anti-politics to:

put politics in its place, and make sure it stays there, never overstepping its proper office of defending and defining the rules of civil society. Anti-politics is the ethos of civil society and civil society is the opposite of military society (1987: 82).

His use of anti-politics is distant from Havel's ethical civil society; it embodies the idea of constructing a counter-power, far away from the development of a ruling ideology. This is constructed at everyday level, in everyday action and has to lead to a pervasive level of democratization, well beyond the 'periodic exchange of political elites via free and fair elections' (Falk 2005).

The idea of 'parallel polis' derives from the thought of the Czech 'dissident' Václav Benda who argued that the political strategies of anti-politics had hampered further development of the Charter 77 movement.[2] He was advocating the creation of 'slowly but surely, parallel structures that are capable, to a limited degree at least, of supplementing the generally beneficial and necessary functions that are missing in the existing structures' (quoted in Renwick 2006: 291).

The second approach sought to change the state through external intervention. This tendency is to be found in a number of institutional movements which culminated in the establishment of Charter 77, as well as in other similar networks such as the Hungarian *Beszélő*.[3] These movements, together with those centred around the intellectual activity of Michnick and Kuron in Poland leading to Solidarnosc, advocated the need for an alternative organizational structure which could channel involvement from below. The crucial aim in each of these perspectives was to mobilize civil society. These approaches were underscored by the intention to convince (although on different intellectual levels) that the state was oppositely positioned versus civil society, and that engaging with the state meant acting outside of it. Tamás Bauer, one of the leading Hungarian intellectuals of the period, advocated the development of 'pluralism of political interests' representations', which was still seen as the optimal alternative to revolutionizing state structures (Renwick 2006: 298).

---

2   The Charter 77 was a dissident movement originating in Czechoslovakia in the late 1976. The charter originated as a call for respect of human rights and was delivered to the federal assembly of the country, containing 242 signatures, mainly of Czech and Slovak intellectuals. Among them, Vaclàv Havel and Ludvík Vaculík were detained for several months. The document was confiscated, but it circulated in several samizdat copies and was eventually published in major Western newspapers. In spite of further repressions, the document served as a matrix on which to ground dissident and informal activities that continued in the 1980s.

3   This (The Speaker) was the widest read Hungarian samizdat publication, which started in 1981 edited by Kis János and Haraszti Miklós. Conceived under the influence of Polish and Czechoslovakian examples, the Beszélő maintained the policy of disclosing the personal contacts, addresses and telephone numbers of its editors. It was intended to publish unofficial coverage of events, to fight the myth that 'nothing of note ever happens in Hungary' (Falk 2005: 131).

The third approach emphasized the importance to engage with the state within its political structures. This approach was, like the others, characterized by different degrees of political intervention, as theorized in the course of the historical development of this stream of ideas. The first wing of this movement theorized the possibility of acting within the communist state, in a reasonably moderated opposition with it, but in rejection of Marxist ideas. One example was the Hungarian populist movement centred around the magazine *Hitel* (Kürti 1990), edited by Nagy Gáspár, a poet of Catholic faith whose contribution was deemed salient to counterbalance the large presence of Protestant intellectuals who joined, after 1989, the Hungarian Democratic Forum[4] (MDF), the first party in Hungary's 1990 democratic elections. A second wing concerns more radical positions which aimed to subvert state power but were, as easily understood, a small minority within new civic movements. One such example was the KNP (Confederation for Independent Poland), which operated often at the margins of Solidarnosc. Founded in 1979 by the military historian Leszek Moczulski, before the emergence of Solidarnosc, this group claimed to have been the first truly anti-communist political party in Eastern Europe.[5]

The third and final wing was characterized by an approach similar to the ethical transformation of civil society advocated by Havel. In Hungary Kis János had warned that 'the dissident movement must not be political in the traditional sense – must not offer political programs; it must stand in a moral attitude' (quoted in Renwick 2006: 300). As 1989 approached, a similar position was held by the circle of the journal Demokrata (Csizmadia 2005). If in Poland the strength and influence of the Solidarnosc movement became hardly unchallengeable from other parallel movements, in Czechoslovakia in 1988 the Movement for Civic Freedom (HOS) appeared, calling in its manifesto for 'genuine democracy, a system based on intellectual, political and economic pluralism and mutual tolerance' (Renwick 2006: 302). This movement was followed by the consolidation of a number of other democratic initiatives which, unlike the Polish case, were not conceived under the same umbrella but acted separately both in the Czech and in the Slovak territories (see also Kennedy 1992).

As it can be argued from these descriptions, the level at which intellectual and theoretical debates of civil society developed in Central Eastern Europe in the

---

4   The Magyar Demokrata Fórum originated after an informal conference hold in 1987 at the home of the writer Sándor Leszák. The conference included participation of 150 Hungarian intellectuals, divided in two political orientations: the populist group who gave origin to the Democratic Forum, and the democratic opposition called the Alliance for Free Democrats (SzDSz).

5   His leader had been imprisoned several times and because of the 'violent' and radical image of the group, its party scored poorly at the first elections in 1989. In 1991, the political party entering the government coalition was unable to cooperate with the majority parties, especially after allegations that its leader, Moczulski had cooperated with communist secret agents.

1980s is not easily comparable with that of Western European classical debates. The problem emerging with this parallel is that the Hegelian-Marxist-Gramscian stream of tradition could not be found applicable in the contexts of intellectual 'dissident' activists of socialist Europe. Even though this seems easily understood, as some western theorists argue (Kunmar 1993), the point is more complex than this. The emerging contrast between anti-political (and ethical) versus political standpoints suggests two ways of considering critically the influence of the notion of civil society on late socialist Central Eastern Europe. The first is that where civil society was not openly used as an expression of the political arena where renovation and struggle towards democracy could be fought the dialogue with western European thinkers was easier. Among others, Havel's works became very influential in Western Europe, and especially among activist circles, because they constitute a case of this first way of considering civil society. The ethical approach, or the parallel way, functioned as intelligible schema for the west to engage with Central Eastern European reference schema of civil society. Anti-state political engagement was refused by these positions, and this had the initial mitigating effects of leaving space to dialogue with mainly leftists' activist movements in Western Europe, where the notion of civil society had been revitalizing. Of course, when Havel and several other Czechoslovak intellectuals actively entered the political realm of post-socialist Czechoslovakia (and later Czech Republic), their intellectual positions became exposed to severe criticism (Skilling and Wilson 1991). Anti-politics had become a chimera, or, in the words of Tóth Károly, one of the Slovak active intellectuals: 'it became clear that until that time we had been engaging in intellectual level communication, and that was fine. After 1990s a number of us believed that things were to be done concretely, and they sought active political engagement'.[6]

The second way to look at the use of the notion of civil society in late socialist Central Eastern Europe is to consider this as a case-sensitive approach which convoyed two synergies: the need to achieve civic participation and to build consensus, and the quest for a common political action to subvert socialism. This form of active political engagement, which marked the Polish and to a lesser extent the Hungarian case, drew on the aforementioned use of the civil society discourse as an instrument of anti-politics or reformation (Kenendy 1992). Here a common discussion ground with the intellectual and activist movements of Western European origin was more difficult. For one thing, both the Hegelian notion of civil society was, for the reasons described above, unsatisfactory, and the normative approach which dated back to the Enlightenment thought could not be easily tenable in what was going on during those years. The rapid international and national political developments of the long 1979–1989 decade, as well as the different intellectual backgrounds of Polish and Hungarian 'dissidents' contributed to build a less static, less universal and constantly changing notion of civil society which at times served as a 'pressure group', at times as 'anti-political politics'

---

6   Personal communication, 22–7–2007.

and even as 'real political opposition'. Within this panorama, and under different epistemological standpoints than in Western Europe, the second way of conceiving civil society was what, only after 1989, opened space to mutual fertilization, and to the development of a more applied and concrete concept.

Civil society became, after the events of 1989 and the consolidation of the first free democratic movements into political parties, a domain of practice, whereas intellectual debates over the universalist, ethical and self-reflexive natures of the notion remained left in the background. Not only was the political environment rapidly changing, as Havel's election as the first post-socialist president of Czechoslovakia demonstrated, but the flourishing body of NGOs and extraterritorial civic organizations urged for the establishing of a common ground of cooperation and communication between Eastern and Western Europe. This was the point when civil society became gradually a common language in the whole European continent, insofar as the domain of non-state intervention in 'development' or other projects were concerned.

Politicization of the former democratic movements in post-socialist Central Eastern Europe did not mean that the technical usage of 'civil society' superseded the intellectual and ethical. It rather meant that, after 1989, the only common ground on which using the notion between the geographical east and the west was its applied domain. Before looking at different forms of consolidation of this applied notion of civil society, I would like to shed further light onto the problem of how anthropology has dealt with the epistemological and empirical uses of civil society.

The role of anthropology in theorizing civil society

Anthropology has often hesitated to use the notion of civil society and to engage in its study. There may be several reasons for this and some will be outlined here. The first is that there is no general agreement on the definition of the notion, this generates confusion and has led some anthropologists to challenge whether the notion is meaningful at all. The second reason has to do, as indicated above, with the ethnocentrism inherent in the notion, which, taken uncritically, may breed an opposition between 'western civil' versus a 'non-western uncivil' society (Hann and Dunn 1996; Goody 2001; Junghans 2001). Here anthropological unease is at its height, first because the common use of the notion derives from the western intellectual tradition and thus cuts out those regions on which the larger numbers of anthropologists work. Second, policy makers, activists, NGOs and international organizations engaging with civil society in development projects increasingly call for a continuous and urging involvement of anthropology to test the consequences and real applicability of the notion. Applied anthropology, in other words, cannot avoid dealing with civil society, and non-applied anthropology is faced with it in order to establish interdisciplinary communication. The third reason concerns the methodological approach to its study. Framed in a perspective of global transformation, civil society becomes usually adopted as a panacea to denounce and fight transnational 'uncivil forces' such as criminality, corruption, poverty and environmental crimes (Schneider and Schneider 2001). Studying civil society at a global level is a highly contradictory effort (see below), which leaves the researcher who opts for this notion with the creeping doubt that the object of study is indefinable and as such cannot be confined to one single case study. To this one adds the difficulty of distinguishing between genuinely local civic movements, national non-governmental organizations and movements born under wider and diversified umbrella organizations (Hearn 2001).

This differentiation calls for accurate and complex methodologies of fieldwork research which trace the different and plural local origins of these movements, their changes over time, and the different strategies of their actions when confronting with different institutional actors (citizens, state and local governments, NGOs, transnational political forces, the market, international organizations etc.). The limits of anthropological fieldwork, or of participant observation, become manifest in the attempt to study what has recently been called 'global civil society'.

The methodological dilemma with which anthropology is confronted, which becomes particularly troublesome in the context of Eastern Europe, is how to tackle forms of civil society which are born locally, but operate through national and transnational networks of socio-political interaction. The case studies of this book are all concrete examples of this point. This leaves anthropologists with a constant paradox, of dealing with new forms of civil society that cannot be studied satisfactorily at a mere local level, but that, if not studied anthropologically, will continue to be objects of ethnocentric and stereotyped analyses through the use of western-centred, ready-made categories, as it will be illustrated in the final section of this chapter.

The most complete and sophisticated theorization of civil society in anthropology is the work by Ernest Gellner (1994). The Jewish-Bohemian philosopher and social anthropologist started his enquiry into a notion that, he underlines, 'all of a sudden has been taken out and thoroughly dusted, and has become a shining emblem' (1994: 1). He attributed this revitalization not only to the 'brutality' of the socialist regimes, but also to the recognition that Marxist theory had come to a dead end. Gellner argued against the inappropriateness of the standard definitions of civil society, which refer to 'non-governmental institutions strong enough to counterbalance the state' in specifying the link with the modern concept of freedom. One example is to him the case of segmentary societies which, although challenging or presenting as alternative to central power, they nonetheless limit and control individual freedom (see also Goody 2001: 161–3). His focus is not on civil society in the narrow sense of non-governmental organizations, but in a broader sense of social order. Thus he contrasted what, in his view could not belong to the idea of civil society: preindustrial segmentary societies, Soviet communism, Islamic rule and other historical forms. Through contrast with these notable examples of what civil society is not, Gellner is able to construct different and alternative definitions of the notion when, for instance, he argues that compared to Islam 'civil society is an a-moral order' (1994: 137), or 'unlike communism it is the separation of [the polity from the economy], but with the economy not merely dependent but actually dominant, treating the polity as its accountable servant' (205–6). 'What is essential to [civil society] is the absence of either ideological or institutional monopoly: no one doctrine is elevated to sacredness and uniquely linked to the social order' (p. 188). His final answer to the initial question: 'why civil society appeared suddenly luminescent from the obscurity?' is partly a reaction to communism, a monolithic form of social order which curtailed any form of independence.

The issue of the different uses of civil society or its different developments in world regions is addressed by Gellner but not through a cultural explanation, as some political scientists have attempted to do (Putnam is one of the most notable, 1993 and 2000). Gellner recognizes that:

> The condition defined by [civil society] had become highly valued and loaded
> with political appeal. In extensive parts of the world, what it denoted was absent.
> This lack came in due course to be strongly felt and bitterly resented: eventually
> it turned into an aching void (1994: I).

To him, the absence of civil society was the mark of a universal condition in which centralized power and the dominance of a 'single political-economic-ideological hierarchy' constrained people in forms of social order that could not tolerate civic arrangements. Thus, one finds in Gellner's perspective a tension, unresolved for some (see Hann and Dunn's critique below), between the particularism of anthropology's view and the universalism of the view that inscribes in civil society the struggle and resistance against a central totalitarian authority, in the Gramscian perspective. It is not a surprise if the most notable achievement of Gellner's theoretical effort is its openness to interdisciplinary cross-fertilization (see for instance Katz 2002).

Jean and John Comaroff, in the introduction to their edited volume on civil society in Africa (1999) warn about the multifaceted nature of the notion which: 'an all-purpose placeholder, it captures otherwise inchoate – as yet unnamed and unnameable – popular aspirations, moral concerns, sites and spaces of practices' (1999: 3). Civil society is to them an effort to deal with 'positive politics', reviving an old notion which is imbued with methodological confusion. This approach draws from the authors' initial reflections on a number of paradoxes, such as the point that revitalization of the notion became, in some socio-political contexts, attached to 'a populist strive for *moral community* and *social being*' against a background of intruding neoliberalism (1999: 3–4). This paradox has been pointed out by other authors, also non anthropologists, who denounced the unease with a notion that, while predicating the triumph of self-reflexive and pluralist movements beyond or beneath the influence of the state in the 'western' world, it tells about resistance and insurgency against a violent re-occupying of these spaces by the neoliberal state in 'non-western' contexts (see Hardt 1995; Keane 2003).

The commonly detected epistemic problem seems to be that the civil society-state relationship can no longer be dealt with through the classical theoretical approaches on which the notion itself is grounded. The Hegelian/Marxist call for the need to bring in play economic relations and the market may still appear very timely, but it makes an insufficient framework since political society is increasingly formed beyond the state. The Comaroffs argue that this happened in three ways: through the deconstruction of currencies and custom borders, the transnational flow of credits and mobile markets and the transnationalizing trend of the division of labour and migration (Comaroff and Comaroff 1999: 15). Hence, within the eroding state all the localities attacked by the power of global capitalism would have developed a number of counter-phenomena (over)emphasizing the production of cultural, social identities and local practices which challenge, or according to others channel the violence of neoliberalism.[7] In this perspective, the rise of civil society becomes yet another of those reactions/reflections of the rule of global neoliberalism.

Chris Hann has made a similar point, but taking it from a different angle (1996). His view of the use of civil society departs from criticism of Gellner's approach, which he considers borne out of a social philosopher and not an anthropologist (1996: 2). In particular, taking for model the post-socialist transformation in Eastern Europe, he considers the western traditional antagonism state-society as a 'futile' endeavour (1996: 9). The same use of the notion of civil society to back the 'so called anti-political' dissident movements would be at odds with the real political character of the multiparty systems that developed after 1990. A general ambivalence prevails when attempting to apply civil society to describe the post-socialist transformation. This would happen for two reasons: on the one hand, contrary to what is usually assumed, socialism granted local citizens, especially in rural areas, venues of expression of their social identities, needs and aspirations which after the 1990s have been gradually damaged or lost forever (see also Torsello 2003). The socialist state, as a number of anthropological studies have demonstrated, intruded in society, but also built a parallel 'civil society' through support of semiformal and informal networks, circles, associations, foundations which were not necessarily of political nature. These forms have in part been eradicated in the post-socialist transformation, in part they are used as matrixes on which to build new types of reasonably formalized civil society (see also Pine 2002; Kaneff 2004).

On the other hand, civil society, after 1990, had definitively lost 'the emotional slogan' of the late 1980s (Hann 1999: 10). Hence, Hann concludes that the relationship between civil society and the state cannot be relevantly investigated

---

7 Anthropology's engagement with neoliberalism and the effects economic, social and political transformation is extremely rich and well-articulated. Some further readings can be found in the thematic issue of Cultural Anthropology (2010) 25(1): Neoliberalism, subjectivity, citizenship; Hedelman and Haugerud 2005; Greenhouse 2009; Comaroff and Comaroff 2001.

with the notion of civil society if this has come to be 'equated crassly with the expansion of 'non-governmental organization' sector' (1999: 9).

The Comaroffs' and Hann/Dunn's critiques suggest two important points of reflection. The first is that, in order to still be a useful and methodologically valid concept, civil society needs to be conceived of critically, as an outcome of the neoliberal state and of bottom-up forces reacting or adjusting to market and institutional pressures. The second is that anthropologists are wary of improper definitions of civil society to cover a number of cases of formal to informal socio-political action (from religious to ethnic ties, interpersonal networks, unions, neighbours, social clubs, and so forth) which have been traditional objects of ethnographic research. From these perspectives arises, in my view, the substantial need to diversify the field of investigation. Anthropology, at theoretical and epistemic level can contribute to the discourse over the applicability of the notion of civil society in present conditions of global capitalism and conflicting view of the role of the state (withering, integralist or both). At an applied level, however, anthropology cannot lose sight of the reality that civil society is not at all an empty notion, it is the clot of practices and discourses through which locally born movements acquire self-awareness, often under conditions of severe fluidity of formal-informal, individual-institutional, local-global interaction. In this perspective, the point is less whether the state is the intruder (as Gellner and Hardt maintain) or the victim (as Hann suggests), but whether the strategies, language and ideals of the new civic movements are able to reconstruct a semantic relationship with the state.

Attention to the state-civil society relationship is not futile when one recognizes that one of the emerging features of the 'revival' of civil society in Central Eastern Europe is a re-examination of the role of the state. This marks an important difference which has, in my understanding, been so far neglected by anthropology. One of the most temporally consistent emic distinctions between Western and Eastern understandings of civil society is that in the west, following the Hegelian tradition, the notion is framed as a cushion between state and society and hence it became characterized by definition with positive connotations, imbued, as Hann suggests, with informality which have often rendered it invisible to empirical analysis. On the other hand, the Eastern intellectual traditions emerging in the late socialist years have developed a notion of civil society which served the purpose to *make sense of* the state, in its possible semantics as totalitarian, post-totalitarian or democratic state. Anti-politics was, in this framework the only possible way to define the totalitarian state through civil society, at least until new possibilities have been disclosed by the demise of state socialism and the triumph of global neoliberalism. Therefore, some relevant questions remain: how can anthropology contribute to define the applied use of civil society in conditions of neoliberal capitalism? What are the outcomes of the increased tension between locally based and transnationally spreading movements? Is there such a thing as a genuinely local civil society? What are the social and ideological bases on which strategies of resistance to state and global intrusion are developed from below? Which practices are more commonly ascribable to the influence of a past post-socialist condition? Under which conditions does the EU enlargement process foster a general strengthening of civil society in the new member states? What is the role of the state?

Practices of civil society in post-socialist Eastern Europe

There are two apparently conflicting views of the development of civic movements in post-socialist Europe. One indicates a generalized weakness of civil society as a common feature of the transition processes of Eastern European countries. The second argues about the actual dynamism, plasticity and richness of the civil society organizations and movements, although with some relevant differences between these and Western European countries after 1989. These two positions are apparently irreconcilable because they deal with the same problem but under different premises. The first assumes that to study the level of civic engagement in Eastern Europe it is necessary to pursue a comparative, often quantitative methodological perspective not only within this half of the continent, but more significantly with the other half. The second, taking a prevalently qualitative approach, investigates similarities and dissimilarities of the movements, organizations and alike, which are considered as products of the post-socialist transformation and the EU enlargement process. Hence, arguably, the two approaches could positively complement each other, as has been recently achieved in some of the studies reviewed below (see also Torsello 2008). It is beyond the scope of this chapter to present a general and comprehensive introduction of the development of civil society in post-socialist Europe. In what follows I will sketch out some of the most recurrent analytical trends of these works, trying to compare their findings in order to provide a general picture of the way in which civil society 'in action' is studied by the social sciences.

The first position, which denounces the weakness of civil society in Eastern Europe has been put forward, among others, by Howard's influential book (2003). Howard deals with civil society conceived of as 'a crucial part of the public space between the state and the family, and embodied in voluntary organizations' (2003: 1). He begins his theoretical introduction discerning between two analytical approaches to the study of post-socialist Europe: the first focussing on the novelties of the transition in these regions, and introducing a more general comparative framework including, for instance, Latin American countries. The second, the legacies approach, moves from the idea that what has been inherited from the socialist period cannot be completely overlooked, thus this approach actually focuses on differences and novelties in the post-socialist experience. His three case studies include Russia, Eastern and Western Germany, studied through the use of three indicators: contemporary economic well-being, political institutions and civilization. The term civilization, which sounds immediately odd to an anthropologist, is by him introduced with the meaning of cultural factors, or, as the author underlines it: 'different cultural and religious civilizations' (2003: 4). In spite of his claim against a cross-country analytical approach to civil society, Howard often makes use in the book of aggregate-level national data and quantitative indicators on world countries not included in his case studies. One example is the use of statistic data to prove the low level of participation of post-communist countries in politically oriented civic movements, such as parties and environmental groups (2003: 66–7). This is done contrasting three groups: older democracies, post-authoritarian countries and post-communist countries. The result of his analysis points out that the differences among post-communist countries are differences 'in degree' and not 'in kind' (2003: 70) showing that these countries scores much lower than countries of the other two categories (including South Africa, South Korea and most Latin American countries) and that differences among post-communist nations are minimal.

Howard builds his argument from an initial critique of Hann's contribution. Although he declares to agree with Hann's point about the western-central bias of the commonly used notion of civil society, he refuses the possibility to enlarge the sphere of categories of civic involvement when dealing with Eastern Europe. This, in his view, would only lead to more confusion and to an excessive fragmentation of the empirical findings (2003: 48–50). Thus, he suggests that the only productive way to map the actual participation of citizens in civil society and to avoid limiting the analysis to numbers of organizations is to make use of national survey data (such as the New Democracies Barometer, presently Eurobarometer, and World Value Survey). These data collections would allow for a measurement of the percentage of respondents who are members of civic organizations. His results are the following: citizens in post-socialist countries maintain strong feelings of mistrust in voluntary organizations due to their communist experience; they continue to make use of friendship networks that are disincentive to the development of voluntary organizations; they feel generally disappointed with the current economic and political results of their countries, and this refrains them from joining public organizations (2003: 148).

Although one could argue that some of these results could have been reached without thousands of surveys and in-depth interviews by reading some of the conspicuous anthropological literature on post-socialism, it is important to underline the methodology through which Howard reaches such a conclusion. This method is very similar to that adopted by Robert Putnam in detecting the differences in civic engagement between southern and northern Italy (Putnam 1995). The several critiques towards Putnam (Tarrow 1996), as well as to Howard (Badescu et al. 2004) raise two major problems with these approaches. Although Howard agrees with Hann for the need to imply different conceptions of civil society in the analysis he proposes, he fails in doing so, as Putnam failed taking into account the different historical and institutional factors that account for the south-north differences in Italy (Viesti 2009). This leads to another point, the use of culture ('civilization') as the main order of variables that account for the national differences. Howard never precisely engages with this factor, thus the reader is led to take it for granted, as it is in most of the quantitative measures in which it has a coefficient similarly to GDP or political participation. If one takes cultural explanations as fixed variables, such as for instance 'deferent attitude towards authority', the self-reflexive and pluralist nature of civil society becomes rather obfuscated.

In spite of these perplexities, Howard's book has become very influential in the debate over the weakness of civil society in Eastern Europe, judging from the number of works and studies that quote his contribution. In particular, the culturalistic approach has been the pretext for the development of methodological debates over the need to respond to critiques coming from anthropology. One such work, particularly interesting for its open critique to anthropological views of post-socialist civil society is the one by Jan Kubik (2005). Kubik praises Howard's approach especially because it proposes innovative methodological approaches to the comparative study of civil society in Western and Eastern Europe. He underlines the significance of taking into account differences among Eastern European countries such as those countries which joined the EU and those who did not (at the time of his writing), as well as from those where 'generational change' could account for the consolidation of new values in countries less distant from the west (2005: 112). The interesting point of his analysis, at the methodological level, is his proposal of avoiding the common measurement of civil society by number of associations and memberships, and replacing it with measurements based on two notions: the quality and connectedness of these movements (2005: 114). This is done, following the historical approach of Bermeo and Nord on Nineteen century Europe (2000), through four parameters: secondariness, transparency, tolerance and legality. These respectively lead to methodologically assessing the way in which civil society becomes secondary to domestic groups;[8] the accountability of these organizations; their horizontal democratic practices and discourses; their vertical inscription and compliance within state legal and normative systems (2000: 114–16). According to these premises, in order to build a 'non-canonical' model of Eastern European civil society it is necessary to investigate the way in which this allows organizations above kinship level to mediate family-kinship-state relations and counterbalance the state intrusion and monopoly. The conclusion of his argument is that Howard's is the attempt which had come closest to achieve the goals of what he terms the 'project of civil anthropology' (2005: 120).

In a study of civil society in post-Soviet Ukraine, Stepanenko (2006) makes similar arguments to Howard's thesis on the weakness of the notion in these regions departing, however, from a different standpoint. He declares to be more interested in understanding the meaning of this weakness rather than comparing it to western European realities. He assumes the following: that Ukraine is among those

---

8 Anthropologists are for him the best sources for assessing such a separation, although he does not quote any single ethnographic study, but then he concludes that they have been busier in detecting incongruences and ethnocentrism between western and eastern models than at pointing out alternative forms or models.

countries with an 'unfinished revolution', i.e. where energy of the transformation has been conveyed in the creation of a nation-state (574), that in the 1990s there have been a misleading attribution of civic organizations to the establishment of organizations which were heirs of formerly pro-governmental institutions, that almost the 40% of the interviewed people did not know the meaning of the term 'civil society' and finally that in the decade 1994–2004 the number of those not belonging to any form of association remained roughly constant at about 80%. To explore the real meaning of the 'weakness' of civil society in Ukraine he proposes a kind of socio-cultural and psychological approach (he terms it ethno-psychological characteristics). One of these explanations concerns the actual number of organizations in the country, which is not as low as expected, but which does not reflect the number of active associations. This is to him explainable according to the 'cultural propensity' towards being involved in more than one activity, similarly found in informal economy practices. The second example demonstrates the weakness of philanthropic culture in the country, attributed by him to low generalized trust. Finally, he resorts to the 'clientelistic culture' argument (580) which would explain the resilient patronage in a number of these associations, and the actual weak spontaneous development of a number of others. The outcome is that the prevalence of personalized social connections provides socio-psychological support to the dominant atomized structure in which civic organizations are weak and unequal.

A similar approach is presented by Gibson (2001) on the Russian case. Following Banfield's (1958), Granovetter's (1973) and Putnam's (1993) famous arguments, his empirical study of Russian social networks and mutual trust attempts to build predictions over the consolidation of civil society in Russia. Gibson assumes that a prevalence of social networks based on weak ties may become, coupled with a satisfactorily high level of interpersonal trust, the fertile ground for the development of civil society in Russia. On the other hand, 'un-civil' society is characterized by the atomization of its components and prevalence of strong ties, with particularistic and closed networks. In a paragraph titled 'Russia's un-civil society' (2001: 52) he follows common findings in the political science that point out at the lack of two crucial elements of civil society in contemporary Russia: interpersonal trust and a broad array of non-state voluntary organizations. In the end of his empirical analysis, based on surveys and face-to-face interviews, he reaches two conclusions. The first is that Russia would be dominated by large and dense social networks of weak ties, some of them legacies of the state socialism. These should in principle enhance the consolidation and diffusion of civil society, unfortunately, according to his findings; trust is 'not an issue' in these ties. This means that people who form organizations tend to be people who already share high levels of interpersonal trust, thus establishing trust does not constitute a precondition for civil society building.

A somewhat more critical approach to Howard's positions is the one developed by Badescu et al. in their study of Romanian and Moldovan civic organizations (2004). Their position is critical about the comparison between Eastern and

Western Europe because the level of membership in civic associations is different, and the same applies to their activities as well as to the personal profiles of the activists. Their general quantitative findings, however, seem to prove the weakness argument. Accordingly, only 18% of citizens are actively involved in civic organization, and their weekly time spent in the associations is one-third of that spent in Western European countries. They explain the weakness paradigm on a number of case studies from the two countries and present as main factors the scarcity of resources and economic incentives: lower general level of education among members, the short time to dedicate to association activities (also due to the need to engage in secondary economic practices to make ends meet), the 'tension between goals in the future and a materialistic orientation about the present' (2004: 327). One organizational reason for this weakness found by them is in the nature of NGOs which would develop according to the availability of western funds, and hence are not motivated by real local social interests. Therefore, such organizations would remain largely unattached to local society and hence privilege small bases of membership.

A more empirically and qualitatively solid study is provided by Anhaier et al. (2000) on the nature of Eastern German civic movements. The study investigates the development of a number of associations in different social fields and finds an intriguing paradox. On the one hand, a large number of these organizations consolidated as forms of large institutional transfer from Western German organizations (mainly in the fields of health and social provisions). On the other hand, Eastern Germany has also developed a large number of smaller civic organizations, rooted in the local territories and usually characterized by comparatively narrow bases of membership. These later organizations operate mainly in fields which were prohibited or absent during socialist times: political organizations, recreational centres and environmental groups. Although they find a similar West-East rate of membership per population (around 60–40%), the general membership is almost the half in the eastern territories (26% versus 50% of the surveyed cases). The paradox of these two different types of civil society existing in parallel in Eastern Germany is resolved paying attention to the normative role of the state in the Federal governments. Germany has a long tradition of state legal support to the subsidiarity principle. According to this agreement, the state funds a number of locally based organizations which cooperate with state institutions in the welfare and health sectors. This explains the proliferation of a dense network of large organizations deriving from the Western Ländern which operates in complementarity or even within the state sector. On the other hand, those small associations which developed in other sectors do not receive state support, and can be identified as the true products of Eastern European civil society development. Their memberships and activities are, due to lack of support funding, much more reduced, but in a way more spontaneous.

In a qualitative study on Polish women NGOs and other civic organizations Brunell (2002) takes the challenge of investigating empirically the nexus between the third sector, the state and the Catholic Church. Her study confutes the common idea post-socialism created a perverse mechanism exemplified through a zero-sum game perspective of the development of civil society, hampered by the transition from state protection to market predation (Einhorn 1993). Brunell presents two empirical studies from the cities of Krakow and Lodz. In them she notices different degrees of independency and self-reflexivity of organizations established with the goal of protecting women's' rights and psychological health. These organizations are structured according to different strategies and policy frameworks. In the first case, in Krakow, the civic organizations and NGOs are constantly confronted with the Catholic Church, which is often the favourite partner of public administration in promoting projects for supporting women's rights (such as in the case of domestic violence). This happens even though religious charity associations, some of which have extremely large national umbrella of organizations, are not necessarily trained in the special task they file their bid for. On the other hand, in the case of Lodz she found a higher degree of local government's participation in the third sector. This happens because the city has, as in most of Central Eastern European urban centres, a distinct budget for third sector initiatives. In this case, there is a tendency towards the development of 'patronage networks' that allow for an accurate distribution of state (and EU) funds to city-controlled resources (Brunell 2002: 485). In spite of this formal-informal interplay, this system has a wide spectrum of coverage of different activities, especially in the social sphere, which leaves space to small and medium-size civic organizations to establish networks of cooperation on the basis of mixed formal and informal ties.

The study by Cellarius and Staddon (2002) provides an insightful picture of the environmental NGO sector in Bulgaria. The authors follow three theoretical premises: the problematic nature of the state-oriented versus society-oriented approaches to political change and the revival of civic movements, the expected withdrawal of the state from post-socialist societies, and the excessively politicized role of the new movements within national and international funding schemes. Refusing the 'propagandistic' modernity-approach on the resurgence of civil society in Eastern Europe, the authors argue that the nature of these movements and organizations is extremely complex and often amorphous. This complexity is produced by a number of factors that are, in sequence, treated within the article. The first concerns the number and size of NGOs. Although general data indicate the existence (to 2001) of about 206 environmental NGOs in Bulgaria, this number is problematic since many of them are gemmating from other existing organizations in the moment of submitting applications for funding. Concerning size, the general trend is towards medium-small entities, with only less than 20% with over 150 members. This is, also, a matter of concern and emphasizes that people become involved under very specific circumstances and often under instrumental and personal conditions (205). The relationship with the state and public structures is of difficult definition. Cellarius and Staddon indicate that the neoliberal style of supporting civic organizations increasingly through foreign and international donors and organisms is at odd with the spontaneous and local-oriented nature of these movements. Because of the paucity of philanthropic donations in the country, most NGOs depend on foreign aid which is (as in the case of EU funding) often filtered through state or local governmental institutions. This openly shows a flaw of the bridging nature of civic society between state and society, and eventually render it further dependent on the state. On the other hand, incomplete and inaccurate legislation of the third sector in Bulgaria at the time of the ethnographic investigation is another factor which accounts for the difficulty to trace a clear distinction between state and civil society competencies, range of activities and mutual responsibilities.

These, and a number of other empirical studies on civil society in Eastern Europe have pointed out at the complexity of dealing comprehensively with the problem. One important conclusion seems to be that the operational use of civil society is much more useful a platform for comparison among these countries, both between them and with western European countries. If the application of western theoretical models is, to say the least, at odd with many of the social phenomena, movements, institutions and organizations which developed in this half of Europe since the 1990s, at applied level use of the notion of civil society is more justifiable. This happens because, as some of the mentioned cases and those present in the volume illustrate, the nexus with international organizations (sponsors and other civic organizations) is actively sought to counterbalance two important conditions of shortage: the general public's low participation and concern for the civic organizations and their activities, and the lack of independent and private funds. The interplay of these two conditions alone points out at the major difference, so far, between western and eastern civil society at the operational level: the stronger degree of state dependency of the latter versus the former.

Chapter 3

The Ethnographic Study of Corruption

Scholars and academics may like it or not but corruption has become one of the most studied notions in the social scientific disciplines. This trend is well-rooted in Western intellectual debates over the relationship between the state and society, the state and the market, formal and informal, legal and illegal, black (grey) and white practices. Theorization attempts have followed different shifts in the course of these last three decades, moving from an evolutionary concern for the historical forms of corruption in the western world (Scott 1972; Heidenhaimer 1989) to its influence on political factions and parties (Della Porta and Vannucci 1999; Kawata 2006), its anti-normative, functional role in political systems (Leff 1964; Huntington 1968; Montinola and Jackman 2002), its nexus with democracy, civil society and development (Bardhan 1997; Rose Ackerman 1999; Doig and Theobald 2000; Johnston 2005). In spite of the different perspectives, most of these works agree on the idea that corruption is a pervasive phenomenon of the present times. The best exemplification of this being the number of scholarly (not to mention of course strategy and policy) papers and books written on corruption in the last two decades only.

One of the most striking features of the corruption boom in the social science is the absence of anthropology. A World Bank review (2006) notices that anthropological studies dealing with corruption cover about 2% of the relevant scientific literature. The loneliness of this drop in an ocean has its own justification, as I will argue below, and more importantly, ethnographical accounts of corruption are badly needed, as not only scientists, but policy makers and think-tank organizations denounce it (Andvig 2001). For one thing, corruption is a social practice, other than a narrative (Kerby 1991), and, especially considering the recent critiques to the efficacy of large-scale, quantitative analyses, and the need to complement them with qualitative research, ethnography can play an important role in filling this gap. Having said this, there are a number of problems with which anthropologists confront in the study of corruption. First, there are basic ethical concerns that fieldworkers raise when dealing with the study of such practices, stemming out of issues such as the anonymity of informants, the use of gathered data and the role of the anthropologists as 'intruder' in the social reality he is observing (see Atkinson and Hammersley 1983; Clifford and Marcus 1986). Second, although most of social scientists agree on the damages of corruption, it is not always absolutely clear what corruption is about. Anthropologists have been at unease with western-centred ideas of corruption, and this is immediately reflected by the reluctance of some of them to engage with it. Third, corruption is not a genuinely endemic phenomenon, as much of the modernist literature seemed to point out some decades ago. Today there is increased awareness, both on the side of specialists and of policy makers, that corruption is fostered and generated by foreign aid, development projects, international relations and global capitalism. In increasingly blurred political arena ethnographic fieldwork is not an easy undertaking. The very nature of fine-grain ethnography develops in the constant interaction of the researcher with local inhabitants, the construction of mutual trust within social groups and personal networks with whom he shares a significant part of their daily lives. The ethnography of translocal places is a much thorny effort, in spite of the several (and also partly successful) attempts in recent times (Melhuus et al. 2010). Again, not only is the focus of investigation enlarged and difficult to grasp, but access to information becomes a delicate matter of difficult resolution.

In spite of all these problems there have been, at least in the last fifteen years, a steady increase in anthropologically informed works on corruption. This chapter provides a critical review of a large part of this literature, an effort so far neglected. I do not intend to provide an all-exhaustive review, also because a number of publications are not directly dealing with corruption, and it would be problematic to enlist them thematically. My aim is to detect a number of themes which are the most recurrent in the anthropology of corruption and which, to my view, are relevant to this volume. These themes will be dealt with attention to the detailed (and often neglected) contributions that ethnographic studies have provided to the debate on corruption.

Methodological issues

Arguably, while the other social sciences were already struggling with worldwide denounces of corruption before it came to be declared as to be one of the worst diseases of mankind (OECD 2005), anthropology stayed silent. The word 'corruption' had not been used in any title of books in anthropology after James Scott's famous contribution (1972) and until 2004. Moreover, it is only after 1995 that corruption becomes present at a highly irregular base in titles of articles in academic journals. What are the reasons for this silence? I think there are two explanations, one of which is currently used to distance the discipline from mainstream – mainly political science and economics' – corruption theories, i.e. the Eurocentric nature of the notion. Anthropologists dealing programmatively with corruption have all underlined that the common understanding of the notion is not easily applicable to the sociocultural contexts they have been studied since the beginning of ethnographic fieldwork in the early 20th century.

One of the most common definitions of corruption is 'the abuse of a public office for private benefits and gains'. This definition is problematic in its very essence for anthropology: the dichotomy private-public, informed by the Weberian rationality of the western bureaucratic machinery is context-specific. Anthropological studies of pre-capitalist societies, as well as those of postcolonial societies, have raised abundant evidence to the point that the opposition public-private is, to say the least, blurred in these societal contexts. From whatever side one wishes to take it, the public sphere is not easily defined, rationally, in opposition to the private one, where economic and political strategies, structures and representations constantly bring about the primary necessity to bridge, or to find a constant contact between the two spheres. Institutions are rules of the games also in anthropological evidence, but they are so in that they are made up by people, through their agencies, discourses, ideas which do not necessarily reproduce the kind of artificial reality present in a vacuum that the Weberian rationality called for. Hence, anthropology cannot feel at home with such a definition for the practical reason that virtually all the anthropological scholarship on non-western societies proves the incongruence of this point.

This brings to the second point, the less evident one. Anthropology has remained rather silent about corruption through the past years not because it snubbed this notion, but because it was actively engaging with other concepts that form the bread and butter of corruption. Anthropology's earlier accounts of gift exchange processes, solidarity, reciprocity, redistribution, informal economic practices and transactions, moral economy, clientelism and patronage, nepotism, cronyism, networks analyses are some of the most evident fields in which the discipline was actually the pioneer rather than the latecomer. All these fields, as has come clear today, are the lymph of corruption practices, and not only in non-western societies. Zinn (2001) has argued that anthropology has chosen, after raising the dust on these topics, to remain silent partly for fear of cultural essentializations, partly for a feeling of responsibility on the misuse of some of its discoveries that have contributed to increase the ideological gap between a 'modern', 'rational' and 'transparent' West and the rest, as Sahlins famously remarked. I think the problem is slightly more complex than this. Anthropology continues to engage actively with all these fields (exception due perhaps with clientelism and nepotism), because they are part of the social realities the ethnographer faces while doing fieldwork. The difference is that these practices and ideas are no more labels of the non-western world only: after anthropology has moved into the field classically dominated by sociology, after the end of the colonial period and the disastrous war events of the 1960s, it has discovered that many of these themes were actually, under different spoils present also in less exotic societies. Anthropology, thus, has not discovered directly corruption, because the idea is a western one, and the discipline did not have the methodological and epistemic tools to deal with it in the way other social scientific disciplines were doing.

Common research fields

The study of corruption is an extremely complex endeavour particularly from a methodological viewpoint. The two disciplines that have contributed most actively to the theorization of the notion are political science and economics. Each of the two has departed from a set of assumptions which serve to delineate the field, to build fences outside which one can no more be dealing with corruption. The complexity of this endeavour is best understood when one considers the current difficulties of governments, international organizations and anti-corruption movements to make a clear picture of the situation. In spite of the several founded research projects, international conventions, the recent cries of World Bank, United Nation, OEDC and the EU for a common act of fight against this global disease, one thing has become clear: there is no such a thing as a remedy to this phenomenon. The most eloquent example is the work of Transparency International (TI). Anthropologist Steve Sampson has recently pointed out how TI, through its regular issues of the famous Corruption Perception Index (CPI) has raised public awareness, shaping the way how nations and leaders should think about their responsibilities towards the world (Anving 2001). It is however, no more than that, as Sampson (2010) stresses. One may easily wonder how can the CPI be trusted when a country scoring almost regularly among the top 20 positions, Japan, is inherently corrupt in its informal, legal and semi-legal political practices so to feel the need to issue a number of official publications and manuals (among which manga) for public officers who do not know the real nature of corruption. Another observer may also wonder about the usefulness of a ranking which esteems the assessed performance of countries over the years and present a picture for some of them, for example Central Eastern European countries, which every two-three years move up and down the list losing or gaining twelve to sixteen places. Even the most attentive economist may realize with displeasure that among the top-eight economies only two (Australia and Canada) are listed in the top-twelve CPI positions, among the least corrupt nations, is this alone a sign that efficient market capitalism is not the cure for corruption? Or yet another demonstration that corruption is both dysfunctional and functional to economic performance, as the case of Italy brilliantly suggests?

If grand theories on corruption such as the modernity approach, the market efficiency approach or the democracy approach have failed, it is in micro-level and fine theoretical understanding of the notion that interdisciplinary communalities can be searched for. Even though not always recognizing it, the social scientific disciplines have discovered through the years a number of fields in which their operationability intersect. I am thinking about the role of the state, the moralities of corruption and anti-corruption movements, the distinction between ideas and discourses of corruption, the difference between grand and petty corruption and the so-called cultural features of corruption. Each of these elements or fields of study presents a real challenge to the scholar who wishes to empirically test the applicability of the notion of corruption to the analyses of socio-political practices. I argue that ethnographic studies dealing more or less explicitly with corruption have been actually able to raise a number of points which have proved of significant contribution to the understanding of this phenomenon and of its consequences. This has happened, although at different extent, in all these thematic fields which will be here treated, for the sake of the review effort, separately.

The role of the state

There is scarce agreement in the mainstream literature whether the state plays a major or a minor role in relation with the diffusion of corruption in society. Some theorists argued that a strong state can be seen responsible for the presence of corruption, especially when it tends to function as a totalitarian or monopolizing agent. Putting the argument very simply, a strong degree of state control and of intrusion in social and economic institutional relations is not a deterrent to corruption. This argument has been 'traditionally' used to explain the widespread presence of corruption in authoritarian regimes, as well as in monopolistic states, what economists call 'kleptocracies', 'rent-seeking states' or 'predatory states'. Corruption is conceived as an outcome of widespread interpenetration of the economic and political sphere, which reduces competition and increase privileges, facilitating the creation of powerful elites and cliques operating as, to use a popular term in Italian politics, castes (Sun 2004; Johnston 2005b; Varese 2005).

On the other hand, a weak state is also breed for corruption. Here the African case is paramount: the dissolution of the colonial and postcolonial states is considered the historical origin of the everyday presence of corruption at all levels of social interaction. Here, again, some catchy concepts have been developed such as that of 'neo-patrimonial' state, or 'belly-state'. The weakness of the state structure is seen as providing porous interstices to the multiplication of power battlefields and actors. As in the strong state argument, no single solution against the phenomenon can be envisaged.

Anthropology has provided sophisticated ethnographies of the state in relation to a number of political and social phenomena and cultural practices (Sharma and Gupta 2006). Following the influence of Foucauldian interest for issues of power, knowledge, discourses and governmentality (even though sometimes neglecting government, see Holmes 2000; Wilson 2000), ethnographic accounts of the role of the state in relation to corruption have taken different standpoints. One has been to analyze the legislative functions and spaces in which the state deals with corruption in different societal contexts. This approach is evident in Pardo (2004) and in the recent book by Nuijten and Anders (2007). Nuijten and Anders have entitled their edited volume 'The secret of law', stressing the idea that the common western-informed notion of corruption as dichotomic between public and private also applies to the dichotomy state-society. In this perspective, they argue, there is no space for a positive ethnographic contribution to the study of the notion, since it cannot be grasped by the traditional western legalistic understanding. Because the possibility of transgression is always present in law, corruption is to them the very secret of law, which defines its fields of application and intervention, but meanwhile allows for its depletion in society. Hence a normative approach to corruption, departing from a law-making state at the top is misleading because law is plural. Therefore it is only through sensibility for its pluralism that corruption can be successfully detected through its nuances as alternative form of legal order.

Pardo (2004), and within his edited book in particular the contributions by Prato, Humphrey and Sneath, Gledhill make a similar point but from a different angle. For him the conceptualization and definitions of political and legal nature on corruption are marked by inherent ambiguities. Unlike many of his colleagues (see Haller and Shore 2005 for instance) Pardo, who conducted fieldwork research in southern Italy, recognizes that anthropology is confronted with the difficult balance of historical and ethnographic variations and universal aspects. He understands that one of the main limits of the anthropology of corruption has been its cultural particularism, and proposes two roads to overcome this impasse. The first is to look at morality (see below) as a conflicting battlefield in which social ideas of legality and illegality collide with universal claims and values. The second is to investigate the role of the state which, in his view, can be above the corrupt game, or more significantly part of it, participating 'through institutional blindness to allow the interests of the elites' (2004: 6). The state may even legitimize the ambitions of those corrupt politicians, who, claiming to re-attribute morality to political action, eventually make use of law-making to render more opaque the borders of legality and illegality. The state is in this perspective an active and not a passive agent undergoing the effects of corruption. Law is the sphere of significance and legitimacy through which corruption is accepted or rejected, conceived of and exploited by those in power.

Shore and Haller support a second perspective of the role of the state. Following the Foucauldian tradition, corruption is one of the ways in which people make sense of politics and of the state, like a conversation, a ritual or for some even like sorcery (Bubandt 2006). The issue is not whether the state has been able to set the boundaries between what is legal and illegal, morally acceptable or not, neither whether the state makes use of corruption to obtain public (other than private) legitimacy. Here focus is on the discursive practices and strategies that render corruption a semantic of governance. This approach is present in Gupta's ethnography of the Indian case, one of the most refined and earliest contributions in the anthropology of corruption. Gupta is interested in addressing ways how local citizens in India use corruption as a form of discourse (see below) in order to achieve access to particular benefits that are scarcely allocated. The strategy, he describes through two examples, is that of seeking information on ways to bribe properly, on the amounts of money to be paid and under which interactional conditions bribe are needed to access services provided by state officers of local governments. This is one form of discourse (information seeking) about corruption. The second is the way through which ordinary citizens address corruption in their everyday. The state is commonly denounced a 'profoundly corrupt' in this public talk. In spite of this, Gupta shows that the state is approached by ordinary citizens through personal relations with local officers who are able to make use of clientelistic networks to perpetuate their power at local level. This is alone a form of contradiction in the general western view opposing state and society: corruption is the space in which the state dissolves at local level and is replaced by a plethora of socio-cultural practices and relations. This underlines that the state is much more disaggregated and decentralized than it should appear. However, constant reference to corruption in public discourses (opposed to the private practices of bribery and patron-seeking) brings the state back into play: corruption becomes the venue in which the Indian state is constructed and given meaning in public talk.

This point is stressed by other works on the Indian continent, such as in Wade (1982), Kondos (1987), Price (1999) Ruud (2000, 2001). Sewanta, in an empirical study based on questionnaire survey conducted in Nepal (2009) has demonstrated how corruption is used by local citizens at discursive level to differentiate among the performance and capacities of a number of institutions from the police, to health services, the school and the post. As Gupta, he suggests that this discursive use does not necessarily lead local citizens to avoid engagement with state officials, but it actually works as a frame of reference to establish a flow of communication about best practices.

Conflicting moralities

The issue of an alleged lack of morality in those public officers who seek their own interest through bribes, gifts, favours and alike is another point of wide debate in the ethnographic approaches to corruption. As in the case of law, morality is not accepted as an homogenous underlining explanation of corruption by most anthropologists. Pardo's book is an exception: he insists on the importance of treating corruption through the analysis of different, often conflicting moralities that reflect the hierarchies and constellations of power through which corruption is deployed. Morality, is however, always used in plural by him and the other anthropologists who emphasize, theoretically or methodologically, the relevance of the ethical approach. This stems out of the idea that there is not a single morality on the confutation of which corruption is constructed, because moral stances are in continuous transformation and very much context-specific.

This perspective seems to contradict the classical approach of western political science and political philosophy which, drawing on Aristotelian traditions, has attempted to explain how and why certain societies are able to produce accountable, 'rational', and transparent forms of government whereas others cannot (see also Rothstein and Eek 2009). Morality is of course not the only answer, but it plays a major role in building what some have called social contract, others trust, cooperation, modernity and so forth seen at the core of democratic government. Moral claims are, however, undeniably important for the study of corruption. Anthropology's downplaying this aspect is not to be seen as intentional, but rather expression of the methodological approaches of ethnographic studies. On the one hand, the too often simplistic relationships that some of the northern American scholarship has through the years drawn between morality and development, social trust, social capital and civil society (Banfield 1958; Fukuyama 1995; Putnam 1995, 2000) has been theatre of long debates in anthropology, sociology and even political science (Silverman 1965; Miller 1974; Muraskin 1974; Tarrow 1996;

Meloni 1997). If the ethos, in Banfieldian terms, becomes *the* answer to socio-economic problematic phenomena, among which clientelism and corruption, then there would be little need of ethnographic and empirical works on these issues. It would be sufficient to establish some measurement scales for morals and values and to apply them in different regional contexts to detect variation patterns of corruption. However, one of the most problematic aspects of corruption is that it is highly social specific a notion, and it is almost impossible to draw generalization about its moral undertones. Although tempted to do so, there is not a single way a scholar could fruitfully apply the amoral familism paradigm to contexts as different as Latin America, Eastern Europe or Africa, and within them to different regions all affected similarly by this phenomenon. This is not to support the well-known anthropological claim for particularism, but it is to underline that methodologically the ethos approach alone does not work. The role of the state, the local tradition of social movements, the role of identity building ties, of informal networks and practices of exchange all have different meanings which, as Yang underlines for the Chinese case (2002), spring out of different cultural backgrounds at different strategic time points.

On the other hand, if morality plays a central part in ethnographic investigations of corruption, the problem is that it is a polysemic notion. Visvanhatan (2008) puts it in a vivid manner when he underlines the 'warm nature of corruption' against the 'cold of bureaucratic rationality'. Anthropological accounts of corruption have tended, sometimes even uncritically, to draw on the opposition between rational legalism and moral connectivism. Rational legalism is the framework in which bureaucratic, anti-corruption informed views of the social order should impose an efficient reality in which illegal practices, informality and shadow zones should be completely absent. Although none of the reviewed works explicitly makes use of this dichotomy for methodological purposes, it is present in many of these studies. This makes also a point about the distinction between grand and petty corruption, as below, but here it is necessary to understand the different social fields to which this distinction is applied.

Rivkin-Fish (2005), in a study of corruption in the Russian health care system shows that one of the functions of corrupt practices in postsocialist Russia is, unlike under socialism, not to work side-effectively to fill the gaps of the central planned economy, but to provide venues for generating mutual trust. Market economy, in her ethnography, has brought about what people feared the most: a lack of or a diminished space for social interaction, and corruption is used to fill this gap. In the study of a rural village in Slovakia (2003) I noticed a high degree of ambivalence between people practices and discourses of trust, particularly in institutions. In several cases people who had vehemently reacted against the municipal administration and the agricultural cooperative denouncing absolute mistrust in them, actually turned to these institutions for services and goods. This ambivalence was part of a set of strategies that he termed the need to 'invest in social relationships', which is a slightly different claim than Putnam's recent distinction between bonding and bridging social capital. The morality of actions was at issue there, and its implications for social arrangements: one could feel morally irreprehensible even if he said and did different things because the need not to lose contact with personal networks was generally to be hoped, desired and hence deemed as a value. Similarly, Rivkin-Fish describes how the gift and bribe system working in the health care sector in Russia (and common to all postsocialist Europe) has been strongly affected by the introduction of money in these transactions in recent years. Money can actually endanger the morality of corruption or, as it has been observed in several other mainly African contexts radically change it.

Oliver de Sardan (1999) in one of the most theory-oriented anthropological contribution to corruption makes use of the notion of 'moral economy' to refer to the African case. To him the key for understanding the widespread diffusion of corruption in the African continent is to look at its 'banalization and generalization' in everyday practices and discourses. He sees corruption as a realm of rumour and gossip, where the political and the social become intermingled and semantically determined for the single actors. Thanks to a number of culturally constructed practices (gift giving, brokerage, solidarity networks, predatory authority and redistributive accumulation) corruption becomes banalized, as commonly accepted and esteemed practice. In these contexts, according to him, actions which refuse openly and decisively compliance with such practices are amoral, because they provide space for egoism and lack of care for the others.

A similar point is made by Hasty, in an insightful study of anti-corruption officers in Ghana (Hasty 2005). Hasty had the privilege of being a journalist other than trained as anthropologist and this disclosed to him access to a number of documents and personalities which for 'common ethnographers' would have been easily out of reach. He describes the personal character and actions of an official working in anti-corruption public office who strived to maintain an image of integrity in spite of the many forms of desire that shape corruption as inherently social practices. Self-discipline is used as a counter-morality (my term) to the indulgement in these desires: the official Hasty described refused to take food and drink gifts (except for soft drinks) that are an extremely common in several African contexts, at the expenses of being seen as a bashful, asocial person who lives a retired life, and thus morally suspicious in his social environment. This behaviour is in open contradiction with the morality of corruption, in western Africa called 'to chop', or 'eat', where conviviality and participation in large and lavish banquets is seen as an almost natural consequence of the flow of material (money and wealth) and immaterial (power) desires.

From these approaches it emerges that corruption is often grounded in different, if not conflicting moralities. Not only is the polarization between public versus private good extremely problematic to most anthropologists. Also, the very idea that corruption should be deemed as amoral in an a prioristic perspective is to be rejected. The concurrence of a number of culturally determined, as well as historical (fruits of the profound institutional transformation of, for instance postsocialist societies and postcolonial states) factors and variables is to be taken into account when attempting to map these moralities and the ways they acquire public meaning.

Petty vs. processual corruption

The majority of the ethnographic works on corruption at pointed at the (more or less) hidden morality constructed on types of corrupt practices, which range from bribes, facilitation payments to tokens of mutual solidarity, gift exchange and interpersonal trust. Concerning this typology, one can stress that anthropological accounts have followed two directions. In the first, a number of studies have departed from the distinction between grand and petty corruption which allows anthropology to introduce themes and problems with which it has dealt extensively through the history of the discipline. Thus, petty corruption is the field which ethnographers can more effectively study, whereas large scale corruption deals and scandals are commonly not field of anthropological investigation for obvious methodological reasons. A second approach, however, transcends this distinction. In this approach corruption is the outcome of the conflicting influence of macro with micro forces, such as in development theory, in the process of institutional transformation and also in anti-corruption measures. This is not to state that this approach looks at grand corruption rather than at petty corruption, it rather focuses on a processual perspective of corruption, that looks at conflicting notions of legitimacy, of institutional change and the moral evaluations that different sets of actors attribute to such processes. I will sketch some examples of contributions in the two perspectives.

Among those scholars who have directly or indirectly dealt with petty corruption one can read an almost general tendency to equate this with other social practices about which anthropology have an established theoretical tradition. This equation is understandable from a mere methodological point of view, but problematic from an heuristic perspective. Methodologically, the ethnographer may be often exposed to observation of informality in economic transactions, semi- or illegal practices, clientelism and bribery. He is in the troublesome position to judge whose good are serving those practices. The tendency is to objectivize the meaning of those practices framing them into the sociocultural context of belonging, which leads to the above mentioned distaste of anthropologists for clear-cut categories.

One example is Yang's famous work on guanxi (personal connections) in China (1994). Guanxi, along with the notion of blat in Russia (Ledeneva 1998), has become a famous paradigm of petty corruption used not only by anthropologists. Yang, in a later writing (2002) reflects on the inappropriate use that some scholars have made of her interpretation of such practices which she saw emerging in the times of the Cultural Revolution as a way to shield people from conditions of excessive state inherence in the public life. She is preoccupied to treat guanxi not as a given set of cultural practices, but as historically specific product acquiring different meanings and deployments along ethnic, class, gender and even regional dimensions. Yang reacts to the uncritical use of guanxi and its recent development guanxixue (the economy of personal connections), to describe corruption in China as functional to the socialist and the newly emerged capitalist economies. Her argument is that guanxi has lost its role of being beneficial to many, a sort of civil society, to serve only the interests of few after the interpenetration of public with private sphere brought about by capitalist development in the country. The consolidation of business networks and their influence in politics is what account for the loss of the initial semantic and social use of guanxi, hence petty corruption expands to become a larger process, but to the benefits of mere elitarian powers.

Similarly, Bubandt (2006) offers an ethnographic description of the changing role of corruption in delocalizing Indonesia. Indonesia, after the end of the Suharto regime, has accomplished one of the world's most dramatic processes of decentralization of power, with the creation of a number of regional and local government centres even in areas where transport and communication is still difficult. In Indonesia, as in most of south-eastern Asia, corruption is a well-consolidated topic of public discourse, and increased preoccupation about its outcomes has supported the public call for regional reforms. Bubandt parallels corruption with witchcraft, showing that these two 'occult forces' are 'used as technologies to manipulate and transcend the large power of corruption, affecting the local sphere' (2006: 419). He tells the story of a local politician who, after a long negotiation for establishing a new provincial district, making use of legal and illegal means, became suddenly ill and died under unclear circumstances. The local interpretation for his (and that of two of his colleagues) death has been the use of witchcraft, connected with politics in a socially disruptive way, similarly to how corruption in petty local practices is used for achieving personal goals.

The problem with the petty corruption perspective in anthropology is that it can be used, often unproblematically, outside of ethnographic approaches to classify responses from below that are, otherwise, of difficult categorization. This becomes manifest in the tendencies to stigmatize sociocultural practices as widely attributed to one single nation, or even to cultures. Ideas such those of 'neo-patrimonial states', the 'belly state', 'network cultures', 'gift-exchange cultures' and many others become thus comfortable devices through which the analyst explains what he is not able to in terms of the grand (and western-centered) models of democracy, transparency, maximization of profit, civil society. Anthropologists are right to have remained external to such debates, and this has arguably characterized their distance from the study of corruption as well. However, throwing the stone is something and hiding the hand which threw it is another thing. The difference in approaches to petty and processual corruption is a demonstration that not all anthropologists remain sceptical of the analytical use of corruption, whereas all agree on the importance to maintain a critical standpoint to the universalities of its claim.

One example of the processual approach is the work by Shore (2005) where he analyzes corruption in the setting of the EU civil service. He challenges the Weberian legal-rational model of efficient bureaucracy addressing issues of fraud, nepotism and corruption in the European Commission following the 1999 scandals. The argument is that both institutional and cultural norms matter for identifying causes of endemic corruption at EU level, but the significant thrust is that shared administrative norms and codes of conduct, as well as mechanisms of accountability are missing. Corruption is here an outcome of the process of EU integration, bringing about the need to fuse together different traditions of civil service under the notion of supernationalism. However, instead of achieving a process of Europeanization, according to Shore, EU practices have sometimes become standardized over privileged, cronyistic types of networks which perpetuate their systemic ordering of elitarian systems of governance.

Another field where corruption is treated as a processual force is development. A number of ethnographic works (see Harrison 2010) have suggested that in general there tends to be more perception than real practices of corruption at local level beyond the petty corruption talk (Parry 2000). One explanation to this may be that excessive concern for corruption becomes a pessimistic reflection of the failure of development policies, market liberalization, decentralization and privatization (Harrison 2010). Anti-corruption rhetoric is rendered problematic by these approaches which see it as yet another way to justify western intervention in developing economies. Ethnographies in Africa and the Indian subcontinent portray how the high degree of generalization about widespread corruption and the outraging need for reform and policy intervention can actually mask a real need of more funding and donations to support state and local level intervention (including NGO activities to counter measure the 'corruption eruption' (Tanzi 1998). It is not accidental that the very political agenda of leaders, emerging elites and parties in these regions make of the fight against corruption one stronghold.

De Sardan argues that developmental practices in postcolonial Africa have favoured the spread of corruption and of an assistentialist culture (1999, see also Blundo et al. 2006). A similar trend is registred in Eastern Europe and the Balkan regions, where an umbrella of anti-corruption organizations and movements has mushroomed in the await of foreign aid and funding. Similar claims have been made about Latin American country, where corruption is not perceived as systemic to weak states unable to maintain their grip on local administrative centres and semiofficial figures of intermediaries between public and private authorities, as in the African case, but it is an integral part of the evergreen rhetoric of 'modernization' and 'democratization' by political leaders and their elites. The processual nature of corruption is in the case of development more a function of the ongoing relationship of dependence of these states, and their local governments on western powers as well as international organizations that make of corruption their flagship.

Cultural concerns

The very idea of a culture of corruption is suspicious to most anthropologists. Apart for a few of them (Lomnitz 1995; de Sardan 1999; Shore 2005; Smart and Hsu

2007), cultural concerns about the alleged prevalence of corruption in particular social and political contexts are only marginal fields of analysis. This may seem surprising to non-anthropologists, who are used to situate the contribution of this discipline in cultural analysis. Indeed, this is to my view, shared by Harrison, one of the motives that explain the comparative scarce contribution of anthropology to the debate. The problem is not that anthropology refuses to deal with culture, but that culture has been often misappropriated to draw on oversimplifications and generalizations.

However, it would be misleading to state that culture is absent from ethnographic accounts of corruption. Most of these have constantly engaged with the idea that cultural factors have influenced the ways how informal ties, semi- and illegal practices have been dealt with and gained meaning in societies. Perhaps one of the best examples in this direction is Lomnitz's study of corruption in politics in Mexico (1995). Lomnitz has been one of the few anthropologists (see also Scott 1972) who have seriously engaged with history to reconstruct the role of corruption as a cultural, other than political, practice. She departs from the analysis of the forms of local political power in Mexico under Spanish colonial rule to arrive to the times of national independence in 1917. The Bourbons had attempted to jeopardize the power of local and regional landlords by gaining control on the source of their influence, i.e. tax excision, through the institution of a bureaucratic apparatus depending on the crown for legitimacy and wealth. This process continued after independence, when the state faced the contradiction of having to grant local power as a way to brush up the past and needing to control it. Lomnitz shows that as a matter of fact a real process of centralization never completely took place and the state remained forced to negotiate with local authorities and elites. One of the strategies through which the state sought to maintain control of local elites was the institution of a public sphere of political discussion, which until the beginning of the 20th century was limited to rumour and gossip and did not develop in real horizontal structures of civil society. Thus, the state created, through political parties, associations and other forms of collectivities, a highly ritualized order in juxtaposition of the existing local one, based on vertical, hierarchical and clientelistic structures around influential kinship groups. At this point, however, public spaces became reoccupied by these vertical structures, through the institutions of local festivals (gradually deprived of their original religious meaning) where efforts in keeping alive local identities, especially against the background of an industrialization process, became one of the most effective channels of patronage. This has, according to Lomnitz, caused a general loss of trust in the state, and the consolidation of corrupt networks on local level through the cargo-like institution of local festivals. Therefore, the ritualization of local politics, which gradually took place from the period of the national independence, left the state in the awkward position of, paradoxally, having to foster corruption and patronage to extend its power onto local venues without being able to replace those cultural practices preceding national unification which underpinned corruption.

Lomnitz, as Yang for the Chinese case, is explicit about her use of the idea of cultural practices underlining the consolidation of corruption in Mexico. She does not refer to essential cultural features of the country, or of particular regions. Culture is a product of history, under peculiar social and economic conditions, and as such is subject to change, sometimes leading to expected, others to unexpected outcomes. The question remains, is culture a fruitful explanation for understanding the recourse to corruption? Ethnographies of corruption are not explicitly suggesting an answer to this question, what they have proven so far is that corruption practices and ideas are often rooted in more profound forms of social interaction that leave space for their deployment. This is made possible because of the concomitance of a number of factors which accompany profound institutional transformation be that in a postcolonial, postsocialist or neo-liberalist regimes. What is fundamentally relevant of these approaches to the study of corruption is that local level responses constitute developing strategies and not given sets of answers imposed top-down from a range of political choices. The political agency that corruption restitutes to people is one of the most interesting and promising fields of anthropological contribution, in spite of the attempts to reduce this field to mere stigmatization of cultures of corruption.

The power of words

Ethnographic studies of corruption have opened a new field, until recently highly neglected, that of discursive practices of corruption. Emerging out of the methodological limitations imposed by the fieldwork experience, anthropologists have faced issues of corruption often unexpectedly. In several cases ethnographers have confessed that their encounter with corruption was not intentional. Rather corruption was part of the expressive and communicative strategies of local people that the researcher could not avoid dealing with it (Gupta 1995, 2005). In this sense, as Gupta underlined it, corruption became a narrative, or at its extremes, a meta-language through which communicating anxieties, concerns and ideas of the ideal world. One should not overemphasize the discursive power of corruption, particularly under the intruding conditions of fieldwork. The presence of the ethnographer, quite often of foreign nationality, is what stimulates the verbal performance of the discussions and interviews with informants, hence overt denounces, often highly emotional, about corruption should be taken with a critical standpoint. However, a sensitive analysis of the ways in which discourses match or oppose to practices of corruption is highly contributive.

Ethnographic accounts of corruption have revealed another nature of the notion. Speaking about corruption is good, for two reasons. One is that this is a type of social practice that may contribute to build emotional ties of belonging, sharing and common identity (Zerilli 2005; Anders and Nujiten 2007). The same force of conviviality that ethnographers attribute to different forms of social interaction is sometimes observed in the case of corruption talk. Corruption talk, however, as some anthropologists have pointed out, have another important goal, that of permitting access to information. Corruption is about the management of information, about whom to bribe, how to bribe and at what extent (the amount of bribery). Only those who gain access to this information are able to get better deals out of common practices. This fundamental problem is often resolved through time-consuming interactions among clients or those who are in the position of paying bribes. One of the point confirmed by most of the ethnographic accounts on discursive practices of corruption is, in fact, that the briber does not ask the bribed how much he wants for his services (this may not be the case in corporate corruption though). Thus, common and public discourses on corruption have the second aim of disclosing and rendering accessible, often in an indirect way, information on the successful strategies to bribe which can commonly be acquired only through prolonged social interaction.

The discursive power of corruption is one of the most recent findings of anthropology in the field. It seems acceptable to affirm that there is indeed little to wonder about the stronger role that this theme will play in the near future on the debate over the cultural, national and regional differentiation of corruption. The most challenging aspect of this debate is perhaps that public perception of corruption can be measured not only against the kind and degree of bribes taken, and how the knowledge of these bribes is shared by the general public. Conversely, the kind and degree of corruption talk can provide an insightful framework for future analyses of corruption that take seriously the qualitative aspects of this phenomenon. In spite of the insightful ethnographic treatments on this line, there is nowadays a crucial need of more empirical research.

Following this final perspective, in the case studies presented in this volume I am interested to analyse the strategies through which corruption becomes a language that identifies, under particular temporal and spatial conditions, a language that identifies the environmental discourse. This will be done following two approaches. The first considers the ways in which environmental movements make use of allegations and facts of political and business corruption to communicate to local citizens the meaning of their forms of public protest. The second concerns the impact of generalized public talk about corruption, mainly initiated by media reports, on the local perception of the damages of corruption. This aspect will add to the efficacy of the environmentalist discourse as far as its open political stance is concerned.

Chapter 4

Case One: The Motorway Transport Project in Považská Bystrica, Slovakia

This chapter addresses the problem of how civil society engages with environmental damage brought about by a EU-funded structural development project in Slovakia. Slovakia has been considered as one of the "success stories' of economic development and civil society building among the post-socialist countries in Eastern Europe. One of the main keys to this success is the geopolitical location of the country, 'in the heart of Europe', as some leaflets wrote in the early 1990s, which has accounted for the attraction of vast foreign capital investments. Since its peaceful split from the Czech Republic in 1992, Slovakia's governments have followed contrasting political orientations which alternated initial phases of cautious liberalization with steady democratization and privatization in the second half of the 1990s. Following EU accession in 2004, the country is among the most dynamic economic realities in Central Eastern Europe, although several problems related to corruption, clientelism and political populism still persist.

The Slovak case is indicative of how local forms of civil society can gain strength and establish public legitimacy thanks to the growing divide between national and local political orientations. The main questions to which this chapter will seek answers are: what are the political and dialectical strategies pursued by local interest groups in order to buffer the damages of globalization? How far can corruption be used by civic organizations to question the credibility of local governments? Does the transnational scope of transport development projects affect the functions and form of civic organizations?

Collective engagement is often difficult in social and political contexts that are undergoing profound transformation, and measuring the extent of this engagement is a delicate process that needs an attentive social analysis. The danger is to follow theoretical models that are unable to be applied positively to empirical data collected on the ground. The case study deals with the implementation of one EU funded Trans-European Network project for the completion of the D1 highway crossing Slovakia. The project directly affects the environment and the rural landscape around the town of Považská Bystrica, as well as one inhabited section of the town itself.

The Trans-European Transport Network

Under the terms of the Maastricht Treaty, signed in 1992 and enforced in 1993, the European Union elaborated a complex plan of development of its transport network, named the Trans-European Transport Network (TEN-T). The project, which became operative in 1996, aimed at improving the transport of people and goods among the European Union states and along two main axes: the Mediterranean and Eastern Europe. The early project list, which included ameliorations to highways, speedways, bridges, sea and river transport, airports, harbors, included 14 interventions, all located in the western European member states. In 2004, following the EU Enlargement, the TEN-T was extended to include a total of 30 priority projects, half of them involving Central Eastern European countries.[1] Up until 2010 only 5 projects have been accomplished and 4 more have been completed only partially (all of them in Western Europe).

Although since 2001 the concern of the TEN-T development projects has sensitively shifted towards environmental pollution and the preference for transport systems alternative to road, presently about 70% of freight and up to 84% of people are still transported by road (Final Evaluation Report 2007: 21). Central Eastern European countries play a major role in this trend as most of the projects located on their territories are road projects.

Since the early stage of the projects funding has, constituted a major problem. By 2007 only one third of necessary investment had been made (Implementation of the Priority Projects... 2008). Therefore, the TEN-T financing scheme was corrected to increase its budget over the following five years. It is calculated that about 600 billion Euros will be needed, to accomplish the projects by 2020. The initial amount scheduled was 225 billion Euros, around one third of the amount presently considered (Mid Term Review 2010).[2]

The funding scheme has been improved since 2004 to include different sources of financing, from EU to private sources. One of the major actors in the funding process has been the European Investment Bank, with a turnover of 75 billion Euros in the period 2007–2013. Again, finding the ways to obtain funding is not an easy process. The slow path of the TEN-T is also explained by the complex trajectories that each project must follow in order to be approved and be prioritized. These steps include informal communication about the project, pre-application, a detailed application, and evaluation. Since 2004, approved projects receive a six-year funding scheme, with no need (as before) to re-assess the project and refund it year by year. This has helped to speed up certain projects, but has also led to many substantial

---

1 Of these projects, in 2005, 18 were railway ameliorations; two are inland waterway projects; one a sea transport project and the remainder highway, motorway and multimodal projects. The projects envisage the building of a total of 89,500 km of road, 94,000 km of railway, 11,250 km of inland waterway involving 210 inland ports, 294 seaports and 366 airports by 2020. See Implementation of the priority, 2008.

2 The overall budget for TEN-T is esteemed at 8.013 billion euro, of which 580 billion are to be contributed by the European Union. This is divided approximately into 500 billion granted through the Loan Guarantee Instrument (LGTT) sponsored by the European Investment Bank, and 80 billion through the Marguerite Fund, to support projects following Public Private Partnership (PPP).

problems. It has been assessed that this system proves particularly effective for large projects, that already foresee large budgets, whereas it tends to slow down smaller projects or make them less effective. The second order of problem is of a political nature. The informal negotiations which precede the project application tend to lack transparency. Also, since each country follows a different political itinerary in planning, assessing, funding and building, transnational projects tend to be delayed for bureaucratic problems. Delay in a project becomes the major cause for lack of EU funding, and it is no surprise if few projects, especially those involving the Corridors, can be carried out within schedule.

The third order of problem concerns the assessment of the road project's impact. One of the major concerns of the TEN-T projects is their environmental impact. Even though the TEN-T legislation is clear about the need to assess the potential damage on the environment, satisfactory assessment for each project is seldom achieved, often at a high cost.

A recent report has identified some of the main weaknesses of the TEN-T policy guidelines in the EU. Among them the following are particularly relevant to this volume:

- The concept of common/European interest as expressed in the Guidelines is vague and not operational and does not sufficiently emphasize 'European added value'.

- The current network is mainly identified in a bottom-up approach. In addition, projects also lack focus which leads to dilution of resources, this in turn results in a failure to achieve a 'network' perspective [...] In addition, TEN-T projects do not always focus on areas with the highest transport demand and are not always based upon reliable traffic predictions

- As the lion's share of investment (73% between 2007–2013) has to come from national budgets or private financing, public budget restrictions and inappropriate prioritization lead to project delays and sub-optimal investments.

- The Guidelines do not provide sufficient flexibility to reflect changes/ evolution in transport policy; there is also no provision for establishing common datasets for the monitoring and evaluation of the TEN-T network, negatively affecting policy formulation and the setting of priorities.

- The current Guidelines are unable to focus on chronic bottlenecks in cross-border areas, which prevents network optimization (Final Report Expert Group 2 2010: 7–8).

As will be seen in the four case studies in this volume, all these points are relevant to the unfolding of diverse strategies of an economic and political nature that see a confrontation between political layers (from state to regional and local governments) and civil society.

The far-reaching character of the TEN-T scheme is best understood when considering that it is not a transport system limited to the EU member states, but that it actually aims to integrate the old and new members with future potential members, as well as with Russia. The overall transport scheme is organized around ten corridors which connect Western Europe with Eastern Europe, the Balkans and Turkey. In this study the section of Corridor V are taken into exam. The corridor is planned to reach the Ukrainian border through three branches: Venice- Ljubljana-Budapest, Zagreb-Budapest and Sarajevo-Budapest. One additional branch, the one being examined, connects Bratislava with the Slovak-Ukrainian border, cutting across the whole of Slovakia and interconnecting with Corridor VI, which runs from Brno-Katowice to Gdansk and from Žilina to Katowice on the Slovak-Polish border. The project being examined in this chapter belongs to Priority Project 25,[3] the Gdansk-Brno-Vienna-Bratislava motorway (TEN-T Priority Axes 2005).

Slovakia is characterized by a marked regional disparity in economic and structural development terms between the western and the eastern regions. The western part, where the capital Bratislava is situated, has a GDP per capita that is higher than the EU average, whereas the eastern regions are well below average. Considering the proximity of the Bratislava region to Vienna, Budapest and Brno, it is no surprise if 32% of existing national roads are concentrated in this region, whereas the eastern part has fewer than 10%. Therefore, the motorway development projects in the country focused on reducing this gap, and on supporting the creation of a triangular corridor system linking these two regions with a northern connection to the Polish border. This case study lies in the proximity of the vertex of this triangle.

Regarding its portion, in 2007 Slovakia reached an operational agreement on transport development with Brussels for a total budget of 3.8 billion Euros (one third of the overall EU investment for the country in the period 2007–2013). The scheduled projects include railway (around 34% of the funding) and road infrastructure development. The projects will cover the modernization of about 170 km of roads and 200 km of railway. The TEN-T scheme is expected to fund approximately 1.8 billion, and the remaining 1.4 billion will come from the EU Cohesion Fund (Operational Programme 2008).

The case study: the Považská Bystrica highway

Považská Bystrica (hereinafter PB) is a town of 42,000 inhabitants in northern Slovakia. The town is located half way between the two industrial centres of Trenčin and Žilina in the area where Slovakia borders Poland and the Czech Republic.

---

3   In 2008, 443 km of the project were completed out of a total of 1185 km. The overall cost is esteemed at 6.85 billion euro (Implementation of the Priority Projects 2008).

Under the former regime, its region constituted one of the most important heavy industrial centres in the country, but nowadays it has much less to offer in terms of jobs, save for the recently developed KIA manufacturing plant in Žilina (see below).[4] It was in the first half of the 1970s that the earliest plan for a highway, crossing Slovakia from Bratislava to the Ukrainian border, was conceived. The Slovak highway was planned to circumvent the town of PB, as there was no other way to cut through the valley in which the town lies.

By 1996 seven different variants of the highway traversing PB were under discussion. The problem was to find a solution which would balance the environmental impact and the costs, since it had become clear that it would not be possible to avoid to go through the town. 1996 was also the year when the long battle over the highway started. On the one hand, the municipal and county offices had to find a quick and feasible solution in order to be able to apply for the EU funding scheme which was due to be made available after 2004. On the other hand, changes in the local and national political attitudes towards the case instilled in some of the town inhabitants the idea that a dangerous game was being played against their will.

In December 2006, a group of citizens led by two key figures, a teacher and an engineer, founded two environmental organizations to protest against the highway project. The creation of the NGOs[5] ((Dialnica a ludia, Dialnica a priroda, The highway and the people, The highway and nature) was the first formal step towards the mobilization of local civil society, and thanks to them the focus of the protest shifted from informal to formal meetings where local authorities were asked to shed light onto the project. The main line of the protest concerned two points: the environmental impact of the planned highway on the town and the rural landscape and the dispossession and expropriation of land, houses and shops which happen to be located under the highway. In fact, while the road variant proposed under socialism did not actually cross the town, the city of PB passed a second variant (V2a) in 1996 which envisaged a flyover bridge of between 22 to 34 metres high which would cross one section of the town. The result would entail the removal of at least two town streets, and the construction of 500 new flats destined to compensate the dislocated families. Moreover, for those who lived in

---

4   The KIA manufacturing plant was established in the Slovak town of Žilina, 33 km from PB, in 2007. This constitutes the car manufacturing company's first assembly plant in Europe, creating almost 10,000 jobs in the region with a production capacity of almost 300,000 cars. The Slovak government conceded financial aid of 43 million euro for the development of the plant, as well as transport facilities (a completed highway from Bratislava) and special living facilities for KIA managerial staff.

5   Throughout the text the civic organizations that are object of analysis will be also denominated as NGOs. Although I am aware of the limits that this denomination bears, as well as of the methodological dangers of equating uncritically civil society with non-governmental organizations, I decided to follow this use merely focusing on the economic and technical aspects of these that are all non-profit and formally acting outside the state institutional apparatuses.

flats above the fifth floor, new anti-noise windows would have been installed. The NGOs, backed by research reports commissioned to academic experts, proposed two other variants which would bypass the town, one of which via a tunnel.

Meanwhile, a first petition[6] was signed by some 1600 people, who asked for a reassessment of the city variant. In 1997 the first Environmental Impact Assessment (EIA) required by national and EU laws took place. The three ministries of Transport, Environment and Traffic recommended four variants, none of which was the one proposed by the city. A second EIA was undertaken in 2001, producing three recommended variants. In spite of the results of the EIA, the municipal administration decided for the city variant, excluding those which recommended that the highway bypass the city. The explanation given to this decision, which contradicted the initial recommendations of the Slovak government, was twofold. First, it was stated that the flyover bridge variant would allow for a saving of about one third of the cost of the tunnel variant. Secondly, the mayor of PB at the time explained to me that the main problem was of a technical nature. As of 2007, the appointed building company did not possess the technology that would allow for the digging of a tunnel below or around the city, as the environmental activists had suggested. The difficulty of digging a tunnel was also supported by the argument that due to the presence of the River Váh and to copious underground water, the tunnel would be a hazardous option. The environmental organizations, on the other hand, alleged that the environmental assessment had not been performed by a completely impartial institution and hence its results could be questioned. One of the first criticisms of lack of transparency comprised the idea that the EIA, in the initial stages of the project, had allegedly been conducted by experts close to the local government. The conclusion that building the tunnel variant would have needed a technology which was not 'at hand', did not convince the environmental activists. They maintained that if 'local' contracts could have been issued to drill the tunnel, PB 'would have been crossed not by one, but by a series of tunnels'.[7]

In 2004 the protest grew bitter, with efforts to stir public awareness and the submission of a number of formal complaints by the two NGOs to the County Building Office and the County Government. Both complaints and the above mentioned petition were rejected. The only issue which the County agreed to discuss was the improvement of the EIA methods, including the calculation of expected noise pollution. The NGOs had indicated, using a study by an academic from one university in Bratislava, that the expected noise production would exceed the allowed levels by 5–10 decibels. The study was taken into consideration but later was lost by the county offices. Instead, there seemed to be less talk about air pollution. The issue was problematic for both sides. The city government did not wish to proceed with a detailed assessment of the gas level emissions

---

6 In the ten years of the protest I have been studying, three petitions were drawn up, the second and the third, however, had a bad fate because they were used against the civic associations (second) or they failed to collect a significant number of signatures (third).

7 Interview 6–5–2007, Pál, 54 years old.

above the city. On the other hand, heavy traffic (mainly trucks heading for Poland and Ukraine) crossing the city had steadily increased since 2004 causing air and noise pollution to become a sensitive issue. This was a 'natural' outcome of the completion process of the D1 national highway of which the 9.6 km section in PB was missing. Hard to believe, the entire highway traffic was diverted, because of the missing link, through the centre of the town, crossing four traffic lights and at least six pedestrian crossings. During this period the number of accidents is reported to have increased, the town traffic congestion worsened, greater difficulty in finding available parking spaces. The only positive note was the increase in the number of daily guests at local restaurants and coffee bars, which in recent years has produced a sensitive increase in business. Even though the environmental movements several times reported the need to build a road diversion route which would avoid the town centre, their request was never accepted on the grounding that it would have been too complex and costly.

In 2005 the Slovak government entrusted the newly founded Highway Society (DS) with all the projects related to the improvement and modernization of the national highway network.

In 2006, ten years after the first public discussion, the city organized a public meeting to discuss the compensation scheme. The NGO leaders criticized the move, stating that it constituted nothing more than an effort to improve the image of the local government. Some months later, the DS opened the Highway Info Point in town: an elegant, technologically equipped office, where citizens could learn about the highway project, and view a sophisticated video which illustrated the steps to the building of the 'Highway at our gate'. The use of multi-media techniques allowed the Info Point to make different types of material (cd-roms, pens, gadgets, posters and pamphlets) to promulgate the content and future look of their project. One video clip, in particular, depicted the most characteristic section of the highway, the flyover bridge, in idyllic tones, with the figure of a little girl carrying a mirror in her hands and reflecting the future highway onto the background of the existing town. This video, an informant[8] pointed out to me, deliberately avoided showing the portion of the town where the bridge tower over the houses by some few metres.

In August 2006, the NGOs prompted the international organizations Friends of the Earth Slovakia and CEE Bankwatch Network to send a letter to the Director of the European Investment Bank, through which the TEN-T funds were assigned, to stop financing the highway. The letter claimed firstly, that the initial EIA approved by the Transport and Environment Ministries had been ignored and, secondly, that no clear scheme of compensation for the dispossessed owners had been discussed publicly.[9] Meanwhile, the two NGOs addressed their petition and protest to the

---

8   Petr, 7 years old, interview 11–5–2007.

9   One major problem about the compensation scheme for the landowners was that the land on which the highway was to be built was never, officially put on sale as the TEN-T projects require. Some of the owners, as a matter of fact, still refuse to sell it. During one

National Supreme Court. The effort was successful and the funding process was temporarily halted.

In 2007, after the traffic conditions worsened in PB, it became clear that the battleground had shifted from the highway variants to the compensation scheme and the moving of the two streets. Although the Ministry of Transport and the Ministry of the Environment advised not to move the main city road, the city council was not clear about complying with this recommendation. The new mayor, elected in 2006, was seen by some citizens to be in a weaker position to defend the interest of the city to gain compensation for the dispossessed and dislocated owners compared to the old mayor, the real promoter of the highway project. This point was rendered more obscure by the fact that there had been no agreement as to whether the state, the town or the Highway Company should be in charge of compensation.

In September 2008 the Slovak government issued a law package under the name 'Extraordinary measures in preparation of selected motorway construction' which, among other things, allowed highway construction on land that had not yet been purchased by the DS. This law, which is presently the object of fierce debate and criticism since it seems to violate landowners' rights, has predictably speeded up the highway construction process.

On May 31, 2010 the Sverepec-Vrtižer highway connection of 9.59 km, with a 1.3 km long flyover bridge was opened to the public. The outcomes have been various: the transport connection Bratislava-Žilina has been reduced by half an hour, traffic conditions are significantly better in PB, the number of guests and daily visitors to the town has sharply decreased. As for the compensation scheme, although the upper-floors windows in the nearby flats have been changed, not all dispossessed owners have received the promised flats. Less clear is the situation concerning land ownership, following the application of the extraordinary measure, which has been amended and partially suspended under the present government. Moreover, a significant number of town residents in the areas shadowed by the bridge have seen their estate market prices dramatically decrease, but no compensation scheme, up to this day, is foreseen for them.

State vs. local power

The different approaches of the state and local authorities to the TEN-T project are expressions of the power struggle which were consolidated in the mid-1990s. During the years of the Dzurinda cabinets (1998–2002 and 2002–2006), the County of Trenčín, traditionally a stronghold of the opposition party at the time, HZDS, denounced the slow path to which the highway project was being implemented by local governments. The supporters of the highway project

---

of my visits to the DS Info Point I heard local citizens complaining about the lack of transparency in the selling procedure.

accused the state of overlooking the real problems connected to the development of the region, especially after the main city factories were forced to cut down over 10000 workers in the mid-1990s.

In a letter dated May 24, 2005, the mayor addressed the issue of the one year delay in the highway building in starkly critical tones. He overtly denounced the incapacity of the Ministry of Transport to deal with the technical procedures needed to proceed with the bridge building. He pointed out that one year had gone by since the Ministry had agreed to proceed with the city variant (flyover bridge) in 2003, yet they still had not received the proper documentation that the city needed in order to start the work. In his words: 'The state cannot let a handful of city counselors and citizens blackmail it' and must continue its work in a 'just and responsible manner'. [10] In particular, the mayor blamed the Minister of Transport for not taking responsibility for the serious delay in the project.

On the other hand, one month later, the Minister declared: 'I am disappointed. We have waited one year to find a solution to the highway question, and more problems are to be expected in order to obtain the construction permissions for the city'.[11] The Ministry of Transport answered the mayor's criticism of the incapability of his office to settle the problem concerning two issues: the highway variant and the compensation process. In the official documents and press reports there is no mention of the NGOs and the civic protest; the stalemate was mainly imputed to the city itself.

The power struggle between the mayor and the minister was not simply an expression of their contrasting political orientations, as mentioned above. The highway is a priority within the EU structural projects, and is also influenced by the state commitments towards the Korean investors. In the eyes of the mayor, this explained the pressure made by the Ministry of Transport to adopt the cheapest variant, irrespective of its considerable environmental impact. This was explained to the public only in 2006, during the public meeting in which a hundred city inhabitants took part. The NGOs followed the indications of the Ministry of the Environment, dated 2001, which recommended three variants, the most environmentally harmful of which was the variant chosen by the city. The NGOs not only denounced the choice, but also protested that the construction plan had started in 2002, without the necessary permission and an agreement for the compensation scheme.

One of the two NGOs' leaders blamed the municipal administration under the former mayor for the environmentally harmful choice. According to him, the problem had arisen since the mayor changed his standpoint from an initial criticism of the city variant to his unconditional acceptance of it. It is not clear why this happened; evidence from statements reported by local and national media, which in the years 2005–2007 provided wide coverage of the protest, indicates that initially the state (governing majority) had been accused of hampering the project, and the

---

10   Považské Noviny, 21, 24–5–2005.
11   SME, Dial'nica pre Kia nebude načas, 27–6–2005.

economic development of a region traditionally of a different political orientation. Afterwards, following the electoral results of 2007, the new ruling coalition was more sensitive to the issue, at least in the eyes of the local government. The activists, on their side, did not see any concrete difference between the attitudes of the two government coalitions, if not for the modalities in which the project was promoted to achieve public legitimacy. According to Ján[12] the attribute which best describes the conditions of PB inhabitants is 'exhausted'. The over ten year-long battle has, through wide and hot media debates, exposed the town to national attention and made it looke like a 'bad example' of resistance to development and economic progress. In this the state-local government confrontation has surely played a significant role.

Indirect pressure was exerted on the state to complete the project also by the above mentioned establishment of the KIA plant, which in 2007 started production in its first car plant in Europe, located in Žilina. The plant, worth some 1.3 billion dollars, is the largest foreign investment in Slovakia and, as such, has caused several political scandals in the last five years. As in PB, the local government in Žilina has also been pressurized (by the KIA-Hyundai group) to hasten the process of construction and overcome the resistance of a number of landowners who refused to sell their land at the price set by the Ministry of the Economy. Here construction was started even though some 500 landowners had still not agreed to sell their land on which the plant was to be built.

In 2007, the KIA plant, designed to produce 300,000 small cars a year, was twinned with a Hyundai plant built in Moravia, some 70 km from PB. Among the several concessions that the Slovak government made to the Korean investors in order to win the deal and beat the Czech and Polish competition, was that the highway system would be complete by the time the plant was ready. This was unfeasible until 2010, since the highway from Bratislava to Žilina was ready save for the 9.6 km section around PB. In an interview, the chief director of the KIA, said he was 'slightly disappointed' by the failure to complete the transport network, even though he admitted he had expected problems and delays. The Žilina case has been used in newspaper and web articles by the two PB's NGOs as an example of authoritarian use of state and local power vis-à-vis the interests of the citizens, and as one of the hidden causes that made the city accept the worst highway variant. On the other hand, those supporting the highway project justified state action suggesting that, in a small country like Slovakia, if many have to listen to the suggestions of a minority, then economic development will suffer.

There are different ways in which the struggle between state and local institutions can be interpreted. One way is to analyze the choice of the highway variant and its public meaning. In the mid-1990s, when the Dzurinda cabinet started the highway investigation, the city of PB responded tepidly to the possible variants and eventually opposed the one which was to cross the inhabited area. The former mayor used the Ministry of Transport's suggestion to choose the least expensive

---

12   43 years old, interviewed on 6–6–2007.

and technologically most feasible variant as a weapon to justify its distance from the project. For 7 years, until 2003, the town engaged in a ping-pong game with the Ministry with mutual accusations of delaying the construction for lack of documentation and technical assessments. The town administration, at this stage, was still not seen to be directly responsible for the project, as the state was to be blamed or vice versa. This was the period when the NGOs' activities were focused on the observation of the political choices and consensus-building among local people. After 2003 the mayor successfully diverted the public attention transferring the full-fledged responsibility of the bridge choice to the state which, in his eyes, had 'blackmailed the city with no possible way out'. In an article dated 2005, he observed 'at that point [when the construction work actually began] it was clear that the state had imposed its ultimatum: accept the city variant or fight the law'.[13]

One final analysis arising from the confrontation between state and local government is that the requirements of the TEN-T project (from technical to environmental assessments, conditions of landed property) facilitated the struggle. Legitimacy of the project was sought in terms of economic and structural development on both sides, but the complex bureaucratic machine of the EU funding system was the scapegoat, as well as actual obstacle, used to mask shortcomings on both sides, as the environmental groups reported. The local civic organizations, trapped between this struggle, attempted to gain strength in the eyes of the public in two main ways: diversification of the scope of action and communication, and use of multiple issues of public concern, from environmental hazards, to lesion of property rights and lack of transparency in public administration.

Forms and strategies of environmentalism

Another way of attributing meaning to the local-national-transnational power struggle is by observing the forms of civic protest and unraveling the ideas that local people have about their functions and public achievements.

In 1996, when the two NGOs were established, confrontation with the city administration was still not an issue. The creation of the civic associations was a difficult process justified by the necessity to monitor the highway project from the ground level. The founders of the movement were mainly highly educated people: school teachers, professionals, one retired chemist and two entrepreneurs who shared the interest 'not to lose the important details of the project implementation'. At that time it was not clear to the general public that the PB highway was part of a pluralistic design aimed to improve the infrastructures of the country and to improve EU-level transport. The main concern of the two NGOs was the need to avoid mismanagement and lack of information.

I believe that this was the true aim that inspired the first steps of the civic protest even considering that one of the early activists underlined that it would have been

---

13   'Hovorme o factoch, nie o pocitoch'. *Považské Noviny*, 21, 24–5–2005.

difficult to involve citizens with a clear 'political' aim in mind. He indicated that anything unofficial was veiled with suspicion since, due to the socialist regime; people were not used to thinking that public action could be genuinely borne out by such movements.

The environmental movements operated over a temporal span of 14 years. During this period their activity followed three phases: consolidation, expansion and retreat.

In the first period the two NGOs sought to establish public legitimacy aware of the delicate power game being played in the context of the project by the different institutional actors.

The early meetings of the two NGOs were carefully organized and avoided spreading the idea that the associations were openly opposing the state and municipal authorities. It was counterproductive to instill in the citizens the impression that fighting on a public ground could have brought concrete results, since it was not clear whether the protest should be addressed versus the state or the local government. This finding demonstrates most of the mainstream debate over the difficult consolidation of civil society in Eastern Europe, as illustrated above. The NGOs' leaders had to find alternative venues for public expression, as they seemingly avoided official confrontation with the state authorities. The vagueness of their official standpoint allowed them to penetrate the citizens' uneasiness with the city politics. It was exactly the absence of a clear public expression of the protest, as well as their strategy to act in informal channels, that allowed for the creation of the two NGOs. Following a snowball method of involving friends, relatives, neighbours and acquaintances, the two associations proceeded through informal meetings, telephone calls, pub chats, emails, web forums and simple text messages. They established a meeting point where, thanks to fax and internet connections, they were able to make their activities known and to arrange more regular meetings and general public participation slowly grew. The main outcome of this period was to inform the general public and to strengthen awareness of the potential environmental damage of the project.

The reason why formal occasions of interaction were avoided was actually twofold. The first justification was that the socialist experience had taught people to be wary of those forms of protest which were arranged formally and gained specificity through open confrontation with local authorities. Second, however, over-exposal of the civic protest could have undermined its inspiring minds because of the risk of being accused of speculation in the compensation business. The problem was that the initial drive for the protest also came from, among others, landowners and entrepreneurs directly involved in the elimination of the two central streets in which they had their businesses. This was actually used in subsequent denigrating campaigns against the activists in general with the claim that their real interests were speculative and of an economic nature rather than environmental.

The leader of the NGO The Highway and Nature, on two occasions, admitted that having two associations constituted a deliberate strategy to avoid being stormed by the attention of the local media, and also to divert criticism and the legal attacks made by the local institutions. The city administration, in the years when the public battle grew fierce, used the petition campaign launched by the NGOs as an instrument to undermine their function as civic movements. The local media denounced that the work of one of the two NGOs was no more than a cover for a small group of its members who were trying to obtain private gains from speculation on land property. The defamatory campaign forced the association to avoid further public confrontation, as they feared that any direct action would be interpreted as instrumentally directed to private gains rather than aimed to seek the public good.

On one occasion, in 2004, the environmental organizations proposed a list of three alternatives to the city variants, accompanied by a petition signed by most of the land and flat owners on the three streets that were to be removed. One of the variants suggested that the highway be diverted to the nearby settlement of Jašlové. The city used this petition to prove the little regard the NGOs had towards the inhabitants of Jašlové and eventually presented a counter-petition with signatures from the inhabitants of Jašlové asking for the end of the public protest by the NGOs. The feature of civil society movements emerging in this case is one in which the state is seeking to appropriate the very strategies of the movements in order to debase their effort to maintain public consent.

Since 2005 the forms of public engagement have changed appreciably, and have entered a second phase, marked by expansion of the scope. The decade of civic battle over the highway project had brought about contradicting outcomes. As far as the project was concerned, the two NGO leaders had to slowly accept that their chances of winning over the conflation of interests between local government and the state governments after 2006 were severely reduced. It became clear that the flyover bridge would be built; it was only a matter of time. This was, however, not perceived by the environmental movements as a defeat, but as the natural consequence of the general exhaustion about the traffic conditions. The steady worsening of traffic conditions in the city prompted a number of people to give up the protest and abandon their ideas of collective action. Several citizens felt that, at this stage, it was better to have a bridge as soon as possible rather than not have one at all.

The tone of the criticism towards the civic movements became gradually more hostile in that period, as can be noticed in the several blogs in local forums. Following 2006, after the conflict between the state and local government over the project had died down, there was increased media pressure on PB inhabitants to accept the highway. If until that time national and partly local television[14] had given space to the protest, afterwards more emphasis was on publicizing the need for the highway. This can be interpreted as a consequence of the worsening

---

14   Of the three television channels in the region at the time of my fieldwork two received aid from the local government and one was more independent. Although until 2006 all of them had screened reports or interviews with environmental activists and local citizens, after that year relatively little space was dedicated to the protest.

traffic conditions in the urban centre, but nonetheless it was another omen of the diminishing public concern for the protest. The two NGOs came to be presented as stubborn activists who, in the pursuit of personal interests, were hampering the development of PB.

The civic organizations adopted a dual strategy. The first was to avoid formal confrontation with local government authorities and even with the general public. Since the autumn of 2007, the voice against the highway on a local level had become rather silent.[15] Even those who had been extremely active, back at the end of the 1990s, became less keen to manifest their ideas of collective action and public protest. As one informant, the owner of a pizzeria who lost his restaurant and house on one of the two streets affected by the bridge construction, commented: 'Protesting, these days, has turned us against our fellow citizens'.[16] Tired and discouraged by the heavy highway traffic which had crossed the city every day since 2006, more and more local people had gradually become convinced that those activists who opposed the city variants were to be blamed for the delay in the construction of the bridge. Some activists still hoped that the bridge, as a visible sign of the absurdity of the project, would again instill fear and uneasiness in the population who had turned its back on the civic protest, even though at that point it was clearly too late to react.

The second strategy adopted by the civic organizations was to expand their activity beyond the town. The local forms of public protest at this stage sought active connections with global forms of civil society. Three web sites which contain a long list of documents, journal articles and pictures about the highway project were created. The local NGOs were linked to larger environmental organizations such as Ekoforum, Central Eastern European Bankwatch Network and the Friends of Earth[17] (CEPA). These are among the largest non-profit organizations that, in Eastern Europe, address issues of environmental protection and defense of civil rights.

It is thanks to this connection that the local NGOs succeeded in halting, although only temporarily, the funding of the highway project by the European Development Bank in 2006.

During this phase, there was a shift in the activities of the local environmental groups towards what they defined as less 'work on the ground' and more 'paper work'. What could be termed as the bureaucratization of the environmental movement came as a response to the general loss of legitimacy at local level. On

---

15   Demonstration to this was that I found it more difficult to obtain interviews with some of the NGO leaders. In one case, in late 2007, I was asked to meet one of them in some woods situated on the outskirts of the town. This gave me a vivid idea of the difficulties encountered by these forms of civil society at that time.

16   Fero, 48 years old, interviewed on 23–9–2007.

17   These two organizations are presently unified by common aims. Friends of the Earth is a civic association which originated from the formerly called Center for Environmental Public Advocacy (CEPA) and supported projects which relate to environmental protection and awareness, social justice, civil society.

the other hand, increased awareness, on the part of the activists, of the irregularities that had been committed in the development project, instilled in them the idea that what seemed to have been lost at a local level could still be achieved through trans-local activism. It is in this period that the main focus of the protest shifted from the construction of the highway, mainly of the bridge, to the compensation process and the defense of the ownership rights of those directly affected by expropriation. However, after the law on urgent public works was approved in 2008, these activities lost momentum too.

In the final phase of retreat, at the end of 2008, the enlargement of the spatial scope of the environmentalist movement was not matched by a consolidation of ties with local society, as had been hoped. True, when the municipality started to organize the first well attended public meetings about the highway project in 2006 it had found that many of its citizens were perfectly aware of what was going on behind the desks. The degree to which personal communication, interaction with the NGO leaders and transmission of information affected the public protest is one of the most important factors of the protest.

Along with the efforts of environmental activists to bridge local, trans-local and global forms of protest, it was the complementary formal and informal strategies which had given strength to the movement.

The temporary stop in the funding of the TEN-T process was perceived as a positive achievement by the NGO members. Moreover, the very fact that the highway debate was regularly reported by local and national newspapers, suggested that there could be a way of reacting to unjust political manoeuvres. Unfortunately, this success did not last long and did not bring the expected outcomes. In the last phase of the public protest, citizens' involvement diminished dramatically.

The local civic groups opted to follow a policy of retreat: they avoided other forms of public confrontation (even though all public meetings were regularly attended by their members) with the local inhabitants. Once the EIB started financing the highway again, international concern for PB decreased. Contemporarily, the focus of the public protest itself became limited only to the cases of the two streets whose residents were to be dispossessed. But the protest against the elimination of the streets could not remain on a public level as it had done in the early years. Today, although the two NGOs formally exist and continue their activity on the web and via small-circulation publications, it is mainly those members who will lose their property who remain active within them. Many have lost interest in the problem or are simply tired of following it. Among those who are keeping up the protest there are families who, tired of being interviewed and addressed as 'rebels', have decided to isolate themselves and avoid public contact. One man, the owner of a small garage, bought two large dogs to keep journalists and curious people away from his premises. Another, the owner of a small shop, simply refuses to talk about or comment on the highway issue any more.

Since the opening ceremony of the bridge, the environmental movements have kept up their task of monitoring traffic conditions, of presenting regular summaries of media reports and updates on the compensation process on their website.

Another particular field, to which their actions and communication strategies is still dedicated is the transparency of the implementation steps of the project

Corruption allegations and the reactions of the civic movement

In this case study corruption is exposed but only cautiously by the civic organizations in the course of their struggle to improve their political negotiation power at local level. Although corruption is not made a catchword in order to increase the legitimacy of their protest, the organizations have been attentive to maintain an open role of monitors of bad practices, in different fields related to the implementation of the project.

The first overt mention of corrupt practices in the highway project can be found in a web article dated 2002, written by one of the NGO leaders, who denounces the 'lack of transparency' in the early decision over the land where the highway was to be built on the outskirts of the city territory. According to the writer, this land was already destined to the construction of a large shopping centre, owned by a foreign retail company, even though a formal decision had not been taken.[18] It is unclear, from the article, if there had been instances of corruption, but there are suggestions that incentives might have been paid by the company in order to obtain building permission. The main problem was that on that portion of land the environmental movements had envisaged the construction of the tunnel in the V7 version of the highway variants. This version had been considered less environmentally harmful than the one adopted by the Ministry of the Environment in 2001. Therefore, the decision to concede permission to the retail company to build on that land was interpreted as a significant step towards the choice of the flyover-bridge variant.

In the course of my interviews with some NGO members the word 'corruption' arose several times. Even though it was never associated with one person in particular, and any attempts of mine to discover an association with someone were unsuccessful, it was used implicitly to describe some of the motives which led to the controversial choice of the flyover bridge. Accusations of non-transparent practices concerned two main areas. The first regarded the land on which the highway was to be built, the second the flats built by the city as compensation for the dispossessed families. The problem of the purchase of the land on which sections of the state highway could be built was an issue that was discussed at length. The problem was that some portions of the highway had already been built on land which had not been formally purchased from its owners. Some activists interpreted this as mismanagement of the project, as it was not clear whether the purchase of the land should have been the responsibility of the city administration or of the National Highway Company. This ambiguity, according to some exponents of the civic movement, constituted actually a cover-up for some murky practices which have accompanied the whole process of land allotment for the highway building. Some

---

18   http://www.mynoviny.sk/clanok.asp?cl=1585418.

of the owners also lamented that the initial price of the land had been lowered significantly. This justified the discontent people felt with the mayor elected in 2006, who, although more sensitive to the protest, had been seen paradoxically as less able to take a firm position on the compensation scheme.

The issue of the new flats is also linked to non-transparent practices by the local government, according to some of the informants. The former mayor, in his promise to grant the families who were about to lose their houses with new apartments, received a budget to build a complex of 500 new flats. The building of the new flats was a slow process with some irregularities along the way. First, the flats were built in conjunction with the highway, forcing a number of citizens who lost their homes to live for months within a vast construction site which not only surrounded, but worse, hung over them. The local environmental groups were very active in denouncing, through picture collections and videos, this state of things, but they could not get access to larger media sources. Second, a portion of these flats, according to the interviewed NGOs' members, was assigned to families who were not affected by the bridge building. This allegation has never been proved. Although it constituted a case of lack of transparency, the civic movements did not use it in their communications with the local citizens because most of those who received forms of compensation were active members of the movement themselves. At a time when public legitimacy had significantly weakened, the conflicting interests were perceived as a threat to the messages conveyed by the movements.

Corruption comes as a discourse which has not, however, legitimized the civic action of the two organizations. There was never any real public talk about corruption in PB. Most of the internet campaigns over the highway issue do not use the word 'corruption' at all. Even during the scheduled meetings of the NGOs and their legal battles over the compensation scheme, mention of corrupt practices was avoided. Most of the allegations about corruption are actually linked to political choices at a local, regional and even state level even though the NGOs never overtly used them as instruments of activism. The leader of one NGO declared that everybody in the town guessed that the suspicion of corruption behind the choice of the variant was not completely unfounded; nonetheless, it had become too difficult to use this as a strategy of resistance. In the early stages, caution with public exposure of the corruption argument was sought in order not to let the environmental movements being involved in the state-local government struggle over the competencies and planning of the road project. In the second stage, when corruption allegations could have been used more overtly, the organizations hesitated, and this attitude was used as an argument against their legitimacy.

Another more recent issue concerns the contracting process of private companies in the building and compensation scheme. Also here, the environmental movements did not (or were not able to) openly address more general concerns about corruption in this field. Their allusions to the modalities of the process of contracting were very subtle and never direct, as in the case of the tunnel variant. As time passed, when completion of the bridge was approaching, a number of small companies, privately owned or with the participation of members of the local government, became contractors of the project. The share was not particularly large, ranging from the provision of heating systems in the new flats, to changing the windows in the flats around the highway and providing other forms of technical assessments. However, one finds, mainly in the webpages of the movement, several comments referring to these cases of interpenetration of the public and private spheres. At some point the town (again no personal or concrete reference is provided) was accused of favouring the interests of local companies and of acting in their good, rather than in the interest of its inhabitants. Sensitive as these cases may be, they have not been used, in recent times, to strengthen the protest, and further evidence of these allegations was not directly sought.

Conclusion

What is the role of civil society in this case study? Caught between political forces (transnational, state and local), civil society occupies the sphere which embraces people's reaction to what is decided above them. In this there is no evident difference between this case and others in western Europe. A protest movement arises and gains momentum when the opposition between local and national forces becomes more evident. The state is unable to impose its decision on the city, and the city becomes increasingly unable to defend its 'virtuous' political choices. The establishment of the two NGOs makes up the novelty of the process of forced negotiation of the decisions over the flyover bridge. It is not a coincidence that the initial activities of the civic associations are conveyed mainly through informal channels. I believe that this is due not simply to the lack of civic tradition in post-socialist countries.

The activists soon understood that the only way for them to gain consensus was to engage in the protest with the same rules of the game being played by the state and the city. The existence of the conflict between these two parties legitimized the creation of the two organizations. However, initially they were mainly preoccupied with communicating with citizens to broaden the base of legitimacy rather than with engaging in real action. This is why allegations of corruption made against local politicians could not be used with any success to strengthen the protest, since discourses on corruption are still largely based on ethical consensus rather than on the actual impact of corrupt practices which remain unknown to the general public for a long time. Even though, in the first stage, they were successful in gaining local support, their choice to avoid public confrontation and overt condemnation of corrupt practices allowed their opponents to gain back trustworthiness and to blame the protest movements for the delay in the construction of the bridge.

Civil society occupies the layer between households and the state and it is increasingly looking for different, more extensive spaces in which to devise strategies, make decisions and choices. All this is fruit of the post-socialist transformation and of the EU enlargement. However, the same transnational dynamics of development leaves room for poor planning, wrongdoing, environmental damage and corrupt practices. This case study suggests two points. The first is that civil society can be strengthened by the outcomes of the implementation of EU funded structural projects. The second is that, among these outcomes there is also increased political fragmentation, as observed in the struggle between local and national power, as well as in the attempts to debase the civic movements. Corruption and civil society, two central notions in the theoretical debates of the social science disciplines, can be used meaningfully from an empirical perspective if attention is paid to the practices and discourses that centre upon them and to the social circumstances which allow their emergence. At that point a highway bridge built over a city tired of fighting is the most striking symbol of an EU policy that aims to connect people globally, but indeed ends up by dividing them locally.

Chapter 5

Case Two: Road Transport Development in the Czech Republic – The Brno-Vienna Highway

The most evident expression of the need to balance transnational with national interest is in the EU ideological apparatus, finely constructed in the contrasting discourse between communality and subsidiarity. In the Maastricht Treaty (1992) the preamble indicates the resolution of the founding members to 'achieve the strengthening and the convergence of their economies and to establish an economic and monetary union'. This is further stressed by Article B which underlines the aim to 'promote economic and social progress which is balanced and sustainable, in particular through the creation of an area without internal frontiers, through the strengthening of economic and social cohesion and through the establishment of economic and monetary union'. In spite of the strong idealistic thrust towards cohesion and cooperation, the same Treaty, article 5, reports:

> The Community shall act within the limits of the powers conferred upon it by this Treaty and of the objectives assigned to it therein. In areas which do not fall within its exclusive competence, the Community shall take action, in accordance with the principle of subsidiarity only if and in so far as the objectives of the proposed action cannot be sufficiently achieved by the Member States.

The principle of subsidiarity has been more firmly outlined in the Treaty of Lisbon (2007) which contains 4 article paragraphs (Article 3b) defining the limits of the EU competences, versus the above illustrated article which constitutes the only mention in the Maastricht Treaty. A further stipulation was added to the above mentioned article with the signing of the Treaty of Lisbon:

> the Union shall act only and insofar as the objectives of the proposed action cannot be sufficiently achieved by the Member States, either at central level or at regional and local level, but can rather, by reason of the scale or effects of the proposed action, be better achieved at Union Level (Article 3b paragraph 2).

As Holmes (2000) and Shore (2000) have pointed out, the principle of subsidiarity delimitates the decisional powers of the EU, being de facto at odds with the ideology of the EU founding fathers. It is one thing to envisage the benefits of common policies and objectives, and another to avoid intruding into national political and economic decisions. This is precisely what makes the EU a controversial project since it embodies the most basic tensions of the globalization process. The TEN-T is an exemplary on this point. It is the main structural development scheme in the Union since it sets to improve connectivity among states and regions, promoting multilevel economic development. Hence it becomes particularly significant to analyze how far the global economic crisis will affect the tension between transnational, national and local political forces within the planning sphere of this scheme. This approach, in my view, can help to shed the lights onto the actual utility of some of the globalization theories, as well as to put into question the role of the state.

The case study: the Brno-Vienna motorway axis

The motorway portion examined here is a section of the multimodal (road and railway) corridor VI which connects Danzig to Vienna and Bratislava. The corridor includes a road portion as well as modernization and amelioration of the existing railway network among the four countries.

The case study concerns the priority axis 25 in the section Vienna-Brno in the transnational context Austria – Czech Republic – Poland, or Vienna – Katowice. The most problematic portion is the connection between Brno and the Austrian border. This portion can be completed in two ways: either by using the existing 4 lane highway D2 Brno – Břeclav (-Bratislava) and planned bypass of the town of Břeclav, and building just 3 km of an additional road to the Austrian border at Reintal, or alternatively, by building about 25 km of a new 4 lane road R52 to the Czech-Austrian border at Mikulov/Drasenhofen.

This portion, of approximately 25 km, has been the centre of dispute over the last twelve years. The R52 seems to be completely redundant as it would be parallel to the existing D2 highway at a distance of just 12–18 km. The point is that the border connection at Mikulov does not justify the construction of the planned 4-lanes road R52 because of the insufficient volume of daily traffic (about 5–6,000 cars per day[1] against at least the 20,000 needed to justify a four lane road).

The differences among the two variants are several. First, the Mikulov variant directly hits the second largest city of the Czech Republic, Brno, and it needs to be complemented by the construction of a new highway, named South-West Tangent, which would cut through densely inhabited areas. Furthermore

---

1 Study of Traffic Intensities on the Border Crossings of the Czech Republic, October 2008 reports 4800 cars/day at Mikulov Border Crossing, Traffic Intensities Survey for 2005 by the Czech Road and Motorway Directorate reported 6185 vehicles/day, Book coauthored by Director Genereal of the Czech Road and Motorway Directorate (2009, http://www.rsd. cz/doc/Silnicni-a-dalnicni-sit/Dalnicni-publikace/paterni-sit-dalnic) gives a prediction of 8–10 thousand cars/day in Mikulov area. The estimates used for justification of R52 (on Czech side) and A5 (on Austrian side) are strikingly higher.

the regional authorities tried to use this variant to get support of a 70 year old alignment of another highway (R43) which is known as 'old Hitler Highway'. This alignment would cut through parts of the densely populated areas of Brno inhabited by over 40.000 people. These decisions were taken by the regional authorities (Jihomoravský kraj) in spite of the results of expert studies which declared the South-West Tangent road as useless. The following points were made in opposition of the project by local environmental activists.

First, the Břeclav variant does not need a new tangent road in Brno because it does not intersect the city and connect to a 2-lane motorway (R55) which already exists and which is being modernized into a 4-lane motorway in the direction of Břeclav – Katowice (Czech Republic-Poland). Second, although both variants have an impact on the local environmental protected area that belongs to the EU *Natura 2000*[2] sites, an authorized expert study clearly concluded that the Břeclav variant has lower impact. This study has been so far ignored by the authorities. Third, the EU corridor from Vienna via Břeclav to Poland is about 40 km shorter and truly multimodal (it closely follows European Priority Rail Project No. 23 Břeclav – Katowice), while the connection from Vienna to Brno by way of Břeclav is just 10 km longer. Fourth, although there are interest groups which have pushed for the road construction in both variants, the Mikulov variant has been, since the early stages, preferred by regional political authorities. Fifth, the road 52 to Mikulov has recently been improved as a first class motorway, hence its upgrading to highway would render, according to the new R52 opponents, the previous work a monetary waste. Finally, the highway system for the South Moravia region based on the connection to Austria at Mikulov has been assessed to be more expensive than the variant based on the main highway connection to Austria at Břeclav, with a difference raising up to EUR 1.3 billion. Regional authorities and the Road and Motorway Directorate of the Czech Republic maintain that the Mikulov Road would make the Czech Government save between Euro 0.04–0.12 billion. On the other hand, the organizations opposing the Mikulov variant point out publicly that the cost data used by the Road and Motorway Directorate are based on inflated cost estimates of the Břeclav variant and purposely lowered costs of the Mikulov variant. This would not be the first case of irregular use of cost estimates by the Road and Motorway Directorate. The Supreme Audit Office of the Czech Republic denounced in its Audit Report No. 02/10 of 2003[3] that there was a cost overrun of close to 100% on the recent modernization of the road 52 to Mikulov (from CZK 1.7 to 3.3 billion).

---

2   Natura 2000 is a network of protected areas within the EU state members established in 1992 which has not yet been completed due to the EU enlargement. The Czech Republic has ratified the agreement and proceeded to include its sites since 2000, with 38 special protected areas including 863 national sites of community importance. The overall surface of protected land in the country amounts at 7.9 million ha, of which 0.7 million ha are located in the southern Moravian region.

3   Supreme Audit Office Report, http://www.nku.cz/kon-zavery/K02010.pdf, p. 126.

The opposition against the Mikulov variant summoned the activity of at least 24 local NGOs, with the involvement of three transnational NGOs (CEE Bankwatch Network, Friends of the Earth and Environmental Law Service[4]) and a number of Austrian civic and green organizations. As part of the TEN-T scheme, the planning of the highway is subject to EU law and needs to follow particular steps. These include the trans-border strategic environmental assessment (SEA), followed by the trans-border Environmental Impact Assessment (EIA) which should ensure feasibility and provide transparent information regarding the environmental damages linked to the project. To be part of the TEN-T funding scheme, therefore, both assessments have to be completed in a transboundary fashion with citizens and civic organizations of both neighboring countries involved.

Austria, from its perspective, is interested in the construction of a 33–36 km highway section (A5) which would link the Moravian border with Vienna, with plans to complete the first of three segments in 2010. At the time of writing this chapter, the EIA for the two residual segments was not completed.

One major difference, which rendered the NGOs' trans-border cooperation problematic, is that in the Czech Republic the SEA and EIA need to be provided (and commissioned) by the Ministry of the Environment, which acts in cooperation with the Ministry of Transport and the Ministry of Local Development for road planning. In Austria, instead, the passage is different: the Ministry of Transport is alone in charge of issuing the final EIA statement. This may significantly reduce the time needed to continue with the construction, but on the other hand it also potentially reduces the transparency of the project as well as the possibility that opposition emerges at government level. The situation is, on the other hand, complicated by different legal role of the EIA statement in Austria. It can be demonstrated on the fact that in the case of two northern segments of A5 the public hearings took place more than 2 years ago. In the Czech Republic the EIA statement would be issued much faster, typically in one month after the public EIA hearings, and it would be clearly separated from other aspects including land-permitting process.

Austria will be hit relatively marginally by the corridor construction since Vienna has already completed its ring road S1 and S2 and the two variants (via Břeclav and via Mikulov) would cross one of the least populated areas of the country, with no major town present and no Natura 2000 areas. These points greatly affect the kind and degree of civic and environmental protest and activism and it justifies the comparative weakness of forms of relevant civic associations in Austria versus their Czech counterparts.

---

4   Environmental Law Service (Ekologický Právní Servis) is a non-governmental organization that originated in the Czech Republic as a voluntary association of students of the faculty of law of the Masaryk University of Brno in 1995. In 1997 it has achieved full professional status and it works to provide consultancy on legal matters on broad issues such as environmental sustainability, business integrity, democratic and citizen rights.

The response from below: types of civil society

There are different layers of power involved in the development project of the highway. What I mean by layers is, following Gupta's use (1995), the uneven configurations of power cut-crossing groups of actors and that have access to political decision-making processes. These layers reflect the interaction of interests and attempts to conciliate different priorities. This is what makes each layer a power holder in itself, framed within its own strategic vision of the project. Each layer has its own access to information, and to interpersonal networks which can or cannot be shared among layers to pursue a common goal. The civic organizations which cooperate to denounce the environmental negative impact of the motorway project constitute one of these layers. What makes the Austrian-Czech case interesting and peculiar in comparison with the above mentioned Slovak case (Chapter 4), is the high degree of diversification within the civic organizations. These organizations are active on both sides of the border, and count for approximately 35 institutions, 24 of which are Czech. They can be divided into four typologies, according to their structure, goals, strategies and standpoint vis-à-vis the TEN-T operations.

The first type is the small-scale civic organization, typically village or town-based, which has a very restricted institutional body, usually formed by a small number of founders, and a number of associates ranging from 20 to over 150 persons. These organizations, such as Nebojsa, assume a strongly emotional standpoint regarding the aim they wish to pursue. Nebojsa, a civic association based in the village of Bavory, was founded in 1996 and includes about 120 members. This association, which owes substantial part of its activity to the vitality of its main founder was the one that started the protest against the R52 construction. Most of the activities of such organizations are undertaken with personal ties of the founders, and continue through informal networks. Membership is sought, but it is never absolutely binding, since the result of actions is not to be found in what these small organizations achieve, but rather in their ability to communicate and cooperate with other forms of civil society. Nonetheless, these organizations are, in the Czech case, rather active and successful in transmitting information (or counter-information) to comparatively large strata of the population, even though they are seldom called into direct action. Another important function is the ability to stir political support from municipalities. Moreover, the local base of these organizations allows them to spread informal networks with those members of local municipalities who have been sensitive to environmental concerns.[5] Nebojsa

---

5 One argument against the genuine participation of local mayors and municipal counsellors to the environmental protests could be that they aimed to achieve recognition and enhance trust by local inhabitants. Although this might have happened in all the case studies present in this book, one needs to consider the long span of the development projects and the protests against them that severely tested the tue intentions and concerns of these official for the public interest.

succeeded in steering public participation in the protest against the Mikulov Road variant involving (in the first stage) five mayors from the villages directly affected by the project.[6] The association successfully linked with larger regional units and was able to organize a number of local meetings to which citizens were invited and received detailed information on the project and the protest movement. Although citizens' participation was not stable and often scarce, the determinacy with which the leaders of these organizations carried out their disseminative task caused some significant results. This included a petition of collected signatures by 15,000 people from the neighboring villages, which resulted in convincing five local mayors about the real extent of the process (2005).

The second type includes middle-scale organizations with a regional (mainly urban) basis, characterized by more complex organizational structures with a role that is primarily relational. One example is Veronica, established in 1999 as an environmental organization (Ekologický Institut Veronica) in relation with the work of a local magazine founded with the same name in 1986. Veronica is very active in cooperating with other local NGOs and institutions (such as municipalities) and the outcome of this dynamism is its ability to establish and maintain a rather large network of cooperation with other NGOs and local political figures. The importance of networking is linked to the dependence of these forms of organizations on external funding, which make them particularly sensitive to shifting priorities in projects management and design. Although they constitute an important ring of the chain, especially because they are able to balance institutional with professional ties (they have members and personnel specialized on different sectors), this type of civic organization is less incisive when it comes to political decision-making. One might call this a *relational* type of organization, where available information is shared with the other layers. Action, however, is rarely directly called for by these organizations. The principal reason is that they are often involved in too many projects to be able to dedicate their efforts to only one of them, and they need to gain funding for them. Veronica, for example, succeeded in the promotion of different projects aimed to raise the environmental awareness through the participation of school children and elderly people. In one such project (in 2004), the organization took three primary schools and some elderly clubs to the natural reservoir belonging to the Natura 2000 interested by the road project. Although no direct mention was made about the road project, one of the leaders explained that these events were intended merely to raise awareness and improve knowledge of the natural environment.

The third type is made by organizations which are based in urban settings, typically Brno and Vienna, and this location helps them to operate in close contact with a larger network of transnational partners. Those with which I have been mostly in contact in the course of my fieldwork are in the Czech case: OS Brno, Děti Země and PŘÍSO. The corridor Mikulov – Modřice – Brno – Svitavy, except for the existing segment of R52 south of Brno, is covered by many civic

---

6   These were Perná, Dolní Dunajovice, Bavory, Klentnice and Horní Věstonice.

organizations which can within short period activate many hundreds or even thousands of supporters and get their signatures to support various petitions. In the southern Moravian area they managed to collect over 38 thousand signatures to support the petition against R43 crossing inhabited parts of Brno and they have been fighting for a full scale bypass of Brno for more than a decade.

During my interviews with key exponents of the OS Brno and Děti Země, I found some similarities in their structure and strategies. The first is that they are deeply rooted in the institutional context of their action. The number of personal contacts with key political figures, institutions and organizations is high. The second is that the importance given to personal networking is not only explicated in the relational sphere, like the second type of organizations, because the main strategy of these associations is to pursue legal and political action. This is possible since these organizations are led by specialists in the areas of interest: engineers, lawyers and academic experts, hence their role is mainly executive. They make up the core of the project, and thus they can sum up the information collected by the previous two forms and to condense these into action. Third, they tend to be rather small and, as the first type, focused on one or few projects. This, along with their ability to share the broader informal networks among the four types, allow them dynamism and rapidity in decision-making. Fourth, there is an enormous effort on the side of the active members, like in the case of Děti Země, to shoulder the high costs of technical and legal consultancy. These costs, as in most of the civic movements analysed in this volume, are shared among members, or in some occasion covered through public events.

These third type organizations, unlike the second type they usually have a lower degree of visibility, which can be seen itself as a strategy. One of the founding members of OS Brno indicated, that being able to be 'at the right place at the right time', or to know 'the right person' is in these projects far more important than appearing in TV or radio programs.[7]

On the one hand, being a small organization is used as an asset, requiring less time for meetings, workshop and formative events (such as in the case of the second type), and focusing all efforts towards legal and political activities. On the other hand, acting in the 'shadow' of the protest allows some of these associations, such as PŘÍSO and OS Brno to remain external to public and media campaigns which commonly label these organizations as 'environmentalists', without paying too much attention to the political implications of the protest, particularly when corruption comes into play. The so-far successful actions against R52 project by way of Mikulov and their support for the Břeclav variant substantively benefitted of the ability of these two institutions to coordinate the activity with the others and to adopt concrete strategies. These included: informing EU politicians and national ministries, maintaining updated information which is constantly shared among the organizations and the participating institutions, taking legal action and coordinating the transnational cooperation among organizations not only between

---

7   Personal interview, 13–9–2008.

Czech Republic and Austria, but in broader European context. Another aspect of the environmental activism of this third group concerns the organization of bilateral meetings with Austrian civic organizations. During my ethnographic investigation there have been two large meetings (one in Moravia and another in Austria) where civic organizations on both sides of the border met to report on their annual activity, concerns, political outcomes and future directions. In each meeting members of 15 to 20 organizations were present, with a larger Czech component, and their topics of discussion included different aspects of the Brno-Vienna motorway connection: from issues concerning land property to harmonization of strategies for increasing public awareness, to technical and legal details on the project. The language of the meetings was usually rather specialized and technical, and the large participation, as well as constant efforts to maintain active the dialogue among the two countries' NGOs are testimonies of the high knowledge and extremely good organizational capacities of the environmental movements. In this the role of the organization belonging to the third type was pristine, they all possess relational and communicative (including language) skills to be able to effectively share information on the two sides of the border. The same is done presently with constant updates and email communications in German and Czech.

The fourth type is made by transnational organizations, usually not based in the countries where they also operate. This is the case of Friends of Earth, Ecology Law Service and Central Eastern Europe Bankwatch Network. These are among the three largest environmental NGOs in Europe which work on a wide number of fields and projects. CEE Bankwatch[8] is particularly interesting since it is mainly concerned with the development of projects with a potential for environmental harm. This organization has active members from each country in Central Eastern Europe, although it does not always have a local basis. Its main aim is to detect cases of environmental and legal abuses in Central Eastern Europe and mainly correlated to the implementation of development project by the European Investment Bank.

The role of these large organizations is to refine the political and legal activity which is to them filtered by the third type. These organizations are able to access EC commissioners or EP members, as all of them are involved at different degrees with consultancy projects in Brussels. The potential benefits of cooperating with this level of organizations are obvious, although it is not to be taken for granted that they will be willing to help. These organizations are constantly involved in national and transnational projects, unlike the second type, they do not always

---

8   The organization was established in 1995 and soon became one of the leading environmental networks in Eastern Europe including NGOs from 12 countries. The name derives from the main goal of the umbrella organization, which is to monitor the activities of international financing institutions, such as the European Investment Bank, and the European Bank for Reconstruction and Development. Recently the organization has achieved an important political status being one of the main third-sector advisors in EU projects in Eastern European countries.

need to apply for funding or design a project to obtain funds since they can manage consultancy projects from EC offices and ministries. This entails that their direct involvement on each project may be reasonably thorough depending on a number of factors (the entity of funding, the political sensitivity of the issue, the degree of transnational cooperation involved and the attention of members or sections of the European Commission). Of course, positive action cannot be expected by this layer of organizations alone. Rather, it is through their mediation that members of the third type are able to develop personal ties with politicians and specialists in Brussels.

In the course of the project local civic organizations have been able, thanks to the good degree of diversification of strategies and organizational types, to harmonize their activities with the consultancy of these larger networks. These took place mainly in two formal ways. The first concerns reference to reports and official case studies issued by these organizations. The second refers to consultancy mainly in legal matters. Both ways were pursued mainly by local organizations through the filter of third-type organizations, which were ready to present new material and legal advice obtained through consultation with larger networks down to local level. In the Czech case these networks have been particularly active, providing prompt to cooperate among them on reporting about political problems and economic bottlenecks caused by transport development projects. At informal level, however, relevance of this type of organizations has been even greater, although not easily identifiable. I found most difficult to obtain firsthand information from members of these large environmental organizations partly because of their caution with politically sensitive issues (such as corruption), partly because the language used by their members is imbued with technical jargon and has a well-structured, almost fixed pattern that leaves little space for insights into 'unofficial' data and trends. According to the comments of members of third-type civic organizations, however, establishing connections with global environmental networks is a crucial prerequisite for increasing efficiency of the movements, and above all for getting access to advice on how to deal with EU directives.

The interdependency of power layers

The Brno-Vienna project is part of a transnational economic plan which is being implemented following a top-down pattern of power distribution penetrating the several layers of decision-making and action. The building of a road, not even longer than 22 km at Mikulov and/or extension of Břeclav bypass (by only 3 km), an apparent insignificant section of the whole corridor, is an extremely complex process, from the very start, when it is designed in Brussels, to the end when the asphalt is paved and the signals are installed. Within this project, a large number of actors are involved, each with his own specific power position and relation. The very nature of the transnational transport development projects allows this complex stratification of power and indeed attributes a particular meaning to it. The EU, what can be seen as the first power layer, is first the designer of the projects, and later the funder of parts of it, thus as such constituting the original channel through which power is attributed, transmitted and negotiated with the other layers.

The planning of a road within the TEN-T scheme entails a number of initial steps which, for the transnational character of the corridors, should be followed in cooperation by the bordering countries, and within them by their regions. As indicated, the most significant of these steps is the assessment of the roads economic and environmental impact. There are economic and ecological procedures which need to be followed, again in concomitance by the bordering regions, and these are conditional to the application for TEN-T funding. One recurrent problem with these procedures is that, even though there are substantiated by a common EU law, they are necessarily framed within national legislative and bureaucratic contexts, before becoming actual arena of political negotiation. Here is where the TEN-T framework comes across its first obstacles, since planning and implementing timings, frameworks and procedures are rather different among countries. This difference is mainly in kind, as bureaucratic performance cannot be easily paralleled in two countries as different as Austria and the Czech Republic. Some members of local civic organizations have pointed out that the 'young' and 'transforming' nature of Czech (as all Central Eastern European) bureaucracy accounts for responses that are uneasily comparable with those of Western European countries. One frequent example concerned exposition of corruption scandals. The argument that corruption yielded to the realization of the transport projects, and eventually discredited different political layers was presented to me in two different ways by Czech and Austrian activists. The formers argued that one plus of the newly restructured public administration system in post-socialist countries is that it benefits from strict laws calling for transparency of public documents, such as bids, local governments' expenses and environmental impact assessment studies. These documents, according to legislations passed as part of the EU enlargement procedures in Central Eastern Europe, are widely available on the internet, or easily conceded by local bureaucrats, the same, however, does not apply to countries as Austria and, worse, to Italy, where the degree of secrecy of some of these documents is sensibly higher, just as the reluctance of local civil servants to grant public access to them is stronger. On the other hand, Austrian civic organizations pointed out that bureaucracy in the Czech case is less transparent. This opacity is imputed, according to the Czech activists, to two factors. The first is the comparatively low pay of bureaucrats, which, is still the case in Central Eastern European countries. Second, political alignment of bureaucrats is stronger in the Czech than in the Austrian case. Two of the leaders of OS Brno explained this by underlying that in Austria public administrators are less tied, for their jobs and duties, to political factions and parties because they have more solid contracts and legal security than their Czech counterparts. In the Czech regions, instead, political reshuffling directly affects the integrity of local bureaucrats who mostly have precarious offices. This, together with what they defined as a 'legacy of socialist opaque practices' influences the ways in which corruption comes into play in hampering the concrete implementation of transport development projects.

The second power layer is the state, which accepts the projects and includes them in the budget for funding. Approval from the ministries need to be accompanied by a study of the project's feasibility (under technical grounds), apart from the above mentioned assessments. This constitutes the first real field of interaction between the second and third layer: the regional authorities. If it is true that environmental and economic impact assessments can be theoretically delayed or falsified, technical assessment needs to reproduce the reality of the building conditions. At this point the regional (in the Czech Republic the *kraj*, in Austria the *Land*) authorities approve the study and actively contribute to its results. Unfortunately, the proper sequence of steps has not been observed for R52 and public involvement was not properly handled by the Czech authorities. This was criticized in the statements of the Czech Ombudsman.[9] The critical part of the process is the preparation of a Regional Land-Use Plan with a vision for the coming 20 years. This marks the step when the interests of municipalities (village or urban districts) meet or collide with those of the regional governments. When problems are identified from the points of view of the municipalities, as it happened for the R52, there is clear indication that a conflict of interests has arisen. Finally, the fourth layer (municipalities) intersects with the fifth, the landowners and local interest groups such as entrepreneurs and firms, who may act as pressure-groups for speeding or slowing the road construction. Also in this case, intersection among the layers becomes very significant for the time and realization of the project. When the interests of the fifth layer collide with those of the third or even the second layer, i.e. when the landowners are able to effectively act as pressure groups vis-à-vis respectively the regional or national plans of transport development it is clear that the regular procedure may be affected. Both the R52 and the Austrian A5 cases have been known through the years for the concomitance of lobby interests which pushed (at different times) for the construction of the road in one place instead of another, or in both. When there is a strong political and economic pressure at local level it becomes probable that the original road project can become influenced, even to the point of being re-designed. At this point, as it occurred with the R52, the original designer, the EU should be called at stake to reestablish its political role, and this is what the environmental organizations did during their protest. However, the EU is not always ready to intervene and reaffirm the validity of the original project, the most common explanation being the above illustrated principle of subsidiarity.

---

9   The Ombudsman Analytical Report can be downloaded from: http://aa.ecn.cz/ img_upload/213998dd557a6ecf241d80d7748bd811/Ombudsman_VUC_Breclavsko_ zpraa_3_11_06.pdf, and final Ombudsman Report can be downloaded from: http://aa.ecn. cz/img_upload/213998dd557a6ecf241d80d7748bd811/Ombudsman_VUC_Breclavska_ zavarecna_zprava.pdf.

Read in this way, the permeability of each of the power layers becomes extreme and reveals the major problem with the EU funding system in the TEN-T scheme: its creating a number of fragmented and competing layers of power. Not only do these layers compete with each other and may become tied to interests of private actors, but they are unable to gain legitimacy both at local and national level, at least in this case study. The EU is then summoned to compensate for this loss of legitimacy, not only, as it can be expected, because national politicians can influence members of the EU parliament, but because the European Commission is unwilling to interfere in matters which are out of its sphere of influence, being transferred to the decision-making process of each of its member states. Given the complexity of the TEN-T application procedures, and the tight schedules it involves, it is very probable that many projects may be torn down. Austria, for example, did not meet the 31 August 2009 deadline and has lost the last opportunity to obtain EUR 90 million for the A5 project because it presented incomplete material without variants comparison (also due to the lack of the final agreement with the Czech side and proper or even missing trans-border SEA and EIA) and the TEN-T Agency of the EC rejected the Austrian request. These cases are quite frequent in the TEN-T and some of the activists stressed that it may be of little surprise if Brussels avoids to intervene in order to smoothen the realization of its big design, and not to be forced to make dramatic budget cuts.

Corruption: structural vice or short-term strategy?

Political scientists' mainstream theories of political corruption tend to underline two main aspects of this problem. The first is the structural conditions which allow for (or deploy) the consolidation of corruption. Following different perspectives, theorists indicate that corruption is indissolubly linked to some particular structural conditions, be them cultural, economic or institutional (Kaufmann and Siegelbaum 1996; Bliss and Di Tella 1997). Corruption is an outcome of these conditions, and while it is allegedly more influential in some countries than others, corruption undeniably impacts political processes and decisions regardless of location. As such, corrupt practices are seen as structural to the functioning of political (or even social) systems (Della Porta and Vannucci 1995; Shleifer and Vishnt 1998). The second aspect concerns the inherent idea that corruption is a deviation from what should be deemed a public notion of politics. Following political philosophical theory that descends from Hobbes and Tocqueville, the origin of corruption is searched in the incapacity of those in power to maintain the public and the private spheres separated. In other words, corrupt practices are interpreted as forms of personal misbehavior by public officers who seek private gain by taking advantage of their position. Corruption, then, becomes identified with misbehavior, abuse of office, vice and even greed, whereas the fight against corruption is a virtuous course of action (de Sousa et al. 2008). This second position is often used complementarily to the first, with corruption analyzed as both an institutional and an individual-centred phenomenon.

Anthropologists have recently attempted to find a third way between these two perspectives, and eventually to disclaim their apparently unchallengeable analytical strength. One way has been to stress that corruption is far from being culturally or socially grounded, since it is elsewhere, from the top to the bottom entries in the Transparency International Perception Index list (Haller and Shore 2005; Torsello 2005). A second way, as seen above, has been to attempt to bridge the two positions proposing an attention to the moral dimension (Pardo 2004). Corruption becomes a condition for achieving a sort moral order (or plural orders), in ways which are familiar to the actors directly involved, but less to those external to that order. In this position, the vice of being corrupt becomes a 'strategy' not only in the sense of favoring political and economic action, but also in the social meaning of building identities, maintaining factions and cliques, and attaining legitimacy.

The TEN-T is currently one of the most prospective basins for political corruption in the EU territory. It is widely known that corruption practices have been tied with the construction business even in 'culturally more virtuous' countries such as the US, Canada and Japan. Indeed, the construction sector is one of the fields where interest lobbies are easily built and substantiated under ideologies of progress, development, modernization. In the case of the TEN-T the multilayered structure of power and the different strategies (and interests) provide much room for corruption, even if this is not always evident from the outside. One reason is that the intersection between the different layers is not itself a transparent process.

National and local politicians in the Czech Republic were not able to solve (also because being confronted by the civic groups) the issue whether to build connection via Mikulov or via Břeclav. According to the environmental movements in Brno at this point a visible political trick was implemented. In June 2008, the Czech Government adopted a Decree (No. 735) which agreed with both roads. According to some of the members of the local NGOs the 'double design' of the Czech portion of the Brno-Vienna highway is the outcome of the need to respond to the interests of two sets of contrasting entrepreneur and/or politician lobbies in the Mikulov and Břeclav areas. Ironically, this fact was publicly admitted by the Czech Prime Minister in a declaration in 2008 directly in the Czech Parliament. He stated that 'Eventually both lobby groups will be satisfied, the one which purchased land at Mikulov as well the one which purchased the land at Bøeclav ...'.[10] The lobbies (composed of so far not identified individuals) obviously urged to have the highway built around one or the other town to satisfy the demand of land speculators (from entrepreneurs to politicians) who controlled large portions of the land to be bought for the highway construction. The regional civic organizations have found allegations that the land in question had been accumulated in advance, when only those close to the superior political layers could know about the TEN-T design. Allegedly, the Mikulov lobby section seemed better positioned than the

---

10   See http://www.psp.cz/eknih/2006ps/stenprot/038schuz/s038096.htm#r4.

Breclav because of the large availability of desmane land deriving from land which under socialism had been confiscated from Sudeten German families living in the area.

The situation can be, however, more complicated and possibly even more explosive. At a meeting of South Moravia Regional Council on 9 November 2006, the former First Deputy of the President of the Council publicly told the Council that there he was 'personally attacked by subjects paid from Austria.' Despite efforts of Czech NGOs to get the meaning of this statement clarified, they never got an answer.

The Czech Supreme Audit Office also touched on this point to some extent when it stated in its Audit Report No. 08/26 (of July 2009) that the:

> Czech Ministry of Transport did not study he societal aspects of the commissioning of Brno-Vienna connection, but allowed Austria to take over all the initiatives, what resulted in the selection of the most risk-prone road alignment for the Czech Republic.[11]

The most serious official finding in the matter was published in the Official 2008 Annual Report of the Czech Intelligence Service ('*Bezpečnostní informační služba*'), which stated that:

> The Service was also interested in preparation of some important traffic infrastructure project (e.g. road R52) [...] In these cases lobby groups purposely tried to influence decision making of organisations reporting to the Ministry of Transport, including exercising force methods.[12]

Speculation did not take the form of land ownership only. Other efforts include for instance the creation of a large recreation centre (thermal spa, hotel and other amenities) on a spot close to the NATURA 2000 protected area, some hundred metres away from the place where the R52 should be built. The investor received a conspicuous funding from the regional government as part of the scheme for the development of rural tourism, but it is very peculiar that the chosen site is in the exact proximity of the planned road (see the following case study).

The importance attributed to the Brno-Vienna section is itself part of a political willingness to increase the visibility of Brno, the second largest city in the Czech Republic, still too far behind Prague in terms of economic and touristic development. In the local municipalities it is believed that this section of the corridor is the result of the strong determination of several Czech politicians from Moravia who fought to modify the logical and shorter TEN-T corridors Vienna – Břeclav – Katowice and Vienna – Znojmo – Prague to one longer and uneconomical Vienna – Brno with continuations to Prague (to the west) and Katowice (to the east). The problem arose

---

11   Page 201 of document http://www.nku.cz/kon-zavery/K08026.pdf.

12   See http://www.bis.cz/n/2009–08–31-vyrocni-zprava-2008.html, Section 1.2..

when there proved to be little substantiation, according to the TEN-T standards, for the R52-A5 corridor section. Official studies funded by the Czech government, which according to Nebojsa and OS Brno have required excessively large amounts of money to be conducted, have been commissioned to support those politicians' wish to portray the R52 as the most economical and justifiable variant from the perspective of traffic volume. According to environmental activists, these studies, although publicly announced as 'studies for Brussels', were never as a whole sent to Brussels and never provided to JASPERS (the Common Service of the Commission and the European Investment Bank, which allots the TEN-T funds)[13]. On the other hand, 'unofficial' studies commissioned by the civic organizations (but developed by authorized traffic planners and environmental assessment experts) have proved that the opposite is true. These studies were submitted to Brussels and the European Commission pointed to their existence in the correspondence with the Prague Ministry of Transport.

A final point concerns the issue of the need of the Brno-Vienna project in relation with the traffic volume. OS Brno denounced that the Road and Motorway Directorate eventually contradicted itself once a new book cosigned by the Director General of the Road and Motorway Directorate was published in 2009.[14] This book contains a map with traffic intensities predicted for the whole Czech Republic up to the year 2030. It does not show the high traffic values used in the official justifications for R52, i.e. values substantially over 20 thousand vehicles per day, but only 8 – 10 thousand vehicles per day in the Mikulov area and consistently less than 20 thousand vehicles per day for the whole planned segment of R52. These 'new official values' come close to two expert studies commissioned by NGOs since 2007. Thus, the producing of statistical data on volumes of traffic relative to the roads in question would have been flawed of irregularities and lack of transparency. On the other hand, local government sources reject these accusations on the grounding that civic organizations' own studies and esteems of traffic would not be taking due consideration of the enlarging volume of traffic which would be, in the years to come, generated, among many, by the completion of the corridor.

Civil society against corruption

The civic organizations have protested that their assessments have been ignored and that the data provided by the official figures do not always correspond to the reality. It has been questioned whether the specialists (companies) who provided such data are close to personal figures in the regional governments. This protest has

---

13 See http://www.jaspers-europa-info.org/index.php/czech-republic.html.

14 This book was distributed in hardcopy and it was published on http://www.rsd.cz/doc/Silnicni-a-dalnicni-sit/Dalnicni-publikace/paterni-sit-dalnic, but was recently removed from the website.

been forwarded both to the regional authorities and, later, to the EC. Corruption arose at different levels in the planning and implementation of the project, even though accusations and allegations could not easily be proved. Corruption was used by the different types of civic organizations in different manners, usually according to their respective strategies. In the first period such allegations were moved by the third type of organizations, those who had the expertise and personal contacts with policy makers, lawyers and technicians to understand the wrongdoings. Later on, corruption has become a useful instrument also for the first type of (local) organizations, which experienced that it had a much stronger appeal to the general public than the environmental problems. The same mayors who joined the protest were aware of this, suggesting that it is only 'dirty politics' that may interest people. However, it has to be underlined that corruption is, in such a complex case of study dominated by different interlacing layers of power, built and discussed at different levels.

At an upper level, one which is out of reach of the denouncement of the active members in the NGOs, is the 'road business', one dominated by cartels of multinational companies. A number of these have long-established personal networks both within the national political establishment and within the countries' regional governments. According to third-type organizations, in some cases these cartels have already established their areas of competence within the Eastern European, the most attractive construction market within the EU. Once rumors of a prospective project become substantiated, the multinational companies may be able to activate their contacts with local (or even national) politicians to get assurance about their future victory in the contractor bid. The monopolizing power of such cartels tends to become so strong that the nature of the bids can become flawed from the very moment of the TEN-T design. Allegations of corruption in public tenders about construction are very diffused in Central Eastern European countries, as the media have portrayed these episodes. More difficult is, however, to understand what is the public perception of the gravity of such episodes. One efficient way to influence this perspective has been that of denouncing the high costs of the highway, the burden it will have on the taxpayers in the future, and finally its positive impact on those lobbying sections who call for the economic development of the region through amelioration of infrastructures, shopping facilities and recreation centres.

The construction of highways in the Czech Republic has been seen as overpriced for a very long time, but hardly any official steps were taken by the Ministry of Transport and by the Road and Motorway Directorate. Czech National Economical Advisory Group, an expert group (called NERV) established by the Czech Government issued its final report in September 2009.[15] This points to the major difference of construction costs for projects funded by public money and construction costs funded from private resources. The report touches on

---

15   See: http://www.vlada.cz/assets/media-centrum/dulezite-dokumenty/zaverecna-zprava-NERV.pdf

the connection between corruption and public spending,[16] summarizing that the infrastructure projects are 1.62 times more expensive compared to prices level in housing projects. According to the OS Brno, there are two problems which still hamper transparency. First, the Prague Ministry of Transport informed the Czech Government several times since the signature of the Operational Programme Transport that no EU funds are to be used for the Brno – Vienna connection. This means, in the eyes of the civic organizations, that no comparison of variants will be submitted to Brussels for an independent supranational evaluation in spite of Brussels' explicit requests. Second, once the already allocated EU funds will not be used for the projects of European interest and European priority, the EU resources will be used for unimportant projects, what cannot be seen otherwise than a potential misuse and/or waste of EU resources so far employed in the Brno-Vienna axis.

Another order of problems comes from the high stratification of political interests and forces. As long as the motorway project is conceived and mediated within although different, but aligned and non-conflicting, political arenas (from the state to regional and local governments) it is highly probable that corruption will arise, as the interests of each layer move particular strategies and decisions that in the end coincide. The problem arises when civic organizations, which collaborated among them within a similarly multilayered structure, had been able to detect (directly or indirectly) a loss of transparency. At this point these organizations have understood that corruption can be used as an efficient instrument in two directions. The first is communication with EU authorities and offices which was rendered possible by the mediation of the fifth type of organizations, with seats in Brussels. The second is the ability to maintain local citizens and some of the local governments involved in the protest. Concerning the former, corruption became an issue of public debate only at a later stage, when it was effectively communicated by local environmental organizations, and only after the official accusations of misconduct had been transmitted to the EC offices. The positive outcomes of collecting signs for the petitions and arranging public meetings were achieved only after corruption became debated and exposed. Concerning local governments, the allegations of speculation on desmane and private land, and the pressures to have the (redundant) motorway built at high costs touched mainly the two towns of Mikulov and Breclav. Most local villages remained 'clean' partly because their decisions over land use had to be taken after the Regional Land Plan was issued (in 2006), partly because, as mentioned above, a number of local entrepreneurs has already become involved in these maneuvers and these became exposed by media coverings.

It is probably no coincidence that local civic organizations have been constituted where little or no speculative interests originated out of the project. What is more striking is that local government's decisions to become actively involved in the environmental protest has to do with the ability to channel corruption as a

---

16   See pages 31–9 of NERV report.

denounce of strategies undertaken by the town or 'less virtuous' rural communities. Corruption and allegations of speculation over public development projects became fruitful discourses allowing some of these municipalities to maintain legitimacy and eventually gain trustworthiness. This similar strategy was pursued by the environmental organizations when it became clear that such allegations could be used in destabilizing the regional and even national authorities in the eyes of the EU.

Conclusion

This case study, in its complexity, reveals a number of important points that need to be taken into account in understanding the impact of the TEN-T projects at national and local levels. Because of the nature of its design, the TEN-T is a transnational endeavor which aims to improve transport and connectivity among EU countries. Nonetheless, the transnational character of the project is profoundly marked by the national and regional features that allow for its implementation. Not only can regional and local political forces modify the original plan, but, as the Brno-Vienna protest showed, they can even effectively bring discussion of more useful variants to media and potentially stop a maligned project. This alone is a proof of the weakness of those arguments in favor of neat separation of the different layers of power from transnational to local level. The ambivalence in the interaction between state and global forces, the local and the trans-local is here of less analytical importance than the effects of the multilayered structure of power, two of which have been the object of this chapter: civic and environmental activism and corruption. These two are not completely unrelated phenomena. Civic and environmental activism, for the case of the Brno-Vienna highway connection is the outcome of lack of transparency in the implementation process of this TEN-T section, as well as a product of the degree of power stratification. Civic and environmental protests related to transport development projects are not rare cases in the TEN-T scheme, and so are denounces of corrupt practices. What can be learned from this case study is that the inability of the state and of regional government to cope with the environmentally harmful potential of these projects is a striking feature not typical of post-socialist Europe alone (see for instance the protest against the high speed railway in northern Italy). The EU seems unable to comply with its own prescriptions caught in between the need to maintain its commitment towards global goals and the respect of the countries' autonomy. The work of civic and transnational organizations attempts to counterbalance the prevalence of lobbies' and groups financial and speculative interests. However, the different layers of power prove to be porous and easily penetrable by converging interests and forces. Corruption emerges among these forces and gains space in the multilayered structure of the development project, through its EU-originating funding scheme. Nonetheless, corruption is also a powerful narrative which has proved more beneficial than the environmentalist rhetoric not only to spur citizens' prolonged involvement in the protest, but also to maintain a small number of municipalities on the side of the activists.

Chapter 6

Case Three: Railway Transport Project in North-Western Italy – The TAV

This chapter addresses a railway transport development project in north-western Italy, seen through the complex and elongated phases of its planning. The project belongs to the umbrella of the TEN-T Corridor 5, one of the major and most contested of the EU trans-national traffic networks. The case study presents a paradoxical situation in which a railway development plan, which in principle should constitute an environmentally positive alternative to road transport, has stirred a massive and fierce environmental protest by the local inhabitants of one valley (Susa Valley) at the Alpine border between Italy and France. The dynamics of this protest, the involvement of local, national and EU political institutions, the language and rhetoric through which the real contents of the project are revealed to local citizens are strikingly flexible and mutable, showing a strong predisposition towards adapting and readapting to changing needs and conditions from all the parties involved. Although this example (which shows a still ongoing struggle between local citizens and civic organizations against the creation of a fast railway (Turin-Lyon) which would cut across a valley in average not broader than 2 km) has been used by social scientists as one of the best demonstrations of 'participated' versus 'representative' democracy, I will demonstrate that corruption and political misconducts have recently become the most sensitive issues through which choices, strategies and communication techniques of the civic organizations are conveyed. On the other hand, I will tackle the diversification of the form and activity spheres of the civic movements, and their ability to construct discourses of time and space that instil in the local population ideas of belonging, common identity and shared participation.

The first part of the chapter introduces the railway project, framing it within the general technical prescriptions of the Corridor 5 programme. In the second part I will analyse the long chronology of events which have marked the protest and the planning of the project. The third part looks at the civic organizations which have developed, or gained strength through the protest, their strategies, limits and ways of communicating with local inhabitants. In the last part I will deal with the different political arena in which the negotiation, alteration and diverse interpretation of the project takes place. This final part will stress the meaning that corrupt practices come to assume not only for those allegedly involved, but more significantly for the local people.

The Turin-Lyon railway project and the Corridor 5

The Turin-Lyon railway section belongs to the intermodal Corridor 5 planned to traverse eastward from Lisbon to Kiev. Corridor 5 runs across six EU countries (Portugal, Spain, France, Italy, Slovenia and Hungary) before reaching Ukraine and has three planned additional branches which connect Slovakia (Chapter 4), Croatia and Bosnia. The Corridor accounts approximately for 3270 km of railways and 2850 of roads. Negotiations among countries on the project started as early as 1996, when Italy was the first to sign agreements with Slovenia, Hungary and Ukraine, later Croatia and Slovakia joined the table (1997). The original feature of this corridor is that it includes both a motorway and a railway plan, including thus heavy ameliorations, restructuring and building of lines for the transport of passengers as well as cargo trains. On April 21, 2004, Brussels issued the new list of 30 priority projects within the TEN-T scheme, and the axis Lyon-Trieste-Ljubljana-Budapest-Ukrainian border was numbered project 6.

Italy plays a highly significant role in the project, being the natural bridge between the western and eastern Mediterranean regions. In fact, Italian involvement in the project has been very strong since the mid-1990s (similarly to France), also since the permanent secretariat of this corridor is based in Trieste. Since the project emphasizes cross-border cooperation among countries, especially in the case of transalpine communications, including tunnels, it becomes mandatory that countries ensure not only a good degree of communication and technical cooperation, but that are also responsible to balance time schedules in construction. This, together with the complex funding scheme of the TEN-T (Chapter 4), has so far proved to be one of the greatest limits of these projects.

Priority Project 6 (when it was conceived in 2004) was expected to be completed by 2017, while today there are expectations that the Corridor will be fully operative not earlier than 2030. Costs reached much higher levels than foreseen. This is not only due to delay in the implementation process, as all the case studies show, but significantly to the political costs which, as times passes, increase exponentially. For example, in 2004 the estimated cost of the trans-border Italian tunnel section of the railway axis was 5.9 billion euro, while in 2010 it has reached 19.8 billion.

Concerning the present state of the project, in Italy there are only minor sections of the railway and highway systems that are operational. These sections only cover roughly one-fourth of the overall foreseen length and they do not include the more problematic trans-border sections with France and Slovenia. Cross-country agreements are particularly problematic. For example, Slovenia has not yet built any km of the project, while France, on the other hand is pressing for a quick solution to the impasse that the Lyon-Turin section has encountered since its very beginning. Some Italian analysts (della Porta and Andretta 2002; Margaira 2005; Sasso 2005) point out that French eagerness to deal with the trans-border project depends on the favourable deal it struck with Italy in 2004 according to which the Italian side is to shoulder the 63% of the costs of the common project section. On the other hand, the Italian government has in recent years used the argument that the elevation in prices is 'structural' to the implementation process, and that the Italian-French agreement will be renegotiated.

According to the 2009 Project Activity Report, the Lyon-Turin section includes a 57 km tunnel at the French-Italian border and about 47 km of railway connection from Turin to Bussolino to be built. These are both decisive and problematic sections, the former for the strong protest object of this research and the latter for the need to improve the urban railway connection system to the city of Turin and avoid the so-far feared 'traffic bottlenecks'. These cases have raised strong awareness in the local population and different forms of protest are still active both in the Valley of Susa and in the outskirts of Turin to be interested by the restructuring of the railway system. In this chapter I will, however, focus on the first case.

The Turin-Lyon project in the Susa Valley

The Lyon-Turin section of Priority Project 6 has made up one of the most debated cases of ground-level reaction to major EU structural projects. This has happened, as in other corridors, because these projects present serious weaknesses at planning level. First, within an overall scheme of connectivity priority within the enlarged EU, both in Eastern and Western Europe, planning is often blind to the idiosyncrasies of European regions and to the different exigencies of their territories. Secondly, the ambitious project of bringing West and East closer, improving the transportation of goods and people was conceived in an age (mid-1990s) when many of the recent developments in transport were unexpected. One of these is surely the boom of low-cost airlines which, in the last 5 years, have seriously endangered at least one half of the initial mission of the TEN-T scheme. Concerning the transport of goods, little mention has ever been given to the actual environmental costs in term of building railway lines, digging tunnels and connecting cities; even though the EU declared priority for railway and seaways over motorways, which still favours the environmentalists. These weaknesses are often hidden behind the alluring and illusory map of a transnational corridor connecting countries and cities in an enlarged Europe.

The portion of the Lyon-Turin which intersects the Susa Valley is approximately 72 km long. It is divided into two sections, the first which connects the Low Valley (Bassa Val di Susa) at the town of Avigliana with the out-bounding traffic from Turin, the capital of the Piemonte region. The second section connects Avigliana with the French border, crossing the main town of the Mid Valley (Media Val di Susa), Susa, and reaching Modane, where the transalpine tunnel would start. The first section is easier to realize, except for the portion in the Turin urban area, for the reasons indicated above. The second part is the object of a protest lasting over twenty years. The main reasons for the protest is that the second portion of the railway, crossing the Low, Middle and High Susa Valley to Mondane, adds to two already existing motorways (a local road and a highway) and one double-track railway. Considering the geomorphological constitution of the Susa Valley, environmental activists and local inhabitants have judged that a second, high-speed railway line would bear too heavy a weight on the ecological capacities of the area.

The region is divided in three sections of Low, Middle and High Valley, and is inhabited by 113,000 people (data of 2009), presenting a diversified socio-economic structure. The Low Valley is mainly an outskirt of the industrial centres of the Turin province, with a strong activity in manufacturing, tourism and some agriculture. This is the most densely populated of the three sections, and the one which has received the heaviest structural intervention during the last three decades. The Middle section maintains some residuals of the agricultural production of the valley, in steady decline since the late-1980s. This section is of strategic importance for the project since it is here that the intermodal (road-rail) transport exchange should take place, building on the existing rail infrastructure which was ameliorated throughout the 1980s and again recently. Susa, the main centre of this section, is also the gateway to the High Valley, traditionally a favourite tourist destination to many Italians (as well as French and other foreigners) and recently experienced a sudden development after hosting the 2006 Winter Olympic Games. The High Valley has a largely independent economic life, it became able, thanks to heavy investment in tourism from the region and the Italian government (Bobbio 2007), to consolidate its attractiveness throughout the last two decades and is, in that, more directly linked to Turin than to the other centres of the Valley.[1] From this picture emerges that the degree of involvement in the transport project and its outcomes is dissimilar among the three sections, although they are all similarly interested by the construction of the high-speed railway. The Middle Valley, the one with the larger number of communes on its territory (16 on the 43 of the valley), has been from the beginning the most adverse to the project and still maintains this position. On the other hand, some of the communes of the Low Valley and High Valley (mainly of centre-right political orientation) have, in the last two years, decreased their support to the NO-TAV movement.

Environmental concerns

Apart for the fear of further traffic congestion, the anti-TAV (NO-TAV) movement supporters strongly emphasize three points against the project. They are the environmental impact, the economic viability and the political background implications.

---

1 This link has become particularly effective after the High Valley was chosen as one site of the 2006 Winter Olympic Games in Turin. Recent investigations and Italian media reports have pointed out the high costs of the games and partly the usefulness of many of its infrastructures (including sport facilities) which presently stand abandoned or only partially used.

The first is that general pollution is expected to increase following the start of the project. Pollution concerns air, water and noise intruding elements. On December 12th, 1992 in the cinema of Condove members of the NO-TAV movement, together with an academic from the Politecnico University of Turin presented a noise simulation of the TAV train crossing the valley. The experiment was so impressive that the performers had to repeat it several times with dozens of people entering the hall at different times. According to a nonofficial study, the level of acoustic emissions in the Low and Mid Valley would become three times as high following the construction of the TAV line, whereas those of the Low Valley, where most of the industries are situated, would rise by 50–70% (Cancelli et al. 2006).

The most feared, however, are water, air and ground pollution. Concerning water pollution, the digging of a 52 km-long tunnel, which in some particular sections goes as deep as 2000 metres under the surface, will generate a huge amount of waste and will require a similar amount of water for the drilling. The water issue is particularly important for a valley which has still relatively pure mountain water coming from the glaciers and underground. Thanks to the evidence which has arisen from the newly opened (2009) Bologna-Firenze TAV, environmental organizations have been able to stir public concern on the fear that the hydrological balance of the valley be seriously damaged, thus denouncing the dispersion of billions of cubic metres of water. Moreover, the valley has been, in the years following the completion of the A32 highway,[2] subject to heavy floods which consistently differed in intensity from traditional floods, due to the critical alteration of the bed of the Dora River.[3]

The most effective weapon in the hands of the NO-TAV, however, are the risks connected with ground pollution. Following independent specialist studies in the mineral composition of the valley rocks, it has emerged that these contain relevant quantities of asbestos, uranium composites and even radon gas. Each of these three elements, contained in dangerous quantities, would be enough to discourage drilling of kilometres of tunnels, but their presence does not seem to influence the decisions of the region and of the Italian government. On the contrary, a number of official geological studies, following drilling tests undertaken in 23 locations, specify that both the uranium and asbestos presence is within alert levels. Environmental organizations, on the other hand, denounce that these studies are partial, that they reveal serious conflicts of interest between those technicians in

---

2   The A32 highway connects Turin with Bardonecchia, at the French border through the tunnel of Frejus, with a length of 72.4 km. It was completed in 1994, and had further adjustments and ameliorations in 2006 in occasion of the Turin Winter Olympics. The highway crosses the Susa valley accompanied by two national roads, number 23 and 25, and the existing railway.

3   Floods have regularly occurred in the Susa Valley delimited by the Dora Riparia River, which flows into the Po, the major Italian river. In the past century major floods have occurred in 1957, 1977, 1994 and 2000.

charge of the environmental impact assessment and the CP,[4] and that material from the pilot drills has only selectively and partially been examined. Whatever the truth, the fear of radioactive and cancerous material coming to the surface after drilling the soil, or contaminating it and the valley's water sources is enough of a risk to stir public concern and preoccupation with the results of the project.

The second point refers to the viability in economic terms of the project. Feasibility studies sponsored by the Italian Railway Company have repeatedly pointed out that there are two arguments for supporting the TAV line in the Valley. The first is the regular increase in the traffic of goods along the corridor which has been calculated to 37.7% for road transport in the decade 1994–2004. Rail transport (of goods), instead, has lost 21.1% of its traffic in the same decade.[5] This data along with the figures on a prospective increase of traffic following railway amelioration leads one to the conclusion that by 2030 the corridor foresees an average of 40 million/tons per year of rail and road transport together, against the 9.4 million/tons per year that passed in 2000. The second argument, following the application of these estimates is that by 2020 the Pass of Modane (which the existing rail and road lines use to cross the French border) will be saturated with traffic and will hence create a bottleneck to Corridor 5 (Quaderno 2: 64).

On the other hand, 'unofficial' estimates are much more cautious. They point out that overall freight transport along the Lyon-Turin line has steadily decreased since its peak in 1994 when it reached 10 million tons per year. According to recent estimates, in 2006 freight transport (including rail and road) along the Susa Valley was as low as 7 million tons, with a decrease of over 14% in the last 7 years.[6] According to environmentalist groups there is no immediate need to build the TAV line since the freight transport estimates are stable – if not negative – in the coming years. Moreover, they (and on this the majority of the municipal administrations of the Mid and Low Valley agree) envisage that doubling of the existing railway line would be enough to meet the actual freight and passenger traffic.

In summary, the TAV project, which along the EU Corridor perspective was designed to target both passengers and freight transport, has gradually shifted to freight only (from 'high speed' to 'high capacity' as some of the environmental groups point out). The reasons are various; one is that the Lyon-Turin connection is only of secondary importance compared to the Paris-Milan axis, to which much of the recent train traffic has been diverted. The second refers to the allegedly wrong planning policies of the Italian Railway (FS) which has gradually been closing down minor stations in the valley since 2000, decreasing the number of trains

---

4   One point of criticism has been that these studies have been undertaken by personnel who are paid, in other duties, by companies close to the contractors of the project. Such irregularity has been detected in other cases of TAV projects in Italy (Imposimato et al. 1999).

5   Quaderno 2 dell'Osservatorio Torino-Lione, Scenari di traffico alpino, Turin: 2006.

6   These data are issued by the Cooperation on Alpine Railway Corridors (CARC 2006), in conjunct work by Italy, France, Switzerland, Austria and Slovenia.

and other international connections excluding fast trains.[7] The decision has been interpreted by these two associations as a further drive to appease public opinion by acknowledging the necessity of high-speed connections. The unexpected outcome, however, has been the steady decrease of passengers travelling on the Lyon-Turin line which, along with the general decline of circulating railway cargos, produces numbers increasingly insufficient to justify the TAV project on the line. On their side, the Italian Railway denounces that the decline in freight transport is to be imputed to the general economic crisis and expects an improvement in the years to come defending the argument that better infrastructures will cause an increased demand for transport.

The third point covers the political strategies which are perceived to underscore the TAV. A detailed treatment will follow, however it is first important to point out that it constitutes the most recent development of the NO-TAV movement. In the first half of its twenty years of history, the movement addressed political issues only marginally. In the 1990s the TAV was a feared project not only for the environmental consequences, but also because all political parties with very few exceptions (the greens, Verdi and the communists, PRC) supported it. This unusual alignment in Italian politics was itself ominous for the residents of the valley, but nothing more. There were still no allegations of corruption or illegal procedures behind the plans of bringing high speed trains, also because the state and regional authorities presented the project most as a European (and less as national) priority. In the first half of the year 2000, however, the other side of the coin slowly manifested. The government, including the left-wing cabinet led by Prodi in 2006, never stopped to support the TAV, whereas the first stories and data about other TAV projects realized in the country became available, usually through internet and small radio programs rather than in national TV channels and newspapers (Cedolin 2006). Thus, it became, for example, known that the Milan-Naples connection came to be as 5.2 times more expensive than foreseen (from 26.180 billion lire, or 13 billion euro in 1991 to 78 billion euro in 2009 for 1000 km), that the Bologna-Florence 78 km section, made up of 73 km of tunnels has wasted some 100 billion litres of spring-water, drying out most of the spring sources in the Mugello region, causing dozens of cases of landslides among which one of a 3 km section of the tunnel, that the Rome connection of the TAV has left over a hundred families without their homes, forcing them to live in new apartment blocks few metres from the 12-metre tall wall fencing from the railway line (Cedolin 2006: 12–16). Several other scandals have arisen over the last four years involving a number of key political and managerial positions in the TAV business throughout the peninsula, including corruption, abuse of office and collusion with criminal networks and enterprises (for more details see Imposimato et al. 1999). In spite of the cautious treatment of these incidents by national and regional media, their echo has reached the NO-TAV movement as

---

7   This position was developed mainly by Legambiente, operating in Turin, and only later adepte by the NOTAV movement as a whole.

early as 2003, strengthening the legitimacy of the protest at local level, as well as strengthening ties between environmental and other civic organizations and the local administrative institutions which had been protested from the very beginning for various reasons.

The chronology of the NO-TAV movement

1990–2000

The first institutional steps towards the TAV project were taken in 1990 when the Committee for the Promotion (CP) of the TAV line was founded. The CP included members such as the president of the Piemonte region and, among others, Umberto Agnelli of the FIAT car manufacturer. The Susa Valley had already been protesting against a series of projects with heavy environmental impact, among them the completion of the A32 highway (which needed twenty years to be completed), two power stations and, in the past decade, a nuclear power plant, which was cancelled thanks to the strong opposition of the valley. Thus the valley was not new to the environmental protest movement.

In 1990 the association Habitat was founded, which included a number of environmental activists and cooperation agreements with some syndicates. In 1991 the FS and the CP, which had become a vehicle for bringing together most of the region and Turin's entrepreneurs calling for the investment, issued its first study of feasibility after signing a cooperation agreement with the French side. This marked the beginning of the NO-TAV campaigns which included petitions in the valley, public demonstrations, strikes and study meetings and workshops in which academic staff and technicians were invited to assess the environmental and economic impacts of the project. In 1993 the communes of the Low Valley unanimously approved a common document which denounced the TAV and voiced their opposition to any kind of variants of the project. The document was signed by 24 mayors. In 1996 a public demonstration against the project took place at S.Ambrogio, with all the mayors wearing the official insignia and holding the flag of their communes at the head of the procession. In 1995 the region issued the final version of the project, and in response, Habitat and Legambiente, the first active environmental organizations to give voice to the protest, enlisted local engineers to graphically reproduce the project, written in a highly technical language with tens of maps of difficult interpretations. The result was a 12 metres long white sheet knitted from different pieces which faithfully reproduced the map of the valley with the planned interventions. The sheet was used frequently by the activists and unrolled at many demonstrations and public events.

1996 marked the first of the two peaks of violence in the NO-TAV process that lasted until 1998. A number of acts of violence and damages were committed toward the railway electric boxes, power generators as well as TV and telephone antennas in the Valley. The name NO-TAV repeatedly appeared in each of these incidents. What is worse, on March 5 1998, three young anarchists from Turin were accused to be among the guilty persons of some of these incidents and subsequently taken to prison. Two of them committed suicide while under arrest. The third was condemned to 6 years for terroristic activity, but then released in 2001 because accusations against him were found inconsistent. In 1996, the first corruption scandals related to key figures of the FS emerged involving the manager Lorenzo Necci, who was arrested for allegations of corruption of magistrates and false consultancies.

By the end of 1996 all three sections of the Valley had joined the protest and organized a Coordination Committee which met regularly to spread information and institutional updates. This committee worked efficiently to coordinate not only initiatives taken in the single communes (until that moment the Low Valley had been more active, but initiatives spread quickly throughout the valley), but also to create a platform where exponents of the several civic organizations could meet. By the end of 1999 the number of civic organizations in the Valley had reached about thirty units, some of them were apolitical, merely environmental organizations (Pro Natura is one of the most typical cases), while others originated from youth movements (Spinta dal Bass) or from anarchic organizations (Asakatsuna).

On March 24, 1999, a terrible accident took place in the tunnel of the Monte Bianco pass, where 39 people died under the fire and smoke of the gallery. Following the accident and the closure of the pass the Susa Valley became the only transit way to France. Hence, in this year and in 2000 the number of trucks crossing the border at Frejus increased threefold. Protest events however, did not decrease and the environmental organizations slowly sought collaboration and confrontation outside of Italy. In the meantime, similar movements had arisen in France (mainly around Lyon) and in the Basque territories in Spain, where other sections of the Corridor 5 came under serious debate. From this point onwards a number of large demonstrations saw participation of French (and even Basque) activists, and in turn, delegations from the Susa Valley joined their French counterparts on different occasions.

2000–2010

The second decade of the protest can be roughly divided into two sub-periods. The first, 2000–2006, was marked by recrudescence of the confrontation between NO-TAV movement and the national and regional institutions supporting the project. This period also marked the definitive strengthening of public awareness for the protest, and the climax of the positive results reached by the NO-TAV which ultimately, in 2006, suspended its operations. After this year, however, the protest entered a different phase, marked by a deeper interest with politicization and a less violent confrontation with the supporting parties. This process, at the time of writing, is still ongoing and it is deemed to cause decisive results in the following months.

In 2001 a further cooperation agreement (there have been nine up until 2010) was signed by Italy and France with Prime Minister Berlusconi visiting the French counterpart to warm up the cooling interest by the French premier[8] (Bobbio 2007). It is at this time that Italy struck an unfavourable deal with France promising to shoulder the 63% of the costs of the common international section of the line. The two companies, the French RTF and the Italian RFI were created to jointly manage the project and the Italian media strongly voiced the necessity for the country, and above all the north-western regions not to miss this precious occasion of development and modernization. A more vehement public standpoint originated in the Region of Piemonte, when members of the president's staff (of left-wing orientation) starkly denounced the 'backward' and 'anti-progress' positions of the NO-TAV supporters.

Wide-scale demonstrations, strikes and information propaganda actions followed throughout the first half of the 2000s. In 2003, the manifestation *In Marcia per la Valle*[9] (In March for the valley) called for some 20000 participants, which became around 50000 (according to national media 20000) in the largest participation of the protest, held in Turin in 2005. The same year, in June, a number of thirty mayors from the valley met with the Minister of Transport and other political officers in Rome to present the reasons of their opposition. The attempt, like their previous attempt in Turin, was unsuccessful.

The year 2005 was highlighted by an escalation in violence by the opposition. Technicians of the RFI were escorted by anti-uprising special police squads in the sites where they were to start pilot drills according to the new project issues in the same year. Three times in autumn and later in winter there were cases of serious fights between the police which forcedly pushed the protesters out of the designed sites on where they had built permanent camps (presidi). In the operations a number of protesters were injured by police officers, and in turn, some police officers are also hurt. According to the environmental organizations, the opposition of the NO-TAV had remained peaceful during the occupation by the police, and some accounts of the incidents even question reports of police officers 'injured' in the most violent of the skirmishes, the 'Battle of Seghino'[10] (Sasso 2006: 111). After

---

8   In the course of the recent meeting between the Italian and French prime ministers, on 26–4–2011, no direct mention was made to the Lyon-Turin project. Although the Italian parliament has urged a report on the state of the affairs from the Ministry of Transport to be completed in the early months of 2011, so far no concrete step has been taken in this direction.

9   The manifestation, held on May 31, was one of the largest of the movement in the valley. Along with the wide participation from local citizens, all environmental groups, from local to national and transnational (WWF) were present, as well as religious authorities from the local communes and members of the two Comunità montane of the Low and Middle Valley. The manifestation also hit the record of 55 mayors lining in the march from local municipalities.

10   On October 31, 2005 dozens of policemen gathered in the early morning around the small village of Seghino, at 700 m on the Susa mid valley. Facing each other at the two ends of a small stone bridge were military and police forces in assault uniforms and women, elderly and young people holding in their hands the white flag with the red NO TAV on it.

occupying the sites where the drilling was planned to start the RFI authorities built fences and started to bring in the relevant machineries, unfortunately some days later the protesters broke in and reoccupied the sites impeding any further action.

The events of 2005 signalled an important development for the future of the project in different modalities. First, the NO-TAV movement effectively proved its cohesion and inner strength to the country. The media, which up to that point had neglected the actions of the opponents, depicting them as 'anarchists', 'no-global', 'backward' or even 'antidemocratic' were forced to admit that the movement was something more than a handful of violent youngsters. This admission coincided with the increased ability of the NO-TAV to build networks with other environmental movements throughout the country, especially against the bridge over the Messina Strait (see Della Porta and Piazza 2008 for a comparison on the two movements). Until that moment only occasional and scattered information had been conveyed by the mainstream media on the project and, as a result, many followers of other environmental protests were largely misinformed on the Susa issue.

Secondly, the CP and RFI realized, for the very first time, the real possibility of negotiating with local authorities and even some sections of the environmental movement. Negotiation had until that point been avoided, perhaps due to a sort of superiority on the side of the promoters, who underestimated the scope and capacity of the movement. Confrontation, however, was also sought due to two events which alleviated tension on the regional and national sides. These were the organization of the Winter Olympics, held in Turin and the surrounding valleys in 2006, and the national elections held the same year. The actual respite was sought before the Olympic Games, in fear of other major demonstrations through the decision to establish an Observatory for the Turin-Lyon project, commissioned to the director Mario Virano, an architect who had been working in one of the societies cooperating with RTF and RFI. The Observatory accepted in its study groups representatives of the communes of the valley and the president of the Comunità Montana,[11] Antonio Ferrentino, one of the most esteemed personalities by the NO-TAV groups.

They were local inhabitants, forced to look for sloppy and slippery paths to arrive to the place, avoiding the three blockades installed by the policemen. The 'battle' lasted until 5 pm, with different attempts of the police to break the human wall which, with a number of mayors wearing the tricolor insignia, opposed singing and raising their hands. At the end of the day the protesters had gained an unexpected victory, but they have become aware that they could no longer feel safe any time of the day. Since then the blockades became almost permanent, every local inhabitant was questioned daily one or more times for his documents, repeatedly stopped at police controls.

11   The Comunità Montana is an organization of local governments and institutions situated in mountain regions which was established in 1971 and regulated in 2000. Participation of communes that belong to mountain regions in the country is obligatory, the communities participate in the development, social and territorial planning of all the municipalities which belong to them. A number of Italian regions have tried to abolish these institutions which have proved problematic to management and difficult conciliation

Thirdly, the degree of politicization by the NO-TAV movement began to change after 2006. Until then all civic organizations had deliberately avoided clear political implications of pluralism (see below), one of the strongholds of their protest, however after Romano Prodi's victory things started to change. The great majority of Turin's administrative boundary was, at the time, under leftist administrations. The mayors who had joined the Committee were mostly of the same party (the left DS, then turned into PD) of the members of the new cabinet, hence it was more difficult to maintain an overtly colliding position towards the government. On top of this was the violence of the forced occupation campaigns which were undermining stability in the movement. The presence of Ferrentino as well as of a number of mayors in the table of designing the new project were, finally, new incentives to seek a better opposition not only in ideological and environmental terms, but also politically.

The work of the Observatory proceeded relatively fast, with over 2000 pages of publications on feasibility studies, assessments of economic and environmental viability, making the largest and most detailed study among the cases presented in this volume. After 100 weeks of meetings, the final report was issued on July 30, 2009. On the other hand, the Comunità Montana had issued its own report with technicians nominated by it under the name FARE (Ferrovie Alpine Ragionevoli ed Efficienti, Reasonable and Efficient Alpine Railway) in 17–6–2008. The report envisaged all possible scenarios in the TAV line, including the so-called 'zero option', where no new line was to be built. The report was received and commented by the Observatory but, following new elections and the institution of Berlusconi's new cabinet in 2008, the mood for the TAV project had already changed.

The new elections had marked a different approach to the protest. For the first time a number of communes presented electoral lists to NO-TAV, in open conflict with the orthodox position of their (left-wing) party. 14 such lists won the national elections and, in spite of the fact that a number of communes became right-wing administrations, they were still able to gain the majority in the Comunità Montana at the following regional elections on November 2009 with a number of leftist communes. Paradoxically, the result turned out to be much more harmful after Bresso, the former Piemonte region's president (left-wing coalition), decided to reduce the number of Comunità Montane from 46 to 22. This step, which unified the Susa Valley with the neighbouring Sangone Valley and diluted the NO-TAV vetoing power, had the opposite outcome after the NO-TAV lists gained the majority of the unified Comunità Montana. Following this result, and the decentralization of decision mechanisms within the movement, it became clearer that activists could not deal with the process without being politicized outside the boundaries of their movement.

Increased politicization of the anti-TAV movement coincided with a stronger awareness of the weight of corruption in the planning and implementation project.

---

of economic and political interests, but attempts achieved so far have all been declared as anti-constitutional.

Corruption was rarely used as a catchword in the early steps of the movement, especially because it was feared that 'common people would take the distance from a political movement'. After the completion of the other TAV sections in Italy, however, the situation began to change. The environmental organizations began to publish articles about the interrelation of murky political practices and national construction projects on their websites, and then the case of FS and the national highway system in particular. Towards the end of 2008 a giant banner was hung on one of the highest mountains in the valley: 'NO TAV NO MAFIA', which later appeared as graffiti at different sites. No organization claimed them, but they were received with high criticism by the local population who felt to have become politically stigmatized and damaged through these writings. They were removed after some days, but the impact they had was strong. In a general meeting of January 2009, when the Comunità Montana was about to issue a statement against the declaration restarting the drillings, some of the mayors publicly asked if the term '*mafioso*' could be added together with '*fascista*' to characterize some of the most violent dynamics of state intervention against the valley. The members of the environmental associations agreed and claimed that there were 'circumstances to justify such a strong standpoint'.

In spite of the stronger political weight of the NO-TAV, the government's and CP's positions do not show significant changes. In June 2010 a new plan was issued which, according to the committers, reflected some of the suggestions of the protesters. These are mainly relative to the railway section crossing the Low Valley including a reduction of a few kilometres of the tunnel connecting the outskirts of Turin with the valley and in its mid-course following the tracks of the already existing line around the town of Susa to be turned into an international exchange station. Few or no changes were introduced to the last tunnel section in the High Valley (57 km of tunnel reaching the border) and in the mid valley where most of the protest sites are presently located. The new project estimated some 20 billion euro in expenses, hoping to have the line ready no earlier than 2023. The NO-TAV movement confirmed its dissatisfaction with the project declaring itself ready to block any further attempt to drill the soil, if only for pilot tests. The situation is, still uncertain. A number of drilling sites have been established in the province of Turin, and they have drawn material for geological analysis. In the Susa region, however, to this day no further drilling has been successful. Technicians, usually escorted by over a dozen police officers have attempted repeatedly to enter the valley with the drilling machines, but once there they have always found protesters who blocked their operations.

From the viewpoint of the political negotiation, the institution of the Table smoothened conflicts to the point that a part of the proposals made by the FARE group has been incorporated into the new project design. This concerns, in particular, the opportunity to make use of a portion of the existing railway line. The problem remains, however, unsolved, for the tunnel, recently re-measured to 57 km, which should cut the whole valley in an area where environmental organizations claim there is plenty of underground asbestos. Financially, what raises further doubts, and what could potentially provide hope that the line will not be realized in the near future is the fact that the EU will not be able to provide more than the agreed sum of 53 million euro and the 20% of the common (Italian-French) costs of the work, which are estimated (abundantly according to some sites) at 9.6 billion euro, under the condition that Italy will receive its share only if the construction sites will be open and fully operative by 2011. Finally, concerning the viability of the project, accurate studies by the FARE committee have demonstrated that the TAV can no longer be conceived as a passenger transport project, at least in the next two decades. This happens, first because the automatic security system of the French bullet trains (TGV) is not compatible with the standards of the TAV system, preventing the French trains from circulating in Italian territory. Second, the Italian fast trains circulated on TAV lines cannot access the French high-speed railways. Third, even when the new generation of French bullet trains will be ready in ten-fifteen years, they will be unable to make use of the existing stations in Italy, including Milano and Turin. Hence, to the eyes of the environmentalists, the largest public work project of postwar Italy has clearly become an issue of money investment, in either its positive and negative connotations.

The nature of civic organizations

The first civic organization to be formed within the NO-TAV movement was named *Habitat*, constituted in the end of 1991. Habitat was born as a group of friends (about 60) who shared common interests in opposing the high-speed train project, and only a minority of them already had experience in civic organizations. The common theme was the environmental impacts of the project and this focus, without any clear indication about the political and economic aspects of the TAV, helped them to gain quick consent among the communes of the Low Valley. Their first events, dated in the end of 1992 and in the spring of 1993 repeated a pattern which had proved successful in attracting public attention: the simulation of the noise of running TAV trains in the valley. The experiment was possible thanks to the cooperation of two young researchers of the Technical University of Turin (*Istituto Politecnico di Torino*), which provided the instruments and technology for the simulation. During the following years this cooperation proved extremely useful to maintain the competence of the organization due to their technical expertise. As one of them had to say 'it was thanks to our ability to summon, all the time we needed, technical experts that the initial success of our organization can be read'. This cooperation has continued, even when in the early 2000s the organization decided to split in a number of different units. The splintering was not conceived as a defeat by the promoter of the Habitat, but rather as a concrete sign of the diversification of the protest, which coincided with the moment in which the protest was to be organized on different fronts.

From 2001 a number of youth organizations, usually leftist or no-global, had actively joined the front of the protest. The creation of Spinta dal Bass, an organization born after the split of Habitat, was significant in that it paved the way for over forty such organizations located in the different communes of the valley. Spinta dal Bass was founded by a number of young protesters, among them some of the cofounders of Habitat, which was perceived as an important asset by the participants who insisted to maintain a structure which was based on moving committees (*comitati in movimento*) which could constantly bring the protest in all the locations of the valley without privileging municipal orientations. This strategy, as observed by Bobbio (2007), as well as Della Porta and Andretta (2002) has proved particularly successful in the NO-TAV movement. Well aware of the danger of breaking down the protest in a number of local associations which privileged communal parochialism to a general and common aim, the supporters of the first two civic organizations, Habitat and Spinta dal Bass, maintained a high profile, remaining above local interests. This, in a moment in which the protest had been gaining momentum, such as after 2000, did not allow Habitat to remain as the only large umbrella-type of local organization.

After 2002, when the protest had already gathered a large consensus in the whole valley, large environmental associations such as Lega Ambiente, Italia Nostra and the WWF joined the protest and the ranks of its local supporters. In the beginning the role of these environmental think-tanks was mediated by minor environmental associations, such as Pro Natura, founded by a local engineer who had been working in amelioration projects on the railway line of the Susa Valley for several years. The pattern followed by Pro Natura was similar to that mentioned for the other associations. It started with a small number of members, typically based in the valley, and it aimed to enlarge the basis of its membership sharing themes common to the whole valley, organizing joint manifestations, study meetings and a number of public events (see below). After gaining consensus locally the association enlarged its structure, including personnel from the regional centre of Turin. This helped not only to bring the protest outside the valley, but more significantly to find important personal connections with technicians and experts who had been working for the regional offices who could provide information on the status of the project. Networking and providing technical expertise and counselling turned out to be the most important and successful strategy of these organizations (Habitat had done it in the first decade), which occupied an important niche in the overall structure of civil society. They did not aim to increase consent, but to raise the level of the protest by creating the knowledge to be shared (expertise, also on legal matters) for persuading local inhabitants and even local institutions that concrete and trustworthy answers could be provided regarding their various answers and doubts.

After 2003 local organizations mushroomed in the valley, including also the more reticent communes of the High Valley which had been less interested in the protest. By 2005 almost each commune of the Comunità Montana had its own organization, some of which were mainly groups of youths or cultural associations which took the NO-TAV as a common background around which to organize concerts, video nights, festivals and other night events. On the other hand, thanks to the close participation of local religious personalities in the demonstrations that followed the violent police actions of 2005 and 2006, the number of pacifist and catholic organizations supporting the protest increased significantly. Other groups that joined included the no-global, anarchist groups which expanded the protest to a wider repertoire of anti-capitalistic or anti-globalization political and ideological ideas. These groups were, although distant from the majority of the valley population, often in contact with artists and bands who accepted to play in the incredibly long list of valley events.

Another important asset that these groups were able to provide is shared contacts with other similar national groups. It was only after the escalation in violence that the NO-TAV became able to tighten collaboration and exchange of activities with other protest groups in the country. These included the other NO-TAV movements located in Rome, Turin, Bologna and Florence, a number of movements protesting in the territories of Naples and Salerno against the garbage crisis in the region, several movements denouncing eco-mafias and criminal activities related to the environment, and organizations in Calabria and Sicilia against the bridge on the Messina Strait. The number of the events organized jointly with these associations, or during which delegations were reciprocally sent to seek cooperation or share solidarity is very long, however, what is more relevant is that the already existing texture of protest movements in the Italian territories could be accessed through this section of civil society which was also, to many, the most problematic (see Sasso 2005 for a comprehensive treatment). Repeatedly, in different stages of the protest (e.g. 1997, 2005 and 2006), national and regional media denounced the violent and 'semi-terroristic activities' of anarchist movements cooperating with the NO-TAV. During a number of episodes such as the above mentioned damages to railway or electric boxes, finding explosives, bullets at TAV construction sites, the presence of no-global and anarchist sections were used by the press as a synonym of violence. This climate of terror, which escalated in two different periods in 1997 and 2006, and brought a number of police and military officials to the valley to establish a number of stable checkpoints, exerted considerable fright onto local citizens. The civic organizations had to decide whether to distance themselves from anarchist movements, irrespectively of their true or false involvement in the incidents, or to share solidarity with them, risking losing supporters who feared violence and the instrumental use of the protest. The movements chose not to take completely distance from the anarchist organizations, although caution was sought in strengthening ties with the local population increasing the number of public events and celebrations in the times of crisis. Among them, the number of events which included religious functions (processions, mass services and blessing of the different spots of the resistance in the valley) significantly increased in this period. It is hard to judge if this was another cohesive strategy or it came spontaneously from the participant themselves who included a number of priests and religious functionaries, especially in the communities of the Middle Valley.

These mixed and pluralistic strategies proved, on the long run, successful on two grounds. First, when the violence of the police intervention against the protesters became manifest in the episodes of Seghino, the large environmental and other civic organizations were in the position to show their coherence and gained credibility for not having denied their ongoing commitment with other forms of protest. Secondly, after 2006, with the change of government and the Winter Olympics, media treatment of the Susa Valley question became sensibly more cautious. The number of articles denouncing terrorism or violence from the NO-TAV decreased sensibly, and it became increasingly difficult to stigmatize the protest as an affair of a handful of violent anarchists. The large numbers of participants in the demonstrations in the valley and in Turin, bringing together tens of thousands people, did the rest, confirming the position that the diversified structure of the civic organizations, their attention to different sections and the cure of local communication were all positive ingredients for the duration of such a difficult and delicate protest.

'Making home' and 'living at slow speed': spatio-temporal strategies of protest

Anthropological literature of environmental protest movements in reaction to large development projects around the globe is extremely rich but scattered. A good number of anthropological accounts on environmental movements emphasize the dialogic processes through which the construction of shared meanings, temporally and locally close to the populations involved in the protest, or the political dynamics through which the movements are able to achieve public legitimacy, on the one hand, and decision-making power on the other. Following Gerlach's and Brandt insights (Gerlach 1987; Brandt 1997), I will put emphasis not only on the organizational structure of civic organizations, but more significantly on their political strategies, which are coordinated through actions and discursive practices. In particular, in this final section I will deal with some of the most relevant ways in which meanings were constructed and shared in the valley during the NO-TAV campaigns. I argue that to understand the whole nature of the movement one has to look at two different frames in which meanings were constructed and subsequently shared: the space-time perception and the interests. The first refers to the socio-cognitive mechanisms through which the movement has gained and maintained consensus, which builds on a common cultural and identity construction of coexistence in the valley (sharing space) and at slow speed (sharing time). The second refers to the use of corruption as a meaningful semiotic and ideological framework through which the TAV project has been distanced from the localities of the protest and rendered avulse and alien from them.

The Susa Valley movement has so far been indicated in sociological and political science studies in Italian as an exemplary case of successful political participation and democratic awareness from below. A number of scholarly contributions point out at the strengths and weaknesses of the movement, largely overemphasizing the formers (Della Porta and Andretta 2002; Bobbio 2007). The reasons for the success of the civil society movements, is searched primarily in their multifaceted nature. The different and plural manifestation of the protest all convey an organizational ability to embody the expectations, fears and needs of the different social segments involved and to give them voice. The character of the NO-TAV which has so far caught the attention of analysts, journalists and academics is its plasticity. No other civil movement in postwar Italy has been able to mobilize different and multidimensional sectors of the local society. The NO-TAV has involved virtually all kinds of local citizens: factory workers, farmers, retired people, homemakers, intellectuals, academics, young people, local entrepreneurs, religious officials, local administrative personnel, mayors, civil servants, lawyers, medical doctors, artists, unemployed and even local police officers. There is virtually no occupation which was not represented at some point in the twenty years of the movement's duration. This testifies for its strength and potential since, as illustrated above, even in times of crises and violence it has been able to reproduce itself significantly.

The strength and plasticity of the movement is however partly to be imputed to its successful construction and sharing of a common repertoire of identity constructed in time and space. The first civic organizations to invite the local citizenry were surprised by the degree of local participation to their demonstrations, strikes and even peaceful barricades to police and RTF technicians. In occasions such as the violent events of December 2005, the activists reported the 'tenacious nature of the people of the valley' underlining that in those very moments of crisis, during the night or in the early morning of a cold winter day, when temperature was far below zero, people were able to leave their homes to the places in the valley 'that had been violated'.

The valley became the place where its people could join efforts to defend their future lives. It was the construction, both symbolical and shared of time and space that counted for the protesters to be able to transmit the meaning of their efforts, often openly debased by the national media. In contrast with these, local journalists covering the demonstrations underlined how 'the valley became our *familiar* space' to juxtapose to 'their unfamiliar battleground'. Valley inhabitants knew how to reach a place quickly, how to find apparently non-existing walking paths to surround or circumvent police checks and barricades. The valley was both an open-access space, whose common use had to be defended against the violations by all its inhabitants, and a secret space, where only those who had lived for decades, keepers of the historical narratives of the war resistance and the gestures of the partisans could meaningfully operate and move. Police officers and national technicians sent prefabricated fences to the valley which could not, in the eyes of the activists, enclose a space which for a valley inhabitant is anyway 'accessible'. All the time the protesters regained these spaces, which were often occupied during the night or using devious means[12], they referred to them as the

---

12   On different occasions the policemen retreated temporarily in order to be able to regain positions late at night, when most of the protesters had supposedly returned home.

'meadow' (*il prato*), they did not occupy the site of the drilling, but the *prato* which in their words marked a meaningful sign of continuity with the valley.

Meaningful uses of the open, inviolate and inaccessible space is also to be found in the several attempts to build stable checkpoints (*presidi*), like garrisons, at the locations of the drilling sites. These have become, since 2005, the main sites of confrontation, occupied and re-gained, burned down and reconstructed. In 2005, during the most violent moments of the protest, local inhabitants spontaneously gathered in the *presidi*, upgrading them from campsites to mountain shelters after days of hard work.[13] As the *presidi* gradually assumed solid aspects, usually because of the need to shelter the garrison participants from the cold, their presence became legitimized through the expression '*fare casa*' (making home). *Fare casa* became a prerogative not of domestication of the natural space, but of creation of a common socialized space for living, where every home appliance could be found (there were fridges, crockery, furniture, curtains, but also flowers, pictures on the walls, games and books). A number of local villagers took the custom of stopping after work or in the evening by the *presidi*, as they were seen as places in which the old atmosphere of the public bars and even farmhouses could be reproduced, where evening gatherings were the sole form of daily entertainment.

Around each garrison the grass was constantly maintained and watered (as an activist joked 'we are making the grass nice for their drilling'[14]), every morning somebody cleaned the surrounding soil, planted flowers and herbs. These efforts were done 'to not lose continuity' with the valley. It was their way to oppose 'violation of the valley's nature', one of the most frequently used expressions in the terminology of civic organizations, with a familiarization and socializing of these spaces by the valley inhabitants. This is peculiarly expressed as the feeling of 'being at home' by many of those who regularly hung out to drink a coffee, to talk with somebody, or to taste some homemade food.

The protest in the valley is also rendered meaningful through resorting to metaphors of time, rather than space. Time constructions have two expressions: the first is a cyclical time, the second indicates a quality of time, namely its slowdown. Concerning cyclical time, in several activists' tazebao the word 'resistance' is copiously used. In Italian the word resistance, *resistenza*, has the double meaning concerning also the historical period associated with the partisan movement in the Second World War (*Resistenza*). The Italian *Resistenza* had been particularly fervid in the mountain regions of northern Italy, which offered natural shelter and hiding places to large numbers of partisans from all over the country. The theme of the lives and gestures of the partisans, in its temporal and spatial semiotic, has

---

13   Improvements included for instance the construction of a small log house in lieu of the former tent. The house was equipped with portable gas cooker, a fridge and even electric heating system provided through a gasoline generator. In the presidio furniture was not essential, except for a long table where dutiful spaghetti parties and breaks were organized almost daily.

14   Quoted in Sasso, p. 71.

often been used by the activists and the local population themselves. One finds frequently mentioned phrases and sentiments such as 'the way of the partisans' (their gestures), 'the paths of the partisans' (which refers those hidden mountain paths traditionally used during the war), 'the songs of the partisans', 'the heritage of the partisans' and 'the mission of the partisans'. Interestingly, the war period is used symbolically to refer to a similar period of resistance, even if the present movement strongly underlines its peaceful and anti-violent character. Thus the time of *Resistenza* seems cyclically returned, as the actions of the partisan heroes are reinterpreted to give symbolic meaning to those of the present NO-TAV.

Time is also used as a metaphor of slow life by some of the environmental movements. Slow life, as opposed to high-speed and frenzy life styles has been widely used metaphorically by a number of social movements around the globe. Italy has been particularly active in this direction by establishing, in the Piemonte region, the Slow Food Movement[15] in 1989, which has since become popular worldwide (Geoff 2008). Some of the most common and appealing slogans of the NO-TAV movement in the first decade of its existence draws on the dichotomy of 'slow-natural' versus 'fast-artificial', as the two leading dimensions of the project. The fast-artificial dichotomy was introduced by the CP and regional politicians openly speaking in favour of the project. The fast railway was presented as a definitive symbol of modernization, amelioration of transport standards, Europeanization, development of the region, and as a structural intervention opening up to future investment. To this, when the environmental protest became diversified in its scope, towards the beginning of the 2000s, the opposition with slow-natural attributes become easily attachable.

This dichotomy, as one could imagine, did not include the 'valley' versus 'city' aspect. The activists were very careful in avoiding such a mistake, since they had from the very beginning been aware of the importance not to close themselves in parochialism and anti-urban aspects which would have endangered and weakened the consensus bases of the project, also because another contested section of the TAV crosses the city of Turin. Rather, the slow character of life in the valley, imbued with natural and healthy elements (from food to air, water, building materials, colours and tastes), to the 'genuine simplicity' of valley life, were the strongholds of these dichotomic constructions of qualitative time.

15　The Slow Food movement originated in 1986 as a response from Italian activists against the planned opening of a MacDonald's store in Piazza di Spagna, in Rome. The movement gathered enthusiastic members from all over Italy and later from different countries, covering 132 countries today and over 100,000 members. The main objective of the movement is to oppose fast-food with 'genuine' food which maintains the regional characteristics, ingredients and tastes.

The use of public discourses on corruption

Over the years the NO-TAV movement opted for different strategies to communicate its general objectives. The earliest forms of protest emphasized the environmentalist discourse, using the future health of the valley and its inhabitants as the priority goal for which the movement was summoned. This made the most sensitive aspect about which a large majority of its inhabitants were initially well aware. After the beginning of the second decade of the protest, however, political issues became as well-known as environmental ones.

A small-scale qualitative survey conducted in 2008 in the valley demonstrates that 78% of respondents have knowledge of health consequences of the project (Marincioni and Appiotti 2009). On the other hand, however, 46% of respondents cite construction companies as the main beneficiaries of the TAV, followed by politicians (35%). Concerning credibility of the environmental organizations only 13% believe that their demands are very little or unreasonable, whereas 71% believe that national media coverage of the project is not credible (Marincioni and Appiotti 2009: 867–8). Although small in scope, the results of the questionnaire underline that there is a consolidated awareness of the political aspects of the project, apart from the preoccupation with environmental issues.

Corruption and murky business practices have been denounced by the environmental groups as hidden rationales of the TAV project only in the recent years. To understand this choice attention must be paid to the local power dynamic of the mobilization and negotiation process. Some analysts underline that one novelty of the NO-TAV movement in Italy is its ability to summon local institutions which sided with the protest. This alignment makes an unusual case in a country where corruption becomes a social system structuring local politics, and when the common public is aware of these dynamics. In this section I am interested to frame the political strategies of the environmental movements and the outcomes that denounce corruption which have been published over the last ten years in national and local media.

An intriguing case of political participation from below was evident as local police officers constantly attended protests, demonstrations, strikes and even barricades, wearing their three-coloured official sashes, demonstrating an evident struggle of 'the state versus the state.' This stemmed from a general disillusionment with the integrity of local politics following the publication of results of investigations over TAV projects in other regions of the country. A few media reports, following clear political orientations, denounced these forms of concerted protest pointing out at the greed for power and economic shares in the project of these local administrators. This reaction makes sense in a general condition of corruption where, following Banfield's (1958) amoral familist perspective, every administrator is expected to be greedy and corrupt, and every reaction to the system seems unjustified and hard to believe. The common explanation in these media reports is that, in the beginning all local municipalities interested by the project were initially excluded from a piece of the proverbial pie, and hence a lack of communication and local negotiation by the regional and even provincial authorities was taken as a weapon and used as one of the official motives for aligning with the protesters. As in the other case studies present in this book, political fragmentation, and excessive differentiation of the decision-making spheres (from project planning to implementation and management) has caused serious political and economic bottlenecks, including corruption, distrust, a loss of legitimacy and credibility.

Since the beginning of the project in the early 1990s, the state, supportive of the TAV, had to face the opposition, with different waves of a large stratum of local governments. The outcome was that bilateral support was sought through different sets of political networks in the valley considering the two principal orientations (centre-left and centre-right). In the moment when, in the second half of the 1990s, corruption cases were exposed in other TAV projects, the left-wing parties were governing with the majority of the Piemonte region administration being of left-wing orientation. Therefore, corruption was still too sensitive an issue to be brought to the forefront of the protest, with the risk of losing support among mayors and municipal counsellors who could not openly contrast the main streamlines of the party.

In the period 2000–2010, the situation gradually changed with the right-wing coalition gaining supremacy and winning many seats in the region. At this point, corruption became the rallying cry of the protesters, who could only benefit from the presence of mayors and councillors in the first lines of the protest. This was, in the eyes of the communities, what granted credibility and legitimacy to the movement, as well as electoral supports to these mayors, as the positive results of the NO-TAV electoral lists demonstrate.

The situation changed when the local mayors were invited to the table of negotiations after the establishment of the Observatory. This step has been described by some activists as 'the beginning of the weakening of the protest', as well as the choice of its president by the Berlusconi cabinet, a person of centre-left orientation, at times when the large majority of the communes where still centre-left themselves. Indeed it was after 2006, when the operations of the Observatory started, that corruption became a wide subject of debate among the NO-TAV opponents. Each organization has since then dedicated a whole section of its website to corruption and the murky political implications of the project. The most general discursive form has recently become to use corruption as 'the explanation' to the project, providing a final answer to a number of questions which remain unsolved. This answer appears, in the eyes of the local population, overexposed to corruption scandals nation-wide and almost taken for granted. In line with other ethnographic findings quoted above, there seems to be little need of explanation on 'why corruption is at stake', whereas more discursive effort is dedicated to debate the 'technicalities' and details of opaque politics and business.

One of the ways in which local civic organizations tackled corruption was to refer to existing literature on the TAV projects in the country. As they explained, they felt the need to have people confront the 'hidden' political implications of the project, and not simply the general allegations of mismanagement of public funds. The Italian press has been extremely preoccupied with corruption scandals in the last year (2010), ending a silence which lasted from the end of the Clean Hands movement in the mid-1990s (Miller 2004).

Although information access is a fundamental prerequisite of democracy, especially in the recent history in the Italian case, overexposure to corruption scandals may significantly alter people's cognitive perception and even understanding of the problem. Anthropological studies in developing economies have recently showed that corruption, when overspread and copiously dealt out by media may tend to become a discursive form, a 'talk' in the everyday life of individuals (Parry 2000; Gupta 2005). This can influence the way the public good is perceived, as the Slovak case study in this volume has demonstrated. It is difficult to judge if the civic movements which first made use of corruption in a significant way to inform people about the dangers of the project were aware of this cognitive aspect. I doubt they were. However, their initial standpoint was extremely cautious and this provided, in the long run, a good strategy. The very moment in which corruption became, in their words 'the answer' to the doubts raised by the 'absurdity' of the project, was by them perceived as the moment in which 'people needed something stronger, since they were continuously asking for answers.' This moment strengthened and altered the direction of the movement.

If in the first half of the movement environmental and later economic issues were the most frequently used to promote debates and general meetings in all the communes because they were mostly unknown topics, while in the second half there was a larger degree of shared knowledge of these problems. In one meeting on January 2009, when technicians of the RTF were illustrating the details of the new project in Chiomonte, the village from where the 57 km long alpine tunnel was planned to originate, the town council hall was packed. NO-TAV exponents sat silently, wearing their colourful banners and flags, paying attention to the power point presentation on the technical details of the new tunnel. The technician was unable to speak uninterruptedly for more than four sentences, as each time a different person in attendance asked a new question. In several occasions the technician had to strive hard not to lose his patience, and in others he was visibly frustrated and unable to provide answers. Most of the questions were extremely pertinent. Some of the protesters raised technical doubts and problems with clear and substantiated explanations which were hardly given a response. In at least three circumstances the technical expert had to ask the help of his two other colleagues. After half an hour of this presentation, which had turned into less than fifteen minutes of presentation and over fifteen minutes of questions, one of the eldest NO-TAV representatives, Piero, stood up, visibly losing his patience and uttered:

> You are coming to tell us that we have to have no fear of uranium, no fear of asbestos, since you will take care of everything. But then you are unable to answer a lot of our simple technical questions. This shows that you know much

less than what we do about this valley. Have you ever studied its geography, as
you should?

The technician remained silent, then slowly hinted at an answer but he was again
interrupted by Piero.

You know what the truth is? That you don't care about the line and the project,
you are only commissioned to do your job, but here we all know more than you.
And we all know why this absurd project is bringing you here, because a lot
of people, in Rome and elsewhere, have to benefit from it. Not because of any
consideration about transport.

The exceptional degree of knowledge shared by the active participants in the NO-
TAV movement about the technical details of the project is certainly one of the
stronger points of the protest. In other occasions, they have also demonstrated an
ability to understand the political implications involved. On January 2010 Beppe
Grillo, a famous comic actor who recently supported the foundation of an anti-
global political movement[16] visited the valley and talked to the protesters. He was
about to address them regarding some of the potentially harmful problems related
to the illegal use of public money and the abuse of political offices. At one point
an old woman from the spectators stopped him and declared that he did not need to
talk about these things in those circumstances, and eventually offered to explain to
him the reality of the facts. Indeed, Grillo's treatment of the political implications
of the project had been only superficial and showed paucity of details which was
soon discovered by the participants.

It is difficult to judge whether cases of corruption will have a decisive influence
over the future of the movement. One thing to be sure of is that the publishing of
a number of books on corruption scandals related to the TAV line in other Italian
sections have helped to consolidate civic awareness about the project. The most
notable of these publications is Ferdinando Imposimato's study of the TAV in Italy,
entitled *Corruzione ad alta velocità* (Corruption at high speed, 1999). Imposimato
is a judge, who also worked as a journalist in his youth, and, after retirement,
returned to journalism again. His book is a sharp and lucid denouncement of
cases of corruption built around what he terms 'the mother of all bribes', i.e. the
TAV project. In his book he presented an extremely long list of Italian politicians,
large entrepreneurs and *faccendieri* (in-between goers) who benefitted from the
early stages of the high-speed railway projects in the early 1990s. Imposimato's

---

16   This is called Movimento a Cinque Stelle (Five stars movement), established
in 2009. The movement, which follows the anti-globalist and ecologist ideas of Beppe
Grillo, has slowly gained position in the 2009 and 2010 elections. In particular, in the 2010
regional elections the movement has obtained over 90,000 votes (4%) in the Piemonte
region, and in some communes of the Susa Valley it has reached 30% of votes, making the
strongest political force.

book is an interesting piece of widespread literature on (economic and political) corruption in Italy which is not reticent in pronouncing names, associating names with dates, explaining particular choices and courses of the latest Italian history. These publications have a strong impact on anti-corruption movements, since they are the only valid sources to legitimize the nature and scope of these movements. Imposimato's book (one of the few not to receive any legal action of slander), has been widely read in the valley. The author himself was invited and joined the protesters twice, presenting his book and answering numerous questions. Members of the civic and environmental organizations have, since then, obtained his consent to cite parts of his book on their web pages. This has significantly improved the communication of information about corruption among the movement's members.

The language of corruption

If it can be argued that corruption has fruitfully become a theme of communication of the problems and abuses that the NO-TAV movement considers part of the project, it is necessary to pay attention also to the discursive ways in which this type of communication takes place. Corruption is itself a pervasive argument, but it also carries an inherent weakness, that is its vacuity, particular when applied to socio-political contexts dominated by frequent illegal forms of exchange and transactions. As any other important social phenomena, it can be communicated in different manners which relate to the several applicative domains (from law to political parties, electoral campaigns, structural projects, business contracts, bids and so on). Hence, talking of corruption in the case of the high-speed railway project can at the same time mean dealing with the potential irregularities of the bidding process, the private benefits of local, provincial, regional and state political institutions, the networks with criminal organizations and the fiscal irregularities involved in contracting and subcontracting. All these domains are ruled by different types of laws and assume different degrees of gravity in the eyes of the specialists, save for the great difficulty of transmitting this knowledge and rendering it accessible to the general public. Nonetheless, analysis of the discursive forms used by the local civic organizations can help to identify a number of patterns which indicate to which extent corruption has become part of the environmentalist discourses and practices.

The first point is that a rational analysis of cost-benefits is the most used discursive strategy in presenting the general public with the economic damages of corruption. Most of the bulletins and summaries of the NO-TAV protest start with the delineation of four points justifying the protest. These are: the negative environmental impact, its usefulness, poor economic viability, and the imbalanced rapport costs/benefits. This rapport is measured against two parameters. The first is the generalized costs (*costi per tutti*) which are perceived to be much higher than the generalized benefits (*benefici per tutti*). This imbalance is presented as one of the many lies of the supporters of the project who 'make us think that we will all benefit out of the TAV, whereas only some private enterprises, and not workers, will have a real benefit'.[17] The rationality behind this explanation is as straight as the one stating 'the NO-TAV movement deems important the balance of the state and not the gains of some private subject'. Or, 'In reality all the esteemed cost of 20 billion is on the shoulders of the collective. All public money but entrusted to privates'.[18] Corruption is here presented through the dichotomy public-private, where public is at times identified with the state, but more often with the valley as a whole collective.

The second point is that mismanagement of the project is read through projection of its future costs, which will affect the generations to come. Thus corruption is perceived and communicated as a cumulative loss, as it would affect the valley in the long-term. One finds repeated mention to the 'generational debt' that this project will produce, toward 'our children who will be forced to pay without being able to benefit of the services because of the structural deterioration before the debt can be paid off by tax payers'.[19] Also, the state of indebtedness is cited as one of the most feared effects of corruption in relation with the inefficiency of the economic planning. The most quoted figures are those which show the increase of the TAV costs over the years and their comparison with other EU countries (mainly France and Spain). One such study quotes: 'In a project where Italy has an overall cost of 32 million Euro per km of railway versus 10 million in France and Spain, what future benefits can be expected for the regular tax payers?'[20] In a leaflet one reads: 'There are no privates investing in the TAV project. Tens of billions Euro of already contracted debts are charged 'on the state balances' (There our euros payed in taxes will go), until 2060'.[21]

The third approach presents the description of the bidding process. There are different communicative ways to deal with this domain of corruption. One points out the widespread 'distribution of contracts nationwide' or the 'tentacular capacity to outsource', or the ability to 'intercept rain funds' as alleged prerogatives of the committers of the project. Another looks at the ability 'to dig holes in the budget', or to 'behave as the hole band of thieves', or to 'benefit from the black hole in the budget.' Both ways follow the aim of underlying 'opacity', 'obscurity' or lack of transparency in the outsourcing process which, a document quotes 'has been already signalled by the EU as one of the most negative consequences of the Italian system of large infrastructural works'.[22] Another way to point out alleged or feared irregularities in the contracting and bidding processes is to refer to the 'large public works' which have been recently put to the forefront by several recent scandals in

---

17   Carta di Hendaye del 23 Gennaio 2010.
18   Chi usa il cervello, rifiuta i luoghi comuni. NO-TAV, 2005.
19   NO-TAV, Le ragioni tecniche, economiche e ambientali.
20   Chi usa il cervello…ibidem.
21   Viviamo a Torino e siamo NO TAV, 2009.
22   Chi usa il cervello…ibidem.

the country.[23] In this case, 'Public works' or 'Italy's management of public works' are the most used expressions, usually without the need of including any further adjectives or references to issues of corruption. To this point it is also useful to underline that, in a number of speeches and meetings, NO-TAV personnel has referred to the national-scale TAV project as 'the largest public work after Italian Unification', thus following, but not directly using, Imposimato's expression 'the mother of all bribes.' In this case as well, no other explanation is added since the national media has already been saturated with negative images of the public work endeavours, thus the nexus between them and corrupt practices is an easy cognitive effort.

The fourth and final discursive domain related to corruption is the use of allegations about criminal and Mafia networks. This constitutes a rather recent development, but it has gained momentum after displaying the 'NO TAV NO MAFIA' banner in 2008. Among the most frequent explanations are to be found in 'the fear of criminal infiltrations in the contracting process', or 'the already proved link between Mafia and TAV', the 'wild deregulation of the outsourcing process fostering criminal activity', the 'difficulty to monitor Mafia networks' (NO TAV online page). Some of these expressions are used regarding existing documents and investigations, while others have a more general tone, which, as in the case of the public versus private good debate, introduces a dichotomic view of 'good jobs' and 'bad jobs'. In one leaflet one finds that 'the TAV is proposing the local development of the valley. As a matter of fact we are sure about the creation of a number of bad jobs, the same cannot be said about good jobs'.[24]

Even when maintaining a general and elusive tone, the opposition's focus between good and bad practices is used to contrast the descriptions and explanations usually provided by the media. It is to this aim that each written explanation provided by exponents of the movement is often preceded by expressions like: 'It is generally maintained that…', 'Some common explanations', 'The commonplaces are…' By bringing a constantly contrasting level of discursive description of the reasons for the protest, the civic organizations have sought to build different degrees of counter-information, well aware of their incapacity to challenge the power of media.

Corruption has become a powerful argument in the recent days and it is used in a number of tropes which refer to the different domains to which such a complex notion can apply. This approach is rendered possible by the parallel availability of studies, journalistic reports and even legislative procedures which point out the risk of corruption within the general frame of the project. The fact

---

23   According to police investigations, in preparation of the G8 summit to be held in Sardegna in 2009, the bid for the congress center was won by a small construction company (less than 30 employers) close to the family of the chief of the Italian Civil Protection. The contract, 117 milion euro, amounted to over one third of the overall sum (300 million) destined as public work to the event.

24   http://www.spintadalbass.org, accessed on 23–2–2011.

that both environmental and other civic organizations indistinctly use discourses on corruption to communicate their goals and activities to the general public is an important point for understanding the limits of the environmental discourse and how far can large infrastructural policies generate public distrust at different institutional and political levels.

Conclusion

The NO-TAV movement makes a rather complex but illuminating case study which would probably require its own extended analytical treatment. This complexity is due to its twenty years of history, the different roles and rationales of the actors involved and the difficult and avulses interpretations of the political strategies followed by each set of actors. The aim of this chapter was to introduce the main steps of the movement, framing them within the more general process of transport development projects originating in Brussels. As part of the TEN-T framework in Corridor 5, the Susa Valley high-speed railway is a good case study which can be compared with the others in Eastern Europe that were discussed in the previous chapters. They share the complex and delicate unravelling of political dynamics taking place at different levels, from the transnational to the very local. The NO-TAV is a movement from below originated to oppose rigid and artificial schemes of development imposed from above which are built elsewhere and hence poorly compatible with local social, environmental, economic and even cultural conditions. The political arena is the only area in which the battle between the planners, the committers and the opponents can significantly takes place because of these dystrophies with the local environment. This is what some civic organizations seem to have understood recently when they started to make a more regular use of corruption and allegations of economic irregularities in the effort not to lose the strong appeal that the movement had so far obtained.

The NO-TAV movement is, however, a different movement from those analysed in the previous chapters, mainly because of its scope. The tenacious battle so far fought by the valley inhabitants is self-styled, which is enriched by the presence of different types of civil society organizations, with plural aims, strategies and even languages. The strength of the movement gains further significance when confronted with the intransigent and firm response of the national and regional authorities which support the project. This, as it happened after the escalation of violent episodes in 2005–2006, has elevated the protest to a national and even anti-global movement. At this point, when the state has understood the mistakes made so far, seeking 'reconciliation', or even establishing the bases for a negotiation table in the institution of the Observatory, the new political asset of the local administrations had done the rest. Even though the NO-TAV communes have gained an influential position in the administration of the valley community, a number of these communes, now of rightist political orientation, are presently less sceptical about the project. This development coincides with a turning point in the activity of the protesters, who are more ready than before to embrace political arguments, and to make use of corruption as a discursive weapon to support their ideas.

As in numerous other cases of environmentalist action, the NO-TAV has so far been characterized by different stages of public intervention. The environmental thrust of the movement has allowed its consolidation and diffusion over a large majority of valley inhabitants. The degree and kind of local people intervention in the protest is alone a distinctive feature of the movement and testifies how far environmental and health concerns play a highly significant role in shaping people identities and collective action. The impact of developing projects on a valley which has already been the target of a number of heavy intervention projects has produced, again in opposition with the original intentions of the planners, fierce struggles and has significantly lowered institutional trust at translocal levels, helping, on the other hand, to consolidate local identity ties and a strong interventionist rhetoric.

Chapter 7

Case Four: The Budapest M0 Ring-Road

This chapter discusses the implementation of the third case of motorway development projects in Central Eastern Europe, presenting one of the most debated cases in these regions: the M0 ring-road around the Hungarian capital city. Similar to the previous two case studies, the EU planning, the dynamics of institutional intervention, the involvement of civic organizations are all important stages of the project which cannot be analysed separately. The interlocking of these stages, including the different sets of strategies of political actors, meanings, and power configurations emerging out of them, must be unravelled to gain a greater understanding. This case study is particularly significant for the development of two points: the first concerns the susceptibility of environmental organizations to the effects of the political dynamics which configure at state and local government level. The second is the way in which widespread corruption influences public perception of the consequences of non-transparent and unequal decision-making at local level. These two points, which are in different ways common in the findings from the other case studies presented so far in this volume, become particularly significant in the Hungarian road project for two reasons: the complexity of the planning and implementation of this substantially urban project, and the particularities of Hungary's path of institutional transformation after 1989.

The country has been the quickest to attract foreign investments among those of the former socialist bloc. Hungary was also less rigid in central economic planning among the European socialist states: in this country a symbiotic existence of centralized planned economy and semiprivate enterprises was present already since the late 1970s (Hann 1980; Szelenyi 1988; Swain 1992). Furthermore, the presence of a significant stratum of Hungarian intellectuals and entrepreneurs in the western countries, and above all in North America has, after the post-socialist transformation, strongly marked the typology of the pathways of institutional transformation in a rather original fashion, compared to that of their neighbouring central eastern European countries. Hungary has also been characterized, in the last decade, by a fierce political and ideological battle between rightist liberalist forces centred upon the present ruling party, the Fidesz, among the originators of the post-socialist transformation, and a leftist strive towards guarantees of comparatively heavy state involvement in social welfare schemes. This, particularly during the long leftist government (2002–2010) has also contributed to indebtedness of the country which was forced to resort to EU credits.[1] Finally,

---

1   Hungary received a 440 million euros credit in the beginning of 2009 from the EU, available through the European Investment Bank to boost economic performance.

Hungary has experienced a long period dominated by corruption scandals at all levels of the public life. This period, culminating in the last three years of the cabinet led by Ferenc Gyurcsany (2006–2009), has seen a proliferation of media, public and political discourses on corruption which is unique among the other Central Eastern European countries (and comparable more to the cases of the new EU member states, Romania and Bulgaria). All these conditions make Hungary a peculiar case of study, one in which the tension between the economic and social benefits of the infrastructural transport projects and their perceived damage and corruptibility is dominant and widely acknowledged by all the actors of the case, except due perhaps of the EU planners.

I will introduce the road development project following its historical steps of planning, development and implementation in the first section of the chapter. In the second section I will analyse the emergence and consolidation of civil society movements in the environmental and socio-political fields related to the local opposition to the building of the ring-road. In the third section I will deal with the media's covering of the project, looking at the different temporal shifts of a project which, from its initial conception has already spanned over more than fifteen years.

The Hungarian motorway system

In the 1980s Budapest's population exceeded 2 million inhabitants, but the motorways connection with the rest of the country and abroad were very poor. This was not a peculiar trait of Hungary alone, among the socialist countries, but for density of population and location Budapest has historically been the most convenient hub in Central Eastern Europe. In the early 1990s the only existing national highway connected the capital with the famous touristic region of the Lake Balaton. The reminder of the country was crossed by a number of local and regional, usually two-lane roads which formed a radiant with the centre in the capital. The result of this transportation design is that Budapest needed to be crossed in the four cardinal directions by heavy and light vehicles in order to reach different destinations within and outside Hungary. Thus, already in the 1970s the transport planners had originated a plan for building sections of ring roads especially along the most heavily crossed sections southwards (traffic from the Romanian border) and westwards (towards Vienna). Some of these sections were completed, but the volume of road traffic of that period was obviously not comparable to that of the present times.

In its radiant-shaped transport structure Budapest is connected to the rest of the country by eleven national roads that cross the whole country in all directions

Since 1990, Hungary and the EIB have signed agreements for long-term credit lines of more than 8.9 billion euros, aimed mainly at environmental and transport infrastructure, industrial, telecommunications and educational projects.

leaving only an open section in the north-western part, where the Buda hills and natural reservoirs are located.

During the last twenty years some of these main roads have been partially or completely expanded into six highways. Among these the first to be completed is the M1, connecting Vienna and Budapest, followed by the M7 which expanded the already existing section to the Lake Balaton south-westward to the Serbian border and the M5 southwards to Romania. Those still incomplete include the M6 reaching down to Croatia, the M3 eastwards to Ukraine and the M2 of which only a small section exists, north-eastward to Slovakia. All these highways have to meet at centre of the radiant which connects them, thus requiring the construction of a ring-road which would facilitate their junction avoiding the crossing of Budapest. The design of this transport project, which falls within the EU TEN-T scheme, is incontestably rational. Due to the peculiar structure of the Hungarian motorways system it would be impossible to link the country with its seven neighbours (respectively clockwise Slovenia, Austria, Slovakia, Ukraine, Romania, Serbia and Croatia) without a proper functioning ring road connecting these countries to the capital.

Budapest is connected to a series of Trans-European corridors both through railway and motorways. These include Corridor 5 (Venice-Lviv), Corridor 7 (Munich-Constantza), Corridor 10 (Budapest-Sofia-Thessaloniki) and Corridor 4 (Dresden/Nurmberg-Thessaloniki). These corridors respectively coincide, in Hungary, with highways M3, M2, M6 and M1. The progress under which the Corridors' projects have been accomplished throughout the EU is monitored in several official reports and studies.

According to a 2009 ERDF (European Regional Development Fund) commissioned report, Hungary has showed the highest share of road expenditure among the EU-25 countries, exceeded only by the UK (which is not a EU member). Hungary had, in the period 2000–2006 the highest overall allocation of ERDF funding (276 million euro) which were dedicated, again as the highest EU rate for 85% to road construction (Ex Post Evaluation... 2009). The outcome of this massive intervention is that the number of roads grew in Hungary by 67% only in the decade 1990–2000, even though the percentage of traffic volume using car and buses (respectively 62 and 23 per cent) has not changed over the last fifteen years. What is more interesting, the actual increase in number of passengers cars that boomed in the 1990s (92%), substantially shrank in 2000 (21% of increase). This seems to suggest that although Hungary is still one of the countries in which road is highly preferred to rail transport (also considering freight transport), the booming motorways construction industry, and its high costs are not matched by a parallel increase in traffic volume. According to Eurostat, the national volume of road traffic has increased in Hungary by 13% in the period 1999–2005 (from 2.6 to 3.3 million vehicles per year), this is a trend in line with Western European countries, but much more reduced compared to other post-socialist countries such as for instance Poland (39.6% increase in the same period) and Romania (30%

increase)[2]. What do these statistics and trends suggests? The immediate answer is that in Hungary, in spite of the rapid path of development of road construction projects and of the high budget allocated to these projects there is a comparatively lower trend of increase in road traffic volume. This points exactly to the concerns raised by some of the civic organizations involved in the opposition to the M0 northern section: justification for the completion of the ring-road is too weak in both economic and commercial terms. However, as we shall see, the situation is far more complex than this.

The M0 ring-road

The M0 ring-road is planned to connect Corridor IV (i.e. the eastern motorways M1 from Vienna/Bratislava) and Corridor V/Vb (the M7 from Lake Balaton) with Corridor IV (the M5) and Corridor Vc (M6 southwards to Romania) as well as the continuation Corridor V (the M3 going east to the Ukrainian border and the planned M2 (northwards). The planned length is 108 km, of which so far 79 km have been completed.

The history of the ring-road project is rather complex. The initial idea dates back to 1942, when Professor Vásárhelyi Boldizsár of the Technical University of Budapest envisaged the possibility of connecting the local roads leading to the capital through a ring of much reduced length. The idea, back in the 1960s, developed into a project inspired by the Paris model, which would connect an external highway into one of the major inner routes of Budapest, the Hungaria Út, a road with eight motor-lanes and a double tram lane crossing the city in the Pest territory. The project was abandoned in 1974, readopting the initial concept of a ring rather than of a single central highway. In 1982 the first section of the ring was launched, connecting highways M1 and M5, but the works started only in 1987. In 1998 the southern section of the ring was completed, including 29 km of highway (2x2 lanes, out of the originally planned 3x3) that brought to the conjunction of highways M1, M7 and M5. In December 2005 the first sector of the eastern section was completed, at the conjunction of the national road nr.4 and highway M5. In 2006 the *M0 Látogató Központ* (M0 Visiting Centre) was established, presenting facts, figures and historical data on the ring-road to the public. On September 2008 the Megyeri Bridge over the Danube was opened. The huge project, whose costs exceeded 200 million euros, was the first step towards the debated completion of the missing M0 section, from the eastern end northwards to the planned M2. This 29 km road, conventionally termed as the northern section, is the object of this chapter's ethnographic investigation.

Concerning the costs of the M0, it is hard to assess them presently; nonetheless, a short historical comparison can help to understand the rapid and steady increase

---

2   Statistics from Eurostat: http://appsso.eurostat.ec.europa.eu/nui/show.do?dataset=
tran_r_vehst&lang=en.

in the budget of this project. In 2004, the webpage of the European Investment Bank, which is called into intervention for all the TEN-T projects, quoted the following about one section of the M0:

The project concerns the construction of 38.7 km of a new 2x2 motorway on the Budapest Ring-road M0 between trunk no.4 and motorway M3 (located to the south-east and east of Budapest). The southern sections of the bypass linking radial motorways M1, M7 and M5 and trunk road no.4 have already been completed or are in the process of being completed by using local funds. The proposed project would be supported as well by a significant Cohesion Funds contribution. The estimated cost was 500 million euro, with about 70 million of EIB financing.[3]

Two years later, the EIB issued the news that it gave Hungary a loan of 50 million Euro for the completion of 26.5 km of the M0 eastern section.[4] According to the plan, the Hungarian government would provide approximately 100 million Euro for the project. These figures, however, do not easily match with others on the relative costs, particularly those of the more expensive eastern sectors. According to these, the 39.2 km of the eastern section, culminating at the Megyeri Bridge have been completed under 85% of European (Cohesion Fund and Phare) funding and 15% of Hungarian money. The overall cost of this section, including the bridge, is estimated at about 100 billion forints (370 million Euro), that is a little less than the declared overall cost for the project. How to deal with these gaps? First, it is highly unrealistic to build a rough estimate of the overall project which has expanded through the years with respect to its initial plan. One example is the addition of the M31 section, which adds to the ring a 12 km 'shortcut' between the M0 and M3 around the town of Gödöllo, completed in 2009 at the cost of 45 million Euros. Second, each section has its different costs according to the conditions of land, river-crossing sections, as well as to the actual land price. The missing northern sections are deemed to be particularly expensive due to the presence of hilly ground and to unfavourable climatic conditions such as strong winds, fog and heavy winter snowstorms.

Reasons for the opposition

As in the previous two TEN-T case studies, there are a number of reasons which justify local opposition to the motorways project. These refer to the environmental impact of the road, which in its northern plan will cross naturally protected areas, a portion of which is under the Natura 2000 agreement,[5] areas rich of water and

---

3   Details are available at: http://www.eib.org/projects/pipeline/2004/20040042.htm.

4   Confront: http://www.eib.org/projects/press/2005/2005-026-eur-157-million-for-transport-infrastructure-and-projects-of-smes-and-municipalities.htm?lang=-en.

5   Hungary has 10 national parks, 37 landscape protection areas, 162 nature conservation areas and 1 natural monument (2007). Following ratification of the Natura 2000 agreement, 465 protected sites have been proposed and 55 special protected areas.

thermal springs, as well as regions that have traditionally constituted the 'fresh lung' of Budapest, conveying cool and clean winds towards the polluted capital.

The second refers to the economic impact, in particularly in relation with land price. This relates on the one hand to speculations taking place in the localities where the motorway will be constructed; on the other hand, to the building plots which have been recently purchased and inhabited by an increasing number of former city inhabitants willing to move to a cleaner and greener environment, and which are recently losing value due to the imminent road expansion.

The third refers to political issues, a reflection of the complex process of road planning and building where the interlacing of interests (of economic and political nature) often opposes local governments with their national counterparts. All these factors make the M0 a thorny issue which, judging by its wide media coverage and the diversified opposition of the civic organizations involved, is far from being settled.

The first opposition was conceived in the settlement called Káposztásmegyer.

The original plan of the northern section of the M0, including the Environmental Impact Assessment, were prepared in June 1994. This planned route connected the M3 motorway (coming from Eastern Hungary at Miskolc) with the main road no. 11 (coming from the North, on the western side of the Danube). According to this plan, the M0 would pass through an almost uninhabited area near the M3, then connect with the new M2 main road, which the EIB is also funding under the loan. From there, the road would have gone through a 16 meter high, 270 meter long viaduct, which passes within 250–300 meters of the housing estate, called Káposztásmegyer II, where 5000 inhabitants lived. Furthermore, Junction 2, connecting the new M0 to a major arterial in the direction of downtown Budapest, was planned within 150 meters of a nursery school and within 400 meters of the apartment buildings. This moved the traffic backing up on two-lane roads feeding into the junction that is only 15 meters from the apartment buildings, and runs between the local school, the nursery, and the private apartments. According to studies commissioned by local NGOs, the dust and pollution particles generated by the increased traffic on the road will be 25–30% above Hungarian environmental standards.[6]

The construction of the first section of the northern ring started in spring 1998. Local dwellers learned about the project only after machineries and materials started to be stored close to their houses. It was at that point that a concrete opposition initiative took place. The first such was the creation of the Káposztásmegyer Environmental Protection Society (KKK) with the main aims of individuating illegalities in the Environmental Impact Assessment and

---

6 Experimental evidence indicated severe public health-related risks of PM10 exposure, most of which comes from motor vehicles. In every kilometre 2 tons of pollution will be emitted daily. The noise levels were also expected to exceed the limits and reach 70–76 dB in the day, 63–68 dB at night (counted to the year 2008). The officially accepted limit values are 65 dB in the day, 55 dB at night.

subsequently increasing public awareness of the project. In June 1999, thanks to cooperation with the largest Hungarian environmental NGO, Clean Air Group (CAG), a legal suit forced the State Motorway Management Company (SMMC) to suspend works for a few months. Subsequently, the Supreme Court accepted the SMMC request to restart the works and in 2000 the section was completed, with the only modification of closing its arterial which would have crossed the housing estate. KKK and CAG also submitted an investigation to determine the responsibility of the EIB for the project in late 1998, but the reply was that EIB could not be held responsible for national legal cases. At this point, the two NGOs contacted the EU Ombudsman (this was the first time such a case happened for a country outside the EU). Afterwards, a ping-pong match began between the Ombudsman and the EIB presidency which, in several occasions, refused to provide the documentation requested by the ombudsman and decided not to proceed with funding the northern section exception for the bypasses sections. Finally, in 2001 the Ombudsman could find no irregularity in the conduction of EIB exception due to the warning to respect environmental procedures when conceding loans for structural development projects. According to the two NGOs this answer further stressed the idea that the legal conduct of EIA had been violated.

The problem, according to the local opponents to the project, was its initial formulation. The first amount of funds to the project (14 million Euro) was achieved through a Phare project. In this occasion, the project was presented as a bypass to road Nr. 2 to ensure a balanced development of and between national roads, feeder and trunk roads and international links' (Peters 2005: 5). Thus, the direct mention to the M0 development was avoided. Secondly, the environmental organizations claimed that the initial design of the project was made on a map which did not contain a trace of the house estate (Káposztásmegyer II) on which the roads (bypass and trunk of the M0) were going to be built. This was a serious violation that, unfortunately, did not receive attention by the Supreme Court.

It is interesting to notice, in this case, that the diversification of the protest and the ability of environmental activists to take a firm political stance, until then almost unknown to Central Eastern Europe, have attracted the attention of economists and political scientists (Peters 2005; Tarrow and Petrova 2006). In these articles recognition is given to the forerunner status of the opposition by environmental activists, as this is considered the first such case in post-socialist Europe. With this regard, Peters (2005) underlines how the protest constituted an original contribution to the field of Eastern European environmentalism, since it clearly showed how the political boundaries of intervention could be redefined according to the priorities set by civic organizations. What, in his view, was striking in this protest was the ability of the environmental organizations to enlarge the scope of their action even though they did not have the institutional arrangements to do so. The appellation to the EU Ombudsman is a peculiar case of intervention outside the EU sphere, and can be interpreted as a case of trespassing of national competences. Even though the Ombudsman communicated with the EIB and not directly with the competent Hungarian government bodies (Ministry of Transport, Development and Environment), it set the case for a redefinition of the role of the EIB and hence affected the subsequent process of structural funding to the Hungarian State (Peters 2005: 13–14).

Tarrow and Petrova (2006), on the other hand, are interested to situate the M0 protest within a general panorama of weak civil society in Eastern Europe. Following some of the main events of the protest, they conclude that the 'transactionism' demonstrated by these movements is unique in the Eastern European panorama. By transactionism they mean the tendency of civic organizations to engage with mutual relations and connections more than to seek open participation by the general public which is still seen as problematic. Their conclusion on the comparative strength of Eastern European civic movements is even blunter: apparently less free of institutional constraints and less subject to popular accountability they may work successfully, as the Budapest case indicated. This is also because transactional style of politics is similarly widespread among political elites (Tarrow and Petrova 2006: 15).

I have to admit that out of the ethnographic evidence provided in this book these positions seem particularly pertinent. For one thing, what makes these cases worthy of investigation beyond a common-sense NIMBY approach is that they originated in conditions where civil society was deemed to be weak and still in embryo, and they were framed within often poorly accountable styles of policy-making. Thus, unaccountability, lack of transparency and technical deficiencies (both actual and claimed) are key elements to be analysed when trying to understand the real socio-political values of these movements. However, the two positions described above fail to see beyond the often stereotyped perspective that western scholars adopt when dealing with civic movements in Eastern Europe. In other words, what these approaches miss is a grasp of the ground-level strategies and meanings that activists and those who participated in the protest attribute to it. This can be best achieved through attention to discourses and practices and to their transformation in the over one decade long protest. I will introduce the second case of environmental protest concerning the M0 project, the one related to its northern most section about which I personally conducted fieldwork research, in order to shed further light on the issue.

The puzzle of the second northern section

If the struggle on the first section of the northern ring has dimmed out in the moment the new Danube Bridge has been completed, the second section is still an open case. This section should, in the initial project, close the ring connecting the junction points of national roads n.10 and 11, in the north-eastern part of the city.

There are two main arguments in support of the road construction. The first is that roads n.10 and 11 are extremely congested two-lanes routes which connect Budapest with some of the closer touristic and historical spots of the region of Szentendre and Esztergom, along the curve of the Danube. This area, apart from being rich with thermal and open-air camping attractions, includes one territory of the natural reservoir, Natura 2000. Apart from tourism, however, the immediate north-eastern outskirts of the capital have become a privileged residence destination in the last five-six years for relatively rich urban dwellers looking for larger plots to build family houses nearby the city and yet within a natural environment. This trend, visible by the ever growing number of spots (during socialism weekend houses, now two-storey large family houses) dotting the Buda hills, has called for media attention in the last years particularly because the daily traffic to and from the capital has dramatically increased. Thus, having a section of the over 100 km ring-road in the vicinities does not look as an unattractive proposal to many daily commuters.

The second argument, of economic nature, concerns the re-evaluation of the areas. The municipalities in the north-eastern section of the planned ring-road are rather poor in infrastructures, as well as in local enterprises. In spite of the incoming number of city dwellers who are expanding the population of many of these villages, there is a strong contrast between run-down and even non-existing paved roads in the historical nuclei of these villages (some which inhabitant by a German ethnic minority) and the more recent extensions, where the luxurious houses stand proudly. Furthermore, the number of local enterprises is very low, apart from a handful of shops, car service points and other minor small factories; the region has always been out of the economic planning due to its natural limitations. Already in the 1970s the Buda hills were celebrated as the 'lung of the capital', and thanks to the strong northern winds blowing during all the winter season and later in spring, they were an ideal place to escape pollution and chaos of the city. Thus, economic development has been used as rhetoric for justifying transport ameliorations in this region.

In spite of these two arguments, the conception of the second northern section has long remained alien to most local municipalities. Since 1996 all the municipalities to be cut by the section stood against the project. Unlike in the case of the first section, resistance and protest has proved, through the years, to be less organized and concerted. True, by the end of the 1990s, each village and municipality had its own civic organization (or even more than one) which formally joined forces with the others to oppose the project. However, unlike in Káposztásmegyer, few initiatives saw a common bases of participation, it was as they chose to remain locked in their own towers rather than uniting to fight. In the explanations of one of the leaders of a local civic organization, the problem was the concomitance of different interests which, in a number of municipalities (see below) constituted a strong obstacle to the outcomes of the protest.

Completion of the northern section, once strongly opposed due to mere environmental argumentations, is today auspicated by the general public. When in the late 1990s the public disclosure of plans for the first section stirred general local concern for both the usefulness of the road and its environmental impacts (air, noise pollution and alteration of the landscape), none of the municipalities interested by the second section were hesitant to join the protest. Ten years later, after the completion of the southern M0 sections, and the opening of the Megyeri

Bridge, general traffic conditions along the ring-road, both in its southern and northern sections, have worsened. What is apparent to the daily commuters from the northern regions is a scenario of constant cues at rush hours and even during shopping hours. A quick browsing through blogs related to traffic conditions in Budapest reveal that it is a common view that those who oppose the completion of the ring-road are not perceived as realistically aware of the need for this road. Of course, local media and the sectors supporting the M0 take advantage of this position, alternating the card of the economic development discourse with that of daily traffic congestions.

What the daily commuters do not easily notice, however, is that increased traffic along the M0 is also a result of the M0 construction itself. Already in 1998, some NGOs had noticed that the construction of the M0 was favouring the mushrooming of so-called 'greenfield developments' which created more serious traffic problems than the ring road was supposed to solve (Peters 2005: 3). The tendency, extensively reported in Eastern Europe, to build a number of logistic centres, shopping malls and other amenities along ring roads and highways is very strong in Budapest. Very often this development is disproportionate both to the density of local population, and to the transport infrastructure. In merely economic terms, it is extremely convenient both to investors and to landowners who benefit from sudden and steady fluctuations of land price, particularly when land can be converted from farming to building plots (see the Czech case study). Thus, the role of the M0 project seems to have moved from facilitating transport connections from outside to the capital city to providing new commercial and consumption venues for those who already reside within the capital.

Forms of civil society

The project of the northern section stirred public participation when municipalities interested by other sections became their opposition. There are, however, some significant peculiarities in the protest related to the northern section of the M0. These peculiarities depend not on the type of civic movements and on the degree of involvement of environmental NGOs, which proceeded almost in parallel to the different geographical contexts. What changed was the political struggle between local and state power, its tones, interaction fields and outcomes, on the one hand, and the ways this struggle was reflected in the strategies of the protesters, on the other. To reflect on these features it is necessary to introduce the general features of the environmental movements in the northern section.

The environmental protest concerning the northern section started around the mid-1990s. As mentioned above, by 1996 all the communities interested by the project had developed their own civic movements, which in the early stages more or less cooperated strictly to the common goal. These were: *Piliscsabáért Egyesület, Solymári Környezetvédő Egyesülete, SOS Békásmegyerért Egyesület, Van jobb M0 Ürömiek Egyesülete, Ne M0 Pilisborosjenőjek Egyesülete* and

Zöld Gömb Egyesület. In this stage all these organizations were in line with the directives of the local governments that in principle opposed the construction of the ring-road section. This, in the early phases of the project, gave strong public legitimacy to the protest. The following are the cases of two of these movements that I have studied more closely: Van jobb M0 Ürömiek Egyesülete and SOS Békásmegyerért Egyesület.

Van jobb M0 Ürömiek Egyesülete was founded in 1994 in cooperation with the civic association of the neighbouring community of Ne M0 Pilisborosjenő. The two villages, with a population respectively of about 5500 and 3400 inhabitants, were the forerunners of the protest in the northern section. Towards the end of the 1990s they have jointly reached above 3000 members who became particularly active when the general plans of building the highway through a 16 meter tall bridge lying on the territories of the villages became public. This was the time when local population was particularly sensitive towards the environmental issue. Public meetings were organized regularly and, according to the founding members, they were always extremely crowded. The strength of the two movements, which deliberately used 'M0' in their names, was initially due to their success in involving local politicians, such as the mayors and counsellors. Moreover, the fact their meetings were both held in the premises of the municipal offices and cultural halls gave these events the aspect of formal moments of confrontations, to which local authorities, as well as the population, were invited. The presence of the two mayors, who regularly attended, although did not take an open position in line with the protest, was itself a sign of assurance that the movement was not a temporary gesture of dissidence.

In the following years two petitions were gathered in both communities, reaching above 1600 signs for each of them; whereas publicly presented studies on the noise and mainly air pollution impacts of the road had strong effects on raising public awareness. Another issue that raised public concern was speculation in purchase of land which, in the neighbouring community of Solymár, had already alerted the protesters that their action was needed if they wanted to influence political and economic decision-making processes. This problem became increasingly manifest in the years to come as agricultural fields converted into brown fields, and projects for commercial and logistics centres became public (see below).

After 2003, the strength of the movements began to decline. The mayors of the two communities, who had never been openly in favour of the road, and had taken part in the meetings of the local organizations, changed their attitudes. Formal decisions regarding the northern section followed shortly and the protesters felt increasingly frustrated by the poor outcomes of their efforts. This caused a general disinterest in the movement, especially in the second half of the 2000s. Some internal factors had concurred with this development. First, in the last ten years the two communities, and particularly Pilisborosjenő, were targets of large housing developments, which have brought in a number of new residents, coming from the city, mainly of high economic and social statuses (private entrepreneurs, businessmen and professionals). These newcomers, who had their luxury houses built in brand new quarters of the villages, developed strong horizontal ties among them, but less frequently with the native population. It is not simply a matter of coincidence that when the status gap between the rich newcomers and the local dwellers became increasingly manifest the protest lost general visibility. It was clear that the newcomers had a much weaker environmental sensitivity than the local population, and were strongly in favour of the road for personal interests, i.e. their need to commute daily to work to the city seeing that very few of them use public transport means.

Second, the initial strength of the two movements declined when cooperation and communication among them became less smooth and eventually problematic. This, according to local active members, was caused by the efforts by the state and city government to complete the M0 into sections, and not as an integrated, unitarian project, as the TEN-T framework foresaw. The idea of a common project, which was to be communicated to all the municipalities which were interested was never presented by political authorities, according to informants. Because of this local environmental groups were unable to establish a common platform of actions, and were forced into fragmented and uncoordinated intervention. Each municipality and each civic organization became concerned with the particular section of the project which was of its own pertinence. This weakened the general protest (unlike in the Czech and Italian cases presented in this volume) and eventually had the perverse outcome of bringing the communities in conflict over the possible variants, after the completion of the ring-road was officially announced. One significant difference was in terms of the degree of infrastructural investment in the interested localities: Pilisborosjenő and Üröm had to be crossed by the road through a bridge or tunnels, whereas for instance Solymár, which is situated on higher land, was connected to the national roads at a large junction, which had given space to the creation of shopping and logistic facilities. When the opposition of Solymár began to languish, thanks also to prevailing economic interests, this was interpreted as a sign of general weakness of the movement by activists from other communities. Moreover, the solutions providing an alternative by each environmental organization, in answer to the different stages of development of the project, could not be mutually harmonized, since there was not a common plan on which to build. Therefore, at a later stage after 2004, each intervention of local movements could be accused to threaten the interests of the neighbouring municipalities.

Upon inquiring as to the reasons for the lack of coordination among movements, I did not receive a precise answer. Some of the leaders pointed out that local political decisions had, following the last regional elections, jettisoned the creation of a common ground of protest. In Üröm, the new municipal administration had promised direct intervention to support the tunnel versus the bridge variant, and this had been interpreted positively by the local inhabitants. When the decision to choose the tunnel variant was issued the reasons for the protest seemed to have vanished, since this option was constituted as the 'less harmful' of the possible choices, as indicated by the two local organizations. However, such optimism did not match with the general concern about the northern section, that remained strong in other communities, such as Békásmegyer, which, through the help of national environmental NGOs (particularly the Clean Air Group), as well as global organizations such as CEE Bankwatch, continued to denounce the dangers of drilling in the region which is the largest provider of spring water to the country.

The case of SOS Békásmegyerért Egyesület is even more telling of the hardships encountered by the movements when facing changes in local power configurations. The organization was founded in 1998 and its leader was able, with the help of other enthusiastic founders, to organize a public meeting in the town hall, gathering several thousands of inhabitants. The peculiarity of this movement derives from the different political conditions to which it is subject: Békásmegyer, with a population of over 40,000, belongs to the Third District of the capital, to which it was merged in 1950. During the 1970s it underwent a large demographic increase, growing as an outskirt of the Buda section, with over 13000 panel houses built until the last years of socialism. Today it still maintains the distinction between the original village (Ófalu), with only a minor part of inhabitants, and the new section, with a highly urbanized character. This centre is also connected to the city through the railway, and this has garnered much consent for the protest against the new road up until now. On the other hand, in this case decisions at the political level depend on the city government and thus leave comparatively less space for autonomous local action.

A second distinctive trait of this civic organization derives from the figure of its founding leaders. He is a retired civil servant who still has a good number of personal connections with city politicians. During the protest which lasted over a decade he was able to obtain several personal meetings with them, including the new mayor of Budapest, who is also the ex-mayor of the Third District. From these meetings, the decision by the city to go on with the project emerged, particularly after the Megyeri Bridge was completed. However, the movement, through its leader, still hopes to achieve a better deal in terms of the variants proposed.[7]

Third, the comparative strength of the protest in Békásmegyer depends also on the scarce benefits that the project would bring to the local community. Unlike in the villages described above, where the environmental impact is stronger, but not directly and immediately felt by the inhabitants, here the local population fears increase in noise, traffic and air pollution as this immediately manifested after the construction of the Megyeri Bridge. However, no further infrastructural investment is expected in Békásmegyer, which is already saturated by the sudden demographic expansion of the last three decades.

Also in the case of SOS Békásmegyer, the first years of the movement were marked by a strong degree of public participation which, as said, has not yet

---

7   The environmental movement has proposed three road variants. Among them two would avoid the inhabited centre and only one, the less optimal, would pass close to it. This last, although contrasted, is the one presently favored by the city administration because shorter and less costly.

significantly decreased as it did in the other two cases presented above. Petitions and public demonstrations were organized, and until 2008 the presence of local political exponents was constant. On one such occasion, the movement succeeded in collecting over 1400 signatures on a petition which promised to file legal suit if the planned road would cause harm (directly and indirectly) to local dwellers. Also, simulations of noise and air pollution have been publicly presented to the local population with a strong response in their involvement.

Concerning coordination with other movements, some degree of common organization (such as in the case of petitions) was achieved in the early years, but when the standpoints of some of the municipalities in the hilly regions changed, SOS Békásmegyer stopped communication. This has been interpreted, by members of other movements, in negative rather than positive terms, since it confirmed the suspicion that each organization sought its own way to 'benefit' from or reduce the loss of the project. In the words of the Békásmegyer's movement leaders, however, a general apathy towards protest has followed since 2009, after the opening of Megyeri Bridge, and part of the responsibility is to be found in the decreased activity of civic movements and partly in the increased economic opportunities by different sets of actors.

The rationales of local political actions

As in all the transport projects included in this volume, the dynamics of political actions, the different strategies of the actors, the language they use to communicate such strategies to the public and the meanings of these strategies are all influenced by the modality of the project, which belongs to a global design of EU enlargement. As one informant pointed out: 'If there were no EU there could not be any ring-road, and the dirty political games could not be justified in the eyes of the general public'.[8] Therefore, there is very poor analytical value to look at this case study as a NIMBY case. The framework of EU structural and TEN-T funding provides, willing or not, legitimacy to the actions of the different political layers implied by the project.

In order to understand the rationalities of political action here I will not follow the scheme I adopted in other chapters by presenting the layers separately. This approach is of little help in the Budapest case for a number of reasons. First, this is a case where the political interests of urban elites intermingle more evidently with those of non-urban settings. Unlike in the Czech and the Italian cases, however, the urban centre is directly interrelated with the villages and extra-urban municipalities involved in the project, and not simply affected by their decisions. The ring-road is an urban project, and as such has been conceived within a city development plan. Also, the role of key politicians, such as the city mayors must be searched for by looking at the continuity of the political configurations (personal networks and strategies) that marked their careers.

8   Jenő, 64 years old, interview 20–2–2011.

The second point is that in this case the civic organizations are, as seen above, fractured and not harmonized in their actions. Therefore it has little meaning to look at them as a unique, homogeneous field of political action, as in the classical anthropological meaning (Vincent 1978), because they have responded, in time, differently to the ongoing development of the project. Third, as it will be explained below, the same EU has been 'reconstructed' by the meanings that local actors (from political officers to activists and citizens) in different and often contrasting ways attribute to the transport project. Similar to anthropological literature on the EU enlargement project (Abèles 2000; Shore 2000), this case study analyses ways in which actors attribute to local political strategies a power not only to separate fields of actions, but eventually to infer meaning to the state through discursive reference to abuses and lack of transparency in political decisions.

The main nexus between those political layers that has promoted the ring-road project is the role of the city council, and mainly in the figure of the mayor. During the long left-wing mandate under the former Budapest mayor, Gábor Demszky, who stayed in office for two decades (from 1990 to 2010), the M0 was publicly portrayed as one of the main priority projects. Even after a number of corruption scandals and mismanagement of public funds in the second half of the 2000s undermined the legitimacy of the ruling coalition, the mayor maintained a stable political position. His office pressed for the completion of the Megyeri Bridge that, in the opinion of one officer of the National Highway Company, was creating serious connection problems with other national roads, and eventually would contribute to increase the volume of traffic onto the territories of the missing northern section.[9] This choice has been interpreted by environmental activists as yet another example of the 'sausage technique', in the same terms that have been described to me by Czech and Slovak activists. According to the NGOs, the sausage technique is an apparently widespread strategy in TEN-T projects that would allow 'contested' projects to be hastened, because unconnected sections are built along the planned line so to give the impression to the general public that the road *is* under construction (even though it may not be completed, as Czech case shows). More importantly, the bits of roads contribute to enlarge the traffic volume, also thanks to mushrooming commercial centres alongside them and at their bypasses, causing suffocation of the local roads that become interconnected to these sections and therefore increasing the widespread feeling that the new planned roads are badly needed. All of this allegedly takes place within the general thrust for improvement of connectivity and transport of goods along with EU directives.

The city council has been crucial for shaping political decisions of local governments, as well as strategies of the environmental movements. For example, after the election of the new Budapest mayor in 2010, there has since been an increased belief that the northern section will not be completed soon (the new deadline is 2020). Some of the activists even predict that EU funds will not be enough to cover the expenses of the planned tunnel in the Pilis region, and that the

9   In 'A M0 multja and jövője', AAVV 2008.

present right-wing coalition, which owns 70% of the majority in Parliament, is not willing to provide unlimited financial support to the project.

At the local government level, however, the degree of support to the project has been affected less by the political orientation of the mayors, than by their personal strategies. It is highly indicative that in the first half of the protest all mayors and most council officers were aligned with the generalized environmental concern with the damages that the road could potentially bring to the communities. This happened even though most of these politicians belonged to the same coalition parties of the Budapest mayor. Unity in the protest movement by different actors in the local scene was interpreted as one of the key factors for its initial success. During the second half of the 2000s, however, the situation changed. Personal interests seemed to prevail over collective goals, and this was the case of almost half of the communities involved in the northern section.

The case of Üröm is, again, particularly significant. The present mayor, who is an MP in the left-wing coalition, had been initially very firm in his denouncement of the M0 northern section. In 2002, he declared to unconditionally oppose the ring-road on the homepage of the municipality. However, as two NGO leaders commented, that was the time when elections were approaching (held in the same year) and taking a clear stance against the project was interpreted as a positive pre- and post-electoral strategy. The subsequent facts unveiled this strategy: in December 2003 the mayor gave his vote to the tunnel variant in a meeting that included most local mayors and only few of the civic associations. This has been described as an 'original sin' by local activists, a choice which clearly reveals the complex intertwining of rationales that shape decision-making at the local government level.

In a second intriguing case, in Bekásmegyer, the activists denounced the underground activity of the local district council, which following personal connections with the city council, has allegedly supported 'alternative' forms of civil society in open opposition with the anti-ring-road movement. This is a novel and peculiar situation that I have not observed elsewhere.[10] According to local activists, local government officials would have given full support to the creation of at least two civic organizations that were in favour of the ring-road. They have their own home pages and in recent times (since 2009) they have scheduled public meetings to explain their support for the ring-road. I attended one of these meetings, whose title was unequivocal: 'The M0 and Bekásmegyer, opportunities and directions', in March 2011. The meeting was very informal, with a dozen participants and four activists taking the lead, but it was held in the premises of the town's cultural hall. I arrived five minutes after the starting time and as I took a seat I heard that the discussion of the ring-road, the only topic of the evening according to the calendar, was concluded exactly after six minutes of discussion. What followed was conversation about funding opportunities for the association, future projects of environmental nature,

---

10 I registered mention to a similar case in the Italian anti-Tav movement, particularly concerning the urban district of Turin, however, I have been unable to test reliability of this information.

problems with the sewage system, the waste collection and so forth. In several cases some of the participants urged for the achievement of better 'connectivity' with the city mayor and his council in order to be able to diversify the range of projects. In all these circumstances one of the leaders of the organization had his word to reassure his efforts to re-approach the mayor, as he claimed he had been doing all along. My feeling was that this looked more like a business meeting, or at least an internal meeting for the association, and it was surprising that the M0 theme was not touched at all, in spite of the programs.

Although I could not obtain more precise information on this issue, the results of my participant observation, the vagueness with which these activists treated or answered the ring-road issue, and their manifest intention to lobby the city council all suggested to me that this was a rather different form of civil society. One of the leaders of SOS Bekásmegyer told me that these new organizations, originating at the time of the works at the Megyeri Bridge, eventually communicated with Brussels to establish as a sort of counter-movement supporting the completion of the M0 in short times. I have not been able to access documents which prove the actual confrontation of these movements with EU authorities; therefore this remains only an unproved type of data. However, the very fact that these new movements do not oppose the road project, being themselves environmental movements, make an intriguing case in which civil society is not any longer the space between kinship, households and the State, as in the anthropological literature discussed in Chapter 2, but a different political actor, with its own rationale, affected by the EU funding system more than by the State. However, more data would be needed to test this hypothesis.

Corruption and the missed response from the civil organizations

Compared with the other Central Eastern European countries investigated in this book, Hungary has showed, in the last six years, the strongest degree of public condemnation of corruption scandals both in the private and public sectors. Extensive media coverage on corruption cases have marked the last years of the former left-wing government, and this trend largely continues to the present. It is not in the scope of this chapter to deal with the rationales, outcomes and modalities of this anti-corruption public campaign, instead, what I found more important is to underline that wide coverage of these issues has played a role in the dynamics of the protest.

The construction of highways, one of the major infrastructural development projects in post-EU accession Hungary, has been dotted by several dirty spots. The following are only some of the best known scandals. In 2003, during one of the biggest fraud scandals of the past 16 years, the president of the State Motorway Management was sacked and prosecuted for misappropriating large sums of money. In 2004, the Hungarian Competition Council fined the four largest motorway constructor companies almost EUR 30 million because they had been consulting with each other and engaging in cartel behaviour. In September 2006 one Austrian construction company sent money – through intermediaries, as alleged by an independent Austrian MEP – to the governing parties of Hungary. In recent years this company has been involved in two new motorway constructions which were financed by the EIB: the east section of the M0 motorway, between the M5 motorway and road No 4, and the M35 motorway between Görbeháza and Debrecen.[11]

These cases have been introduced to the general public by national and local media, and the two largest environmental organizations in the country, CAG and Friends of the Earth Hungary (*Magyar Természetvédok Szövetsége*) have used them to communicate to the general public through web and written media. Eventually, in September 2006, these two organizations forwarded a letter of complaint to the director of EIB asking to halt funding transport development projects in Hungary. The letter did not have any positive outcome concerning the protest.

Besides these scandals, a number of more recent ones have occured as well, particularly in the fields of public transport and major infrastructural works, severely undermining public trust in institutions and corporate business (see Gulyás 2004; Schmidt 2010). Extensive media coverage, however, did not always provide a fruitful weapon for strengthening legitimacy and consent to the local civil society organizations. One reason for this failure was the lack of coordination among the several movements. All attempts to present a homogenous picture of the fractured movement have been conducted by the large environmental networks which operate at the national level, and at some extent by CEE Bankwatch at the transnational level. These organizations have also used corruption allegations more frequently in their reports and protest letters.

In all the cases of protest I investigated that have produced a consistent and large case study material, reports, petitions, denounces, executive summaries and public invitations in the 15 years of their activities, the dominant idea is that these movements have sought coordination from above rather than from below. This is different from what has happened in the Italian and in the Czech cases of this volume. In Italy the strength of the movement and its ability to make use of corruption as a cementing factor for political and social purposes derives from decisions, strategies and communication originating and coordinated locally. In the Czech case the local organizations benefit from their link to trans-local and international organizations, but they directly communicate with their supporters in the local society. In Hungary, the role of CAG and, to a minor extent, of Friends of Earth to promote ideas regarding a lack of transparency, fraud and general misconduct in the project has been publicly acknowledgeable but never attempted to be communicated directly to the local public. Therefore what was missing has been the semantic contextualization of corruption to allow citizens to make sense of local governments. This was partly due to the coordination role played by the national environmental organizations, which were not interested to make

---

11   From the webpage of CEE Bankwatch, http://www.bankwatch.org/project. shtml?apc=--307250---1&x=2037815&d=r, accessed 13–4–2011.

of corruption a headline case in their denouncement of the potential damages of the ring road.

The inability of local civil society to make overt use of the several instances of lack of transparency in the different stages of the road construction cannot be read in different manners. First, it can be safely argued that complexity of the M0 project has called for different forms and contents of political action by the civic organizations. The main priorities for the movements operating in the southern and eastern sections of the ring were not *in toto* applicable also to the northern section. As it has been showed above, also within the northern section every community was characterized by different problems. Thus, in the hilly region of the Pilis speculation on estate investments, the non-transparent role of municipalities in issuing permissions for sale of desmane land, as well as in converting green into brown fields have been emerging problems. On the other hand, in lowland communities, and in the boundaries of the III district of Budapest, issues of misconduct seemed more linked to illicit bargaining and abuses of office among local politicians and key officers.

During interviews with local activists, the issue of corruption has emerged in different circumstances and with regard to different moments of the road building project. However, the general position I gathered was that citizens are too distracted by corruption scandals, being disclosed to the nation widely every day by the media, to pay attention to them. One of the leaders of the Van Jobb M0 movement commented:

> If I have to repeat to all the people who support us that there is somebody who is benefitting, in his pocket, from these projects then I have to expect that they will follow my words and come to the meetings, the first time I mention this. But the second, third and fourth time is different. People became used to these scandals nowadays and lost sensitivity.[12]

The idea that excessive exposure to corruption scandals, and the generation of what some anthropologists have called 'corruption talk' would hamper sensitivity to the general damages and corruption that has been demonstrated in other social and cultural contexts (Chapter 3). However, if it were so, there would be no point in using cases and allegations of opaque political behaviour in the political and communication strategies of the civic movements until present. In the M0 case, following the letter to EIB, the shift has been from the mere environmental aspects of the protest, to its economic and political infringements. This is not to state that the environmental aspects have been neglected, but that they are presented in a more complex and articulated discursive form which pays constant attention to issues such as speculation on land, private benefits to different sets of actors, missed economic development for the communities and frauds at the planning level.

---

12 János, 48 years old, interviewed on 13–11–2010.

Why then has the movement not been able to use corruption as an efficient discursive weapon? I believe that the explanation about overexposure to corruption scandals is only superficial. There are two levels to be taken into account when analysing the political strategies of the movements in this case study. The first is the confrontation with central environmental organizations, and the second is the ties with local governments.

Concerning the first problem, some activists have rather meekly mentioned the fact that when seeking coordination from above, from the national environmental organizations, they have to deal with the reality of how these groups are funded. As all civic organizations, they participate in public tenders and eventually receive money from public (state) funds (typically of EU origin). Therefore, one cannot neglect the existence of a tie between these, national, civic organizations and state institutions (such as the Ministry of Environment). None of the interviewed local activists have admitted that they fear that corruption allegations might be omitted in the agenda of these movements' protests, as indeed they were not, but they indicated that precise reference to such scandals or allegations could eventually preclude future cooperation between these organizations and state institutions. I cannot know if this has ever been the case because, as stated above, the aim of my use of corruption is mainly to frame it in discursive practices by the civic organizations. I would, here, limit myself to point out that in this particular case study the link between local and state political institutions is much stronger and significant than in the other cases, hence the use of allegations of corruption, as well as the link to other existing scandals in the transport sector which have a much heavier political impact are more difficult to communicate to the general public.

The other factor to be considered when analysing the use of frauds and opaque practices in discourses over the legitimacy of the protest concerns the ties of civic movements to local governments. Again, comparison with the Italian case seems instructive. In the Susa Valley the movements, until recent times, have remained successfully linked with local governments who openly support them. In Hungary this has happened initially, and has indeed provided legitimacy to the protest, but over time the situation has gradually changed. However, if in Italy the cohesion of the different local groups have provided so far a safe strategy to buffer them against the defection of some municipalities of mainly right-wing orientation, in Hungary fragmentation of these movements has hampered political bargaining power. Discredit to local government was seen as a decisive threat towards disintegration of the movement as whole. This is linked to the general understanding of the idea of civil society.

In several occasions, as in the other case studies, I have been told by activists themselves that in Eastern Europe 'civil society' is still not as free, as in Western Europe, when stretching over large strata of public without having to face (or feel) the need of acting informally, or less overtly. The reasons why these local movements have initially benefitted from the presence of mayors and local officers in their meetings is exactly in this preoccupation. Loss of public legitimacy and the need to constantly reformulate the balance between formal and informal strategies have affected the use of corruption allegations by these movements. Corruption has been used by them mainly in informal settings of interaction with supporters and local population. However, at a more centralized level, and even in the context of interaction with the local media, they have preferred not to rely openly to the language of corruption. In this they have become less free to resort to this discursive weapon, comparatively to other case studies, because they feared to lose once for ever their already weakened bases of consent as well as the support from national organizations. This has been interpreted, in the presence of the anthropologist, as an outcome of a widespread loss of sensitivity towards booming corruption scandals. In reality, the underplaying of local opaque practices reveals a true preoccupation, and at times resignation, with the possibility to maintain significant levels of participation in the protest over time.

Conclusion

The M0 ring-road in Budapest is a case in which the interplay of different economic and political factors and the strategies pursued by the sets of actors call for the need to compare it with the other cases in the volume. The significant feature of this case is its large spatial span, including different typologies of political institutions. This is what makes it difficult to understand and wholly grasp the local dynamics of power. The same is true for the environmental movement, born in the different localities affected by the plan, and that has followed different temporal phases according to the implementation and development of the building process.

The main hardship that civic organizations have confronted in this case has been the fragmentation of their responses to intrusive structural development policies. If the movement has consolidated genuinely strong forms of civic protest, as in the cases of Káposztásmegyer, Bekásmegyer and the other communities of the Pilis region, its duration has constituted a main limit. Not only have the plural agents of the movement been unable to concert common action, but they have also dealt with different degrees of public involvement, interest in and even legitimacy of their action. This can be interpreted as a general outcome of the conflicting interplay of political (as well as economic) interests between state and local governments. On the other hand, concerns over a lack of transparency in public institutions and integrity in private sectors have not led the civic organizations to seek a common ground of action. This is again to be imputed to the planning and implementation steps undertaken to break the project into different sections, matched by the failure to achieve a proper monitoring of the main founders of the ring-road by EU authorities.

However, the consolidation of civil society is here not simply aimed to influence the outcome of local and translocal political choices. The genuine thrust from below has necessarily dealt with some of the limitations of establishing participated forms of political action from below in Central Eastern Europe. The choice, operated by all these movements, to maintain adequate balance of formal and informal strategies, and to 'delegate' the coordination role to national organization has proved successful in the short-run, but weaker in the long-run. As it emerges out of this case study, fragmentation of political power as a result of the EU enlargement policies, and loss of legitimacy in a country vexed by corruption scandals, have not left sufficient space for homogeneity and durability of the strategies from below, all of which has rather hastily been celebrated by some political scientists as the most illustrative example of democratic participation and civil society.

Chapter 8

Case Five: Illegal Waste Export
to Central Eastern Europe

This chapter introduces the case of illegally exported waste to the new EU member states, among which Hungary is chosen as a case study. The main argument of this chapter is that changing EU border regulations after 2004, and following the Treaty of Schengen (originally ratified in 1985) have favoured transportation of goods and persons among the member states, but also given momentum to illicit activities such as waste trade. This can be another case of unintended consequence of the EU liberalizing regulations. Another way to look at the increased movement of waste following the west-east axis is as a result of the institutional and legislative gaps and loopholes concerning waste disposal among the EU countries. Following different temporal and spatial trends, illegal waste export has become a major socio-economic problem in countries such as Czech Republic, Poland, Slovakia, Hungary, Romania and Bulgaria. Many of these cases have only been discovered recently, therefore scientific and scholarly works on these topics are still incomplete if not missing entirely. Inspired by these limitations, this case study is intended to partially fill these gaps, providing an ethnographic account of some of the implications, reactions and political steps taken to address the problem.

As already underlined in the introduction to this volume, this case relies on weaker ethnographic support for several reasons: the link of this case to criminal activities, the still ongoing investigations by police and environmentalists and the unwillingness of the environmental movements themselves to comment on this case. Nonetheless, concerning the timeliness of this problem, which relates to unintended consequences of the EU project, added to the fact that the illegal shipping of waste from more prosperous countries to less prosperous neighbours will be a problem on the agenda of international organizations for years to come, I have decided to include this case study in the volume.

This chapter will be divided into three sections. The first section deals with the problem of illegal waste export to different Central Eastern European countries. This section will introduce some of the available data on the estimated volume of the traffic, as well as the main political steps undertaken by Brussels in the last few years. The second section introduces the Hungarian case, presenting a number of episodes which, especially in 2006–2007, have attracted media and public attention, and subsequently raised several doubts about the ability of EU and national institutions to control the phenomenon. Section three will analyse the civil society movements some of which have developed in response to this phenomenon, whereas others have strengthened their public role by seeking direct intervention at the local level. This section will also analyse the interrelation between corruption and the protest movement through attention to local political and economic dynamics.

Trans-boundary waste trade in the EU

The EU generates approximately 2.6 billion tons of waste yearly, and about 90 million tons of this are classified as hazardous waste. Of course, the difference among countries is striking, not only in the amount of annual waste per household, but also in the amount of hazardous waste (Data Availability on Transboundary... 2009). Categorization of hazardous waste is, according to EU Law, linked with three annexes of EU Hazardous Waste Directive 91/689 (Annex I, II, III) and with the List of Waste 2000/532. The first three annexes define the categories of hazardous waste according to their nature or the activity which generated them, their constituents and properties. The List of Waste includes any type of waste that is considered as hazardous by EC directives.[1]

The most sensitive items of trade within hazardous waste are, however, three: electronic waste (e-waste), contaminated waste (containing contaminated materials such as nuclear waste, oils, heavy metals, and other forms of industrial waste) and spare-parts waste (mainly from used cars). These three items constitute the overall bulk of the hazardous material which is shipped around the world daily at increasingly high volumes. Hazardous material is partly destined to countries, within the EU, which have already provided consent to the trade, and partly goes to non-EU, and non-OECD countries to which the shipment has been allowed. This happens even though, in principle, the EC has prohibited to ship hazardous material for recovery in non-OECD countries (EU regulation 1013/2006). E-waste is usually shipped to African countries and South-east Asia (mainly China and Singapore), contaminated waste travels throughout the earth, and used-cars parts ship mainly to Eastern Europe and Africa. As it can be easily imagined, a real assessment of these business practices is impossible, as agents of the EEA (European Environmental Agency 2009) have openly stated. The available data on the illegal trade of hazardous materials are only partial. EEA points out that this may be due to two reasons: the first being that no regulations have been seriously implemented, resulting in the large number of cases of illegality. In fact, EU official figures show an increase from 6000 reported tonnes in the EU in 2002 to 47000 tonnes in 2005. However, this data is difficult to substantiate since it depends on different regulations imposed by each of the member states. Other reasons for the unreliability of the data include an exceptional case in 2005 with a reported 30000 tonnes of hazardous materials and the fact that not all EU states participated in the annual reports, even though they are mandatory by EU law (EAA 2009: 11).

---

1 Details on the categories can be found at: http://scp.eionet.europa.eu/definitions/hazardous.

A more empirically sound study, issued in 2008 by IMPEL (European Union Network for the Enforcement and Implementation of Environmental Law) shows a more concrete picture of the problem. The IMPEL report, to which 22 EU countries participated (excluding Italy, Spain and Greece, three among the EU members to produce highest rates of waste per household, together with the UK) is based on the inspection of 13.777 cases of waste transport, over 2000 of them trans-boundary shipments. Among them, 19% of the cases were in violation of EU legislation which, in about 40% of the violation cases, meant shipment of hazardous materials without previous agreement or to non-OECD countries, and in the remaining 60%, included shipment of waste without proper documents and certifications (Enforcement Actions I 2008: 26). When comparing the percentage of violations with the complete record of transborder shipments overall, the report indicates that there is an absolute range from 0% (England and Latvia), 20–25% (Belgium, Netherlands, Northern Ireland, Poland and Slovenia), 50% (Scotland) and 100% (Bulgaria) (IMPEL 2009: 28). If inspection figures from the non-participant countries (including the Czech Republic which was one of the most hit Central Eastern European targets of illegal waste exports) were added to the participating countries the situation would look vastly different.

EU official figures of the illegal waste trade from its member states are not realistic, as it can be easily understood. The real dimension of the traffic is extremely high and continuously growing, as several media and environmental activists' reports point out. Taking only two Central Eastern European countries into account, Czech Republic and Hungary, we find a more realistic depiction of the overall situation in the EU. In 2006 the Czech Republic detected an illegal import of waste reaching over 30000 tonnes, whereas the same year in Hungary, 4800 tons were reported (Vail 2010; Szylági 2007). Both estimated amounts, in the Czech Republic and Hungary, originated from Germany only, certainly not the only country to ship illegally to Central Eastern Europe.

As for all other sources of illegal exchange, it must be stated that the waste trade is both difficult to categorize and analyse. The problems related to an efficient solution to the problem are partly legal, partly economic and definitely political. On the legal sphere, the EU legislation, which will be discussed below, leaves a number of dangerous loopholes open. Among these are the different national legislations of the countries which, according to the EU prescription on waste management and disposal, should be 'promoted individually' in principle. In particular, the evident unevenness of western and eastern state laws on waste disposal is the first natural threshold of illegal trade. Secondly, since the national legislations of the newly accessing countries have been ratified only recently according to EU standards, it derives that at least until 2004 there were no restrictions to exports of waste to the East, insofar as the importer had agreed to them. Thirdly, after the validation of the Schengen Treaty all new EU members have drastically reduced border controls to adapt to the new rules and financial restrictions. Thus, one of the main ideological paradigms of the EU, the free circulation of persons and goods, can be also applied to the case of waste shipment, similar to the already analysed TEN-T cases. Fourthly, further problems arise due to the complexity of classifying different types of waste. The EU legislation is very rigid on this point and the colour-classification between green (circulating freely among member states), yellow-amber (circulating with special documents, but not toxic) and red (hazardous waste, need extra-certification) types of waste has reduced problems at border controls. The problem persists, however, concerning the destined use of transported waste. In 2005, about 20% of shipped waste was for disposal, and 80% for 'recovery'. The EU has emphasized the necessity to increase the proportion of waste destined to recovery in its unified policy on waste management, hence the 2005 data seems to provide an optimistic perspective on the future. However, the term 'recovery' is extremely ambiguous and subject to different interpretations.[2] In the years following the end of socialism, for instance, large quantities of dangerous waste was shipped and illegally disposed in Central Eastern European countries, all of which officially labeled 'humanitarian aid' or 'second-hand material' (see on Poland POLWASTE 2010). Transport, in those cases, was allowed under relatively ineffective regulations. Afterwards other categories of classification became more widely used, such as 'landfill waste' or what are technically called 'mirror entries', i.e. waste streams which are considered hazardous only beyond a prescribed standard level of concentration, which several Western European countries have recently posed an import ban (Dorn et al. 2007). Recently, the second-hand market of used cars has found increased momentum following the antirecession economic manoeuvres of several western states conceding financial incentives to buy 'clean fuel' cars. One of the outcomes of these policies was the sudden drop of used car prices, and the enthusiastic purchases of an increasing amount of them in Central Eastern European used car shops, and consequentially the increase of waste produced by disposed car parts.

Concerning economic factors, the most obvious is the high attractiveness of the illegal versus the legal market of waste disposal. Again, the situation differs among types of waste, but the rule is that the more hazardous the more expensive the disposal process. Apart from the fact that some of the new member states do not have proper facilities for the disposal of dangerous waste and hence are forced to bilateral agreements with neighbouring countries (EEA 2009), black market prices are often not easily assessable by specialized studies. For example, official reports from the Netherlands estimate that the black market is 200–300% more profitable than the legal market, whereas other estimates reach 400% (Massari and Mozzini 2004, quoted in Dorn et al. 2007: 25). However, from some of the cases studied locally by civic organizations in Central Eastern European countries, it emerged that the illegal trade of hazardous or contaminated material eastwards could be as much as ten times more profitable than the legal shipping among western states. This, in the first years following EU accession, could be partly attributable to

---

2   On more details on the tecnica details of the transboundary shimpment of waste see *Transboundary shipments*...2008; on issues of ecological criminal activities in the new member states: *Organised environmental crime*...2003.

legislative gaps including border controls and national bans. However, after 2007 it is mainly down to the differences in prices of waste disposal between western and eastern countries that made this traffic attractive.

There are, of course, costs to the illegal trade, and some of them are related to widespread cases of corruption related to this type of business. This leads to the political factors: not only are control measures against illegal shipment difficult to enforce due to the free circulation of goods among EU states, but also when detected some of these shipments have 'special protection arrangements'. In several cases, as those presented below, corruption of local administrators allows these exceptions, otherwise it would be difficult to explain how scores of trucks can freely enter a small commune and deposit their waste in an illegal site, under the eyes of all the villagers.

Corruption is related to different levels and political agencies. On the first level there are local companies which seek to establish business connections with either waste disposal companies or directly with industries in Western Europe. On the second level there are intermediaries who operate to ensure the success of expeditions, bribing institutional actors (mayors, counsellors or even border and police inspectors). On the third level there can be (although not necessarily) criminal organizations which control the flux, intensity and typology of the waste traffic (Situ 1998; Brack 2004; Comte and Krämer 2004). On the fourth level there are local officers who provide support to or, in the case described below, even participate actively in the trade. On another level there are, local and translocal, civic organizations and movements which operate to denounce these waste, raise public awareness or even provide legal consulting on issues related to the use of land as sites, the confiscation of waste and even inter-country regulations. Each of these agents operate according to its priorities and strategies, however, the central point for understanding the complex political dynamics underscoring this trade is, again, the role of the EU. To tackle this issue I find it important to start from the description of the general framework of EU legislation on waste management and disposal.

The EU legal framework on waste

The current EU legal framework on waste is based on the directive 2008/98/EC which refers to the previous regulations, namely to the 1975/439/EEC on waste regulation, the 1991/689/EEC on toxic and dangerous waste and the 2006/12/EC general directive on waste.

Each of the previous regulations has been amended several times, in particular regarding the packaging process (1994/62/EC), the landfill directive (1999/31/EC) and other issues concerning annexes of existing directives. There exists a separate directive, on waste shipment which was initially conceived under the 1993/259/EC, then replaced by the 2006/1013/EC, amended in two annexes by the recent 2009/308/EC.

The 2008 Directive includes a preamble of 49 points indicating the general orientations of the EU towards waste policy, management, recovery and disposal. The Directive is structured into seven chapters which contains a sum of 41 articles. The chapters respectively include: subject, scope and definition; general requirements; waste management; permits and registrations; plans and programmes; inspections and records; final provisions. According to the EU summary, the most significant articles are those concerning waste hierarchy (article 4), waste management (articles 15–22), permits and registrations (23–27), plans and programmes (28–33).

The complex regulating legislation of waste management has been developed in relation not only to the geopolitical transformation of the EU legislative domain, but also concerning technological progress in the environmental sciences. The numerous amendments to the legislations reflect the need to cope with these two factors and are therefore expressions of the awareness of the European Commission to maintain a certain degree of flexibility over time. The latest regulation enlarged the scope of the previous one by introducing clearer definitions of not only the types and qualities of waste, but more specifically of the hierarchy of waste treatment procedures. This step underlines the importance to differentiate possible ways of waste management within a general priority for the safeguard of human and animal health, and of the environment. Thus, according to the 2008 Directive, the order of priority regarding waste hierarchy is as follows: prevention, preparing for reuse, recycling, recovery (such as energy recovery) and disposal. This hierarchy replaces the one formulated in the 2006 Directive which prioritized prevention, followed by the recovery and reuse. In particular, the new Directive specifies that waste prevention should be the first priority and that reuse and recycling should be preferred to energy recovery from waste.

The section related to waste management refers to the responsibility of waste management which is in principle assessed to be that of the original producer or holder and that, even in case of transferral, the responsibility for recovery or disposal is not generally discharged from the original producer. In addition, the principles of self-sufficiency and proximity are sanctioned. The former concerns the idea that the Community as a whole should reach self-sufficiency in waste management. The latter refers to the cooperation needed by (especially bordering) member states to establish an 'integrated and adequate network of waste disposal and recovery installations'. Articles 17–22 regulate the control and labelling of hazardous waste and oils. The section on permits and registrations underlines that any member states carrying out waste treatment shall obtain permits which specify: the types and quantities of waste, technicalities, safety measures, method of treatment, monitoring operations and other provisions when necessary. Finally, the section on plans and programmes defines the kind of management plans which have to be issued periodically by each member state following the objectives and provisions of the Directive. One relevant part of these plans concerns waste prevention programmes (Article 29), according to which each member state is expected to establish its own programme by December 2013, indicating existing prevention measures, as well as planned quantitative and qualitative benchmarks for assessing the progress of prevention measures.

Concerning the general orientation of the EU legislative framework, attention is paid to harmonize EU directives with the freedom of each member state to amend the legislation to its particular case. Aim is to 'set general environmental objectives for the management of waste within the Community', or 'to enable the Community as a whole to become self-sufficient in waste disposal and recovery'. Again, a strong emphasis is added recently to 'help the EU move closer to a "recycling society"' to allow each state to become aware of the need of avoiding waste generation and learning to use waste as a resource (Directive 2006/12/EC). These general orientations somehow juxtapose with pluralistic indications over the freedom of member states 'to limit incoming shipments to incinerators classified as recovery', to stress individual states' decision over the use of waste as an economic resource, and to develop states' individual waste prevention programmes. Even the ambitious call for a 'European recycling society' is modulated through awareness that member states maintain different approaches to the collection of household waste and to waste composition, therefore it is considered appropriate that general targets 'take account of the different collection systems in the Member States'.

One particular and very significant case of pluralism in the recent Directive concerns listing waste (Article 7). This section clearly specifies that a Member State is allowed to consider waste as hazardous even though this does not appear in the annexed list (Annex III), as well as to label waste non-hazardous even if the item is missing from the annex. This tension between EU and national interpretations of the EU legislation has often provided space to non-transparent and even illegal practices including the realm of waste shipments.

The introduction of the single market in the EU in 1993 has stimulated the development of transboundary shipments of goods, including waste, thus requiring more attentive regulations. These have followed the expansion of the EU boundaries especially over the last 15 years. There are four main principles regulating the shipment of waste. First, since waste for disposal is considered to bear a heavier environmental burden, the general EU policy is to achieve self-sufficiency, reducing the shipment of waste among member states as much as possible. Second, waste for disposal should be treated in the nearest installations, thereby avoiding long shipment procedures. Third, the regulations concerning shipment of waste for recovery are less restrictive, allowing a higher degree of mobility of this cargo within the EU. Fourth, the export of hazardous waste within the EU boundaries is allowed only following special procedures. Hazardous waste shipment to non-OECD countries is prohibited since these countries are not expected to possess proper treatment capacities. Transboundary shipments of hazardous waste are regulated by the Basel Convention (22/3/1989, entering in force 5/5/1992) according to which the ratifying countries inform the other participants of the list of hazardous waste items by national standards, designate and communicate the competent authorities to control and authorize the shipment, set the relevant duties and rights in the light of cooperation agreements among countries. The Convention has presently been ratified by 172 countries. In 2007 the EU countries exported a total of about 5.4 million tonnes of hazardous waste; it is calculated that only 80% of this amount was notified through the annual country reports, the reminder was assessed. This number shows a constant increase over recent years, whereas the percentage of hazardous waste exported compared to the overall generated waste remains stable (around 12%). This seems to prove that the EU is achieving self-sufficiency in handling its waste disposal activities. The main items of the hazardous waste exported are demolition waste including mainly polluted soil and asbestos, waste from thermal processes, waste from organic chemical processes and oil wastes of liquid fuels.

Illegal waste shipments in Eastern Europe

In spite of the regulations issued by the Basel Convention, the monitoring process of the EEA and the activities of several transnational and national environmental organizations, the number of illegal waste shipments from EU countries is increasing. Official figures on this type of trade are scarce and their significance to the general scope of the problem is extremely reduced. A large portion of illegal waste exported to non-OECD countries is made of WEEE (waste from electric and electronic equipment) a portion of municipal waste,[3] thus not directly classified as hazardous waste, which is constantly increasing in EU countries. Most of this waste is shipped, legally and illegally, to non-OECD countries such as China, African states and the Middle East. A similar case is that of end-of-life cars, another significant item of illegal waste shipment from EU countries. Cars are shipped as second-hand items, thereby avoiding the controls and documentation necessary for waste. The most common destinations are Eastern Europe, Western Africa and the Middle East. The great economic incentives generated by illegal waste trade make this traffic extremely difficult to track, especially in the case of ordinary items such as electronic devices and cars. In the case of the most common types of hazardous waste generated by building and manufacturing it is expected that illegal practices will continue to increase also thanks to the interest of criminal organizations which, in some countries have been reported as participating in the waste trade business.

Eastern Europe has been targeted for illegal shipment of waste from western European countries since the early post-socialist period. In the 1990s a number of reports denounced the extent of the business in Poland, Romania, Bulgaria, Albania, Ukraine and the Baltic countries. In 1992 Poland intercepted 1332 illegal shipments, most of which came from neighbouring Germany (POLWASTE 2010). The trade was boosted by the enormous differences not only in disposal costs, but

---

3   According to Council Directive 99/31, art. 2(b), the European Law defines 'municipal waste' as:'waste from households, as well as other waste which, because of its nature or composition is similar to waste from households'.

also in fines for illegal dumping, from ten to fifteen times lower in Poland than in Western Europe at the time. One famous case implied the shipping of 4800 tonnes of highly poisonous waste chemical in Sarand, a famous and beautiful Albanian coastal town in 1991–1992 by one German company. The shipment was legal on paper since it contained material classified as 'pesticides for humanitarian aid' to be used for agriculture. Initially the German company obtained permission for the expedition by the Albanian Ministry of Agriculture, but when Albanian authorities acknowledged the real content of the cargo, they repeatedly invoked the return of the shipment. However, restitution was legally impossible and the 'pesticides' had to remain stored in different places in one of the most tourist-oriented regions of the country. In the coming years Greenpeace and other organizations repeatedly denounced cases of leakage in different sites where the toxic waste was stored (Albania 1996).

Numerous other cases have been documented on the illegal waste export of hazardous products in the period immediately following the end of socialism. What made this trade possible was mainly the unpreparedness of Eastern European governments and their legislative frameworks to oppose this form of business which, from its early days, has proved particularly fractious. Moreover, the imbalance in decision-making power between western and eastern states, as well as the 'development rhetoric' which justified intervention, humanitarian aid and support programs to the populations of the former socialist state were other factors accounting for the large scale of this phenomenon. Following the EU enlargement and accession of the new eastern European countries the institutional and logistical conditions to curtail this trade had to be set. Enforcement of EU environmental regulations became a major priority of the EC after 2004, and one of the major goals was to homogenize national answers to EU waste management demands. However, the abolition of borders following the Schenghen Treaty and the paradigm of free circulation of goods and people has seriously undermined the results of police action against environmental crimes. Since 2005 the number of cases of illegal transport of waste, as well as those of hazardous waste traded without proper certification have steadily increased following different waves which are characterized by changes of destinations, from the first-round accession towards the second-round accession state members.

A study by Benjamin Vail, a Czech sociologist, presents the case of waste introduced illegally in the years 2005–2006. In 2006, Czech authorities had detected a sum of over 30000 tonnes of illegal waste of German origin in Bohemia. Waste was mainly dumped in open-air sites including fields, in farm buildings, a vacated military air base, warehouses and landfills (Vail 2007: 1200). In one site, the village of Libčeves in northern Bohemia, over 4000 tonnes of German municipal waste were stored in abandoned farm fields and in a barn. The content had been carried by about 200 tractor-trailer trucks. Following denouncements of the case in the region of Sachsen-Anhalt, where the waste originated, they accepted to take back about 750 tonnes and the reminder became landfill in the Czech Republic. Only one person was found guilty of the illegal import and fined, a lone Czech waste hauler, but his company soon declared bankruptcy and was able to avoid payment (Vail 2007: 1201).

Illegal waste shipments to Hungary

The case of Hungary, subject of this chapter, is particularly significant for understanding the origin and modalities of the trade. Between 2006 and 2007 about 4800 tonnes of illegal waste have been detected on the Hungarian territory by local authorities and environmental activists. The most common expedient was to change the expedition colour code which characterized the typology of waste by EU standards. Thus, most of the waste, which belonged to the yellow code (municipal waste) had instead falsely been classified as green (bio-waste). As in the Czech cases, waste was introduced in the country through local companies which were to provide sites for illegal disposal. As in other post-socialist countries, in Hungary the number of potential sites for illegal dumping is high due to a number of reasons. One is the large presence of dismissed private and public infrastructures such as factories, former military bases, deposits and alike. The second concerns the geographic and economic characteristics of the rural regions. In particular, southern Hungary (and the county of Bács-Kiskun) have been the favourite destination of the illegal business due to the traditional presence of scattered farmyards (*tanya*), as well as to the number of dismissed infrastructures from the socialist period (agricultural cooperatives, small factories, barracks and storages). These factors account for the large number of cases of illegal waste disposal which, compared to the Czech case, stored more limited quantities of waste but on more numerous sites.

Once the sites of stocking and the companies responsible for the shipping are discovered, local authorities face three main obstacles to the restitution of the waste and to monetary compensation for the environmental damage. The first is that in several instances expeditions are formally legal for the side of the exporter, thus agreement on restitutions has to be treated more as a matter of political diplomacy than of bilateral agreement between companies or local governments. This imbalance in the resolution process adds to the existing economic imbalance between the sender and the receiver. Secondly, because these cases entail misconduct on the sides of private actors (companies), but also sometimes public officers (local governments, mayors or counsellors), cases of corruption have emerged widely among nations, multiplying the typologies and numbers of investigations. Third, environmental organizations who have mostly denounced these cases to the general public, using local and national media reports, are not always willing to move effective public campaigns on this issue alone. The problem of illegal waste disposal sites is widespread in Hungary, and although the import of Western European waste can become, as it will be seen below, tinged with strong ideological components, it is one thing to denounce it and another to call for generalized public awareness on the treatment of waste, recycling and abolition of illegal practices.

The years 2006–2007 have seen the climax in the illegal import of waste from Western European countries to Hungary. These countries included mainly Germany, Austria and Italy, and some minor cases also concerned Belgium and the Netherlands. In all expeditions several expedients were used to conceal the statuses of the truck loads, and the denouncements made by police authorities that suspected the presence of a dangerous connection between criminal organizations, local governments and private enterprises.

In 2006, calculations indicated that around 4.100 tons of illegal waste entered Hungary from the countries mentioned above. Waste was stored in several sites in the territories of Bács-Kiskun, Kiskunmajsa, Tatabánya, Kerekegyház, Pirtó, Bócsa, and also in the outskirts of the capital city, in Óbuda. In the following year, this number increased to approximately 6.000 tons, with an assessed total amount of 19 illegal sites discovered in the country.[4] The number of cases diminished since 2008, due to different factors: increased police and border controls, higher fines to illegal traders and the above mentioned changed destinations of the traffic, which, according to environmental organizations, was diverted toward Romania, Bulgaria and even Ukraine. Concerning the treatment of illegally imported waste, since the second half of 2007 Hungary succeeded in sending back one-third of the overall amount of waste (mainly to Germany), and another third was returned by the early 2008. It has been assessed, however, that something less than the remaining one-third of the total amount has never left Hungary. Concerning the assessed profit of this business, the Hungarian Environmental Ministry and the competent police authorities have estimated that an overall profit of over 3 million euros has been reached through these transactions in less than one year by the exporting companies. This sum shows the astonishing gap in the disposal price of yellow coded waste, which in Hungary costs one-tenth of its price in Germany, Austria and Italy, and even less in Romania and Bulgaria.

The case of Kunbaja

One of the largest cases of illegal waste import has been detected in the territories of the village of Kunbaja, southern Hungary, in the early days of 2007. This constitutes the best documented case in the country, where different sets of actors have come into play at different points in time.

According to the findings, at least three German companies, one of which acting in the cross-border section with the Czech Republic, took care of the shipment of

---

4   Data are, of course, incomplete and constitute no more than extimations since the actual number of sites is much higher and the amount of discovered waste only refers to the cases officially denounced to public authorities.

about 220 bales[5] of yellow-coded waste to the village of Kunbaja and to other neighbouring locations. Waste was received by one local company, managed by the spouse of the former mayor of the village, which allegedly provided covering to the destination of the shipment. The two Bayern-based companies had arranged for 26 tons of waste to be shipped to Hungary in December 2006, employing a number of occasional truck drivers, who apparently had no established contacts with them. In addition, the responsible person in Hungary was extraneous to the business, although media investigations found out that he had established contacts with politicians from some of the local governments.[6] The waste was transported to one dismissed farmhouse and stored under the consensus of its owner, who received a small compensation for it.

This system of illegal waste transport is extremely complex and is presently the object of international police investigations. The case of Kunbaja is particularly interesting because its small scale represents a microcosm of all those features that belong to a more general and systematic traffic that unfortunately interests all Eastern European countries.[7] The system has been described as pyramidal, where each level, from the bottom upwards, is linked through a number of key contacts, who are, cautiously, related only to some few of those in the immediately upper and lower level. Therefore, investigations are extremely difficult, because it is scarcely probable to be able to quickly gain a complete picture of the whole business and of all the involved levels and actors.

According to media releases, which have only partially found official confirmation through police investigations, the 'pyramid' in the Kunbaja case was composed of the following levels. At the very bottom were a number of casual workers paid to unload the waste in the selected locations. Moving upwards were the truck drivers, then the owners of old farmsteads or dismissed factories, and a number of entrepreneurs who are allegedly linked with the second-hand trade of goods in the country. The upper levels were occupied by the companies which organized the business transnationally, and by their key contacts in the local governments of the shipment destinations. In the Kunbaja business there are allegations that over 11 municipalities were involved in total, although investigations on the actual connections between them are still ongoing. The pyramidal structure would have allowed space for the opacity of the process, concealing the connection among apparently unrelated cases (despite their common trait of German senders) in other communities in southern Hungary. Moreover, as it has become clear after 2009, this traffic would constitute part of a wider transborder shipment that included Hungary not as final destination, but as site of temporal stocking until the new markets (mainly Romania and Bulgaria) would have opened after these countries'

---

5   One bale contains over 900 kilograms of waste; the first shipment of over 80 tons of waste entailed thus arund 14 trucks coming into the village at night to unload.

6   More details at http://index.hu/bulvar/kuka0110/#1, accessed on 15–5–2001.

7   In 2006 Czech Republic was interested in 15.000 tons of illegal waste transported by Germany alone, Slovakia 1300, Poland over 1000 tons.

EU accession. Therefore, it can be argued that the EU enlargement has introduced a number of liabilities to the newly accessing members, facilitating the illegal shipment of unwanted waste from the neighbouring western countries.

Corruption and the role of local governments

The case of Kunbaja is particularly telling of the political dynamics at local level which allowed for the pyramidal structuring of the illegal transport of waste. One thing that has emerged out of the Hungarian cases is that, even though it is difficult to ascertain connections among them, it is also improbable that the disposal of waste could be easily realized without any previous knowledge by local authorities. Even though the locations selected to store the waste were never within the communities' inhabited boundaries, shipping nonetheless entailed an easily visible traffic load, not to mention the environmental (visual and olfactory) impact of this storing in the long-run.

In Kunbaja investigations have found close connections between the former village mayor and the German companies who acted as senders. The mayor was found guilty of corruption and criminal activity for having allowed and organized the shipping with the aid of his wife, who was the legal owner of the company that arranged the transport in Hungary. In 2009 he was convicted to 18 months in prison, banned for two years from any public office and fined with 500.000 forints. Even before this case, however, his position in the local government had been highly contested for other scandals relative to falsified receipts on the import of oil from Serbia to Hungarian companies, for which he was convicted to one and half year of prison-time in 2003. In spite of this scandal, the mayor, who had remained in office already for 8 years until 2002, was re-elected in 2006.

The case of Kunbaja had a wide ripple-effect in national media and was reported on many environmental NGOs' websites. The former were the true originators of narratives focusing on a lack of transparency, even when fact-gathering was still incomplete. The slowness in achieving the official reconstruction of criminal activities, and the impossibility to use the corruption and frauds in a form of public discourse because the accusations had not been officially proved all contributed to make the case epitomic of two crucial aspects: the impunity or scarce vulnerability of corrupt politicians to the application of legal anti-corruption norms, and the injustices related to the EU enlargement project. In the narratives of media there are two positions towards the resolution of the Kunbaja case. National media have mainly portrayed the case as illustrative of the unexpected outcomes of the EU enlargement process, mainly read in the imbalance of decision-making and negotiation power between western and eastern countries. In these accounts, the decision of the district jury has been used as an argument against the idea that EU enlargement process has been only positive for Hungary, as well as for other Central Eastern European countries. This is not simply to state that increased euroscepticism has found momentum in the treatment of these scandals, but it is a way to underline perception of the weaker political (or diplomatic, as some media sources announced) standpoints of the new versus the older member states.

Different is the position of local media sources, the most attentive to the details and implications of the scandal. They have tended to underline more the implication of the illegal waste import onto local societies than the transnational political dynamics. On the one hand, the case of the convicted mayor had echoed one instance of 'civil injustice', where the sentence to one and half years is seen as scarcely exemplar of the gravity of the accusations.[8] In particular, emphasis is on the difficult resolution of the disposal problem, since a large portion of waste is still on the territories of the communities interested by the scandal. Here the absence of a political decision has explained the occurrence of a sort of paralysis of local governments following the arrest of the mayor. In spite of the several negotiation tables with Germany and consultations at the ministerial level in Hungary, almost 1000 tons of waste remained stocked in nine locations in Hungary, and this lingering problem has recently been used by environmental organizations to increase the public's awareness and concern with waste disposal. At the political level, however, the situation seems to be one of open denouncement and discredit towards the present opaque practices, whereas very few steps have been taken to significantly tackle the emergency at local governments' levels.

The environmental movement and the case of illegal waste

The case of illegal waste imports to Central Eastern European countries is of peculiar interest for assessing the strategies, in discourses and practices, of the new environmental movements. There are some basic analogies with the transport projects presented so far, but also some important differences. Concerning analogies, the movements are all framed within a more general panorama of transnational interaction with large environmental umbrella organizations, such as Friends of the Earth, WWF, Greenpeace. These contacts allow them to actively take part in large initiatives, mainly funded by the EU, to which the local movements alone could not easily access. Also, the nature of the local environmental movements is such that they cannot easily transcend the national sphere of political action. This means that they have to come to terms with the state, and with local governments, and for doing this they need to seek some form of negotiation with the ministries involved in the projects. Finally, the language through which these movements communicate their priorities and strategies to local citizens is strongly influenced by the political commitments of the organization, but less by corruption and non-transparent political practices.

There are some other differences, mainly in the structure and forms, between these movements and those related to the transport projects. One such difference is

---

8   See for instance http://www.hetnap.rs/uj/index.php?zg=4903&no=288; http://k-monitor.hu/adatbazis/cimkek/kunbaja/kornyezetszennyezes.

the lack of true local movements, i.e. those forms of civil society which originate in the localities affected by the environmental threats. The second difference is the extent to which these forms of environmental activism seek to establish trust in local citizens. Being mainly national environmental groups they do not necessarily seek confrontation and support by local people, striving to communicate them the meaning of their activity, but rather focus on seeking larger involvement. This is an important difference with the other case studies concerning corruption that have been presented so far. Corruption becomes, in this case study, not a discursive field used to convey a strong political message to local inhabitants, and/ or to delegitimize local authorities. Instead, here environmental movements are in a comparatively more solid position, as national organizations, which allows them to avoid seeking constant public confrontation at local level. To explore this point I will provide the example of the organization that has used the problem of illegal waste disposal to strengthen its legitimacy and public role. I argue, in this case study, that although inserted in the context of transnational environmental policy and programmatic indications, this movement attempts to fill the gap between national and local politics and civil legitimacy.

The environmental organization which has the longest history of monitoring waste disposal and recycling practices is Humusz (Hulladék Munka Szövetseg, Waste Cooperative). It was founded in 1995, which originated from 11 smaller green organizations in its early period and ultimately extended to 16. It is composed of an active member group who, in the last years has established fruitful contacts nation-wide with other environmental organizations. During the years it has also established wider cooperation with transnational organizations, among them CEE Bankwatch and Friends of the Earth. Unlike other environmental NGOs described in this volume, Humusz is particularly attentive to stress that 'it does not follow any kind of conventional political means',[9] even when the range of its activities is rather large: consulting on environmental risks and hazards, organization of awareness-raising events, management of websites of correlated civic groups, publications archive, grouping of experts, educational projects and other public events.

The main feature of this association is its flexibility. Being organized centrally, with the managing nucleus in the capital centre, Humusz benefits from a changing number of members who are selected from all the country's provinces according to their expertise and field of activism. Usually it avoids overlapping tasks among members, even when they have different geographic backgrounds. The central office of Budapest is the most active and the one with the largest number of members, who can be from 8 to 15, apart from a constant portion of volunteers.[10] The activities of this organization are mostly coordinated according with the different projects to which this, or other smaller civic associations with

---

9   See for details their mission at the website: http://www.humusz.hu/bemutatkozunk.

10   In the first years of its activity, Humusz had mainly student volunteers, but in recent years the number of non-employed persons, mainly retired, has increate significantly. The association, thus, is able to benefit also of the services of persons who, due to their previous

which it cooperates, apply. Because of the needs for funding to develop a project, this environmental organization also has a strong 'market-orientation' While this term is not preferred by its members, nonetheless it is one feature which starkly contrasts with most of those environmental groups described so far. In recent years Humusz has split, resulting in a separate section, Humusz Recycling, which is a profit oriented company. This company has co-opted personnel and members from the mother organization, but still works in close cooperation with the original group. Some of the founding members, in fact, belong to both. This is of great advantage to this environmental group, because there is a constant base of economic income that can be used to fuel the need of resources for the NGOs activities. This business activity is what makes the organization a peculiar form of civil society; however, the significance of this strategy must be held in context with the field in which it operates, waste recycling, which in Hungary is still in a developing phase. Moreover, in the recession of the last years and the austerity programs of the current government, several forms of state funding have been cut, rendering the survival of many nongovernmental organizations extremely difficult.

The organization has a solidly centralized structure which is arranged through the figure of its leader, one of the most prominent Hungarian environmental activists: Szilágyi László. This is not to say that there is no coordinated action among its members and smaller organizations, but the figure of the leader appears prominent when the organization deals with delicate political matters. Concerning the German illegal waste scandal, in 2007 Szilágyi has published a scholarly paper, one of the few in English language on the emergency of the illegal export from western European countries, and certainly the only one on the Hungarian case. Apart from the issue concerning the connections and comparisons among the cases in different countries (mainly Czech Republic and Hungary), the paper is significant in two directions. First, it reveals much open criticism towards what he sees as an unintended outcome of EU enlargement policies, as it can be seen in the section titled 'Pan-European dump' (2007: 141). In this regards, Hungary is seen as having been damaged by the post-Shenghen regulations, because it became vulnerable to illegal traffics and unable to use its once efficient border police forces, which have been recently downsized.

Secondly, the idea that the illegal trade has developed a strong economic value is prominent in his, as well as in the organization's analysis of the problem. In coordination with other environmental groups, Humusz has acted as a key speaker in the denouncement of the cases in 2006–2007. These have used mainly web portals[11] to communicate with the general public, conveying information to national and local media sources. On a second level, the movement has been

---

employments, are able to provide different forms of help, from consultancy to various expertise, as well as to share their personal contacts with, for instance, local politicians.

11   The most used webpage was greenfo (www.greenfo.hu), on which the organizations published continuous and precise updates on the case.

consulting with national political institutions, from the Ministry of Environment to the Ministry of Interior. In a press report from 2007, the Ministry of Environment cites Humusz as the only non-governmental organization to take part in awareness-raising campaigns against the illegal waste import in the country.[12] In other national policy reports the organization is included as the main specialist on the delicate issue and this, even though not directly confirmed by the activists, enforces the idea that it has a strong degree of negotiation power in the environmental field with national political authorities.[13]

In spite of the prominent role of this organization in constituting the *trait d'union* with citizens, on the one hand, and state authorities on the other, what it has so far neglected is the connection with local politicians. This can be seen as both a result of the organizational and management strategies of the association, and of its choice to adopt a relative silence on the local political implications of the waste scandals. In spite of the disclosure of corruption scandals in the Kunbaja case, and of allegations of other similar cases in the country, Humusz has only occasionally referred to this side of the story. Direct mention of political opacity is given mainly in press articles published online and it is almost absent from policy papers and reports by the organization. Not only is the word 'corruption' seldom used in these reports, but the very mentions of the outcomes of police investigations are few. The missing link between the opaque political implications which underscore the illegal waste imports in the country and the discursive practices of this civic organization can be interpreted in different ways. On one level is the need, felt strongly by Humusz and by its sister organizations, to propose alternative ways of political involvement for the general public. The use of corruption scandals in the environmental discourse is to these associations one of the examples of how a 'conventional' manner of presenting political arguments can become undistinguishable from the extremely wide sea of media releases on corruption in Hungary. Therefore, avoidance is sought to maintain this organization's distinctive public face of commitment to environmental goals only.

The failure to establish a link, in the discursive strategies, between corruption and environmental crisis, is not however a matter of façade only. The problem, not easily presented in interviews and reports, is that the organization has gained an established position in the environmental activism panorama in Hungary. Its dependence on public tenders for funds, as well as its dual structure which combines non-profit with profit activities render it difficult and unlikely to form a strong commitment to delicate political issues. In addition, the activities related to illegal waste traffic are largely unexplored and poorly dealt with in the EU

---

12   The title of this report is highly significative: 'Return to sender. Be there no more German waste cases', 2007.

13   Further demonstration to this point is that Humusz has recently introduced two among the largest environmental projects in the country, Nulla Hulladék (Zero waste) and Tiszta Magyarországért (For a Clean Hungary), both including extremely complex and well-articulated actions from education, public events, monitoring, media and even arts.

states, mainly because of difficulties to track them, and for the implications related with organized crime. Hence it is not surprising if corruption, which has surfaced abundantly in media accounts, is almost absent in the communication strategies of these organizations. In this sense, their public role seems more, in the classical Gramscian meaning, as that of counter-hegemonic forms to the state, not separated from it, but as appendixes of what Gramsci indicated as 'political society'. Their strategies are discursively anti-political, as it was envisioned by the actors of the post-socialist revolution in Central Eastern Europe (Chapter 2), but in practice they tend to follow tracks not very dissimilar from those of state institutions.

Conclusion

The case of the illegal waste transport in Central Eastern Europe is indicative of how new forms of environmental activism are increasingly trapped in the paradox of having to deal with the general outcomes of the EU enlargement policies and with coping strategies from below. One of the main conclusions arising from this case study is that the emergence of corruption and illegal practices is linked with the improved conditions of connectivity and the free transport of goods and persons among the member states. This is a potentially powerful argument to raise scepticism in the EU project, and it is used by environmental activists to denounce the everlasting disparities between western and eastern states. However, opportunities for enrichment from the trade of waste materials have mushroomed throughout the globe, hence it is increasingly more difficult to impute these phenomena to the EU enlargement *per se*.

The second conclusion is that local citizens become increasingly alienated from their decision-making power when corruption is overtly denounced and exposed. This seems again in line with the arguments about the power of discourses on corruption, but the inability (or unwillingness), of civic organizations to adopt arguments of lack of transparency to involve larger strata of local population must here be read in different terms. Considering the difficult conditions (dangers of exposition of criminal acts, complex intermingling of trans-border and transnational economic interests, opacity of the disposal process due to several dismissed premised and locations, evolving EU legal frameworks and diminished capacities of border control authorities) under which this case of environmental crime has developed it would have been not easy to expect a strong answer from below in terms of organization of civic movements, as it has been documented in the other case studies. However, the fact that the main actor of nongovernmental activism in the field of waste disposal and recycling in Hungary is a highly professionalized organization that has chosen to remain external to local political debates is a finding, in my view, worthy of attention. Moreover, it is also worthwhile to note that prominent members of this same organization, which operate as consultants of the state institution, take a more critical standpoint versus the unexpected consequences of EU enlargement policies than versus corrupt local governments which have allowed the spreading of criminal activities. This case study suggests, in line with some of the findings of the previous chapters, that the revival of civil society in Central Eastern Europe is a complex field of study, and one in which Western-centred theoretical propositions are scarcely applicable. The changing political role of these movements in their local contexts of operation, as well as their process of adaptability to the requirements of the interaction with transnational sets of actors is what renders any analysis of the data presented above as a delicate analytical endeavour.

Conclusions:
Inside the Green Commando

During the fieldwork sessions that provided the ethnographic data to this volume I experienced different types of encounters with people who are, in their countries, labelled as activists. All of them had personal stories behind their formal involvement in the environmental movements, rarely was I able to penetrate deep into these stories. However, the words they used to describe the twists and turns of their, sometimes discouraged and sometimes fierce, opposition to some kind of political design spoke eloquently of their concerns, hopes and ideas. I was tempted to present some of the more significant individuals here, those who vividly characterized the over 5 years of research on which this book is based. Later, I decided not to do this, for one thing because the people who told me of their activities are all in the already delicate position of having to bear the stigmas of the protests, they give faces and names to what have been called in different tones 'green commando', 'green terrorism', 'anarchic activism', 'rebel organizations' and so forth. It would have been all too easy to stigmatize even further those who, for different personal reasons, have chosen, to remain exposed to the free or to the politically controlled media, to play active public roles in the local and national political scenes and, above all, among the people with whom they share their everyday life. This is particularly true for the Central Eastern European green movements described above: each of them has a well-defined public face represented by its leaders. The leaders, for reasons that I find difficult to explain, are the founders, developers, managers of the civic organizations but most of all, in the eyes of the general public, political institutions and often the media, they embody the movements themselves. The Italian case presented in the volume is exceptional in this sense, here the extent of the protest and its long temporal span made it difficult to identify the movement with one, or a few individuals. In the Italian media and political scenes the protest is supported by the NO-TAV movement located in the Susa Valley, not by a single or a small group. Therefore outlining the figures of some of the most active members would be of little analytical significance, in the same way as it would be useless to try to assess the strength and legitimacy of the movement simply from the public declarations of its spokesmen.

The identification of several of these movements with specific individuals meant that it became necessary to consider their relational strategies at endogenous and exogenous levels from a different angle to the ones from which civil society has traditionally been studied. In the contexts marked by a rapid and sweeping post-socialist transformation, and by an even more tumultuous process of EU accession, the newly born environmental movements had to seek strategies that allowed them to strike a balance between continuity and innovation. The preoccupation with gaining legitimacy and public trust very often emerged from the words of those interviewed. These movements assumed at different times also the claim of avoiding 'conventional politics', direct communication with the public, formal meetings, open protests and demonstrations, personal interaction with officers and politicians. These 'avoidance strategies' are all perfectly placed in the two historical processes under examination: post-socialism and the EU enlargement. As fruits of history, these strategies are strictly connected to their context, they more or less distinguish the Eastern European case studies from the Western European case studies.

The case studies in this book would not have occurred without the general EU (legal, policy and ideological) framework. Then why is Central Eastern Europe different in terms of the local strategies through which environmental groups seek public legitimacy? There are several answers which emerge from these cases, but I suppose there could be even more. However, two of them are the most significant for the content of this book. The first concerns the social dynamics which underly the interaction among the group members, between them and local citizens, and with political institutions. The second is the language they use to communicate, legitimize and substantiate their involvement in green politics.

Concerning the first, as both Gerlach (1987, 1991) and Tarrow and Petrova (2006) have pointed out, the strength of the environmental movements which operate in global and local contexts lies in their ability to change strategies when seeking interaction with different sets of political actors. Tarrow and Petrova define these as 'transactional' strategies, whereas Gerlach, in a more sounded anthropological language, spoke of 'segmentary, polycentric and integrated networks'. These views are confirmed by the cases analysed in the volume. The very nature of these movements is such that it is through their interaction strategies, more than through their ideological standings that they seek to pursue their goals. All the avoidance strategies indicated above are aimed at maintaining adequate levels of public trust, and because of this need, they are mainly (transactional) strategies which manage the interrelations among the different sets of actors. The crucial point for these movements is the ability to differentiate between these strategies, not only to gain funding or to influence policy making, as Gerlach argued, but more significantly not to lose public legitimacy. But here national and cultural differences count too. It is obviously hard to understand, in a country where environmental movements are depicted by the media as the norm and not as the exception, why so much emphasis should be laid on the 'transactional' more than, for instance, on the policy-making sphere. It is similarly problematic to adapt the classical notion of civil society, as developed by western political philosophy, to the 'green commando', originating from the stubborn convictions of a handful of (if not of one) people who meet in pubs, make decisions through mobile telephone calls, during picnics or simply at home with a few friends. The same can be said for the inability of many of these groups to gain formal invitation to 'public' meetings, where the future of a road project, that cuts an urban centre in two, is to be decided. If it were not for the informal systems of communication they had so aptly developed, they would not have been able to join, at the very last moment, some of these meetings, and hence they would not have proved to those who support them that they represent an idea, and not just an assortment of personal interests, as their opponents usually affirm.

Transactional strategies need to be pristine when decision-making is not completely transparent and democratically sought, as in both the Central Eastern European and the Italian cases. In order to maintain a satisfactory degree of negotiation power, these movements had to follow closely the strategies of the different political actors. Like in every game that can be successfully played only by becoming a good insider, environmental activism needed a special touch for the ways in which interpersonal and individual-institutional relations were being configured. This meant drawing on both formal and informal practices. The complex picture provided by these case studies is one in which maintaining an effective network of interpersonal relations proved to be a positive strategy only as long as formal political strategies were adopted in conjunction. This meant seeking expertise and technical advice on the different stages of the project, collecting petitions, filing letters of complaint or information to EU and national authorities, and eventually filing law suits.

In some cases sharing informally information on the personal interests of local government officers, entrepreneurs and national politicians (Czech and Italian cases) was turned into an asset, in order to strengthen legitimacy and trust in the protest movement. Conversely, in other cases the movements attempted to follow formal political strategies and discursive practices like the state (case of illegal waste exports) or local governments (Hungarian transport case) in order to stress their face of unconventional political movements, i.e. free of the implications of 'dirty' politics. Or again, there was a situation (Slovak case) in which engagement with the field of formal political intervention was played down and action took place mainly in restricted informal circles in the fear of losing the already weakened public legitimacy. All these cases suggest that in the complex and extremely lengthy conditions of environmental activism there cannot be one common, single set of interactional strategies. The more strategies there are, the better, but also, and more significantly, well-timed counter-action means more than just having firm ideologies and guidelines, as the Slovak and Hungarian failure cases demonstrated.

With regards to the language through which these movements communicated, it is difficult to confute Gerlach's claim on the polysemic and polyfunctional nature of the environmentalist discursive practices. Here, however, I would like to follow another approach, looking at one of the two main thrusts of this volume, i.e. the use of corruption as a discursive strategy of the environmental movements. In different ways and with different emphasis, corruption has arisen in all the case studies, and it has been associated with the negative outcomes of the implementation of these structural development projects. The use of corruption as a discursive strategy is what makes the civic organizations to different extents, new forms of environmentalism. Before elaborating on this, it is significant to stress that not all civic organizations have been able, willing, or skilled enough to use corruption as a dialogic instrument. Indeed, they all started their activities following 'traditional' environmental discourses, presenting them to the local people, seeking expertise on environmental concerns, producing reports and establishing connections with larger environmental networks. The language used in environmental discourses can be both highly technical and élitist, as well as strongly ideological, if not populist. The two styles openly contradict each other, and in a societal context when a true grass-root movement is addressed as a 'commando', confusing them can have a boomerang effect. Thus, as the Italian case has shown, the optimal way is to use both, alternating them according to the times when the movements needed a more 'emotional' basis of consensus, or when formal strategies were preferred to face the apparently solid rationality of the development and enlargement paradigms.

However, polyfunctionality of discourses on the environment cannot be an easy undertaking in the long run, particularly as all the cases under exam (apart from the one concerning illegal waste) were marked by long periods of protest followed by sudden changes, mainly due to the results of state-EU political negotiations to lock or unlock funds. Typically, when, through the strategic use of media sources, public attention was diverted from the environmental risks associated with the project, to the infrastructural needs of the citizenry to solve, for instance, problems of traffic congestion (in reality generated by the projects themselves), the environmental language became obsolete. This posed a serious dilemma for these movements: they all began with environmentalist agendas, some of them openly sought to avoid conventional political action, but they had to deal with cases in which environmental risks were less visible to the public (because they were diluted into the long term) than the consequences of corruption, mismanagement of public funds, embezzlement and the like. The Italian case, comparatively, shows a stronger resistance to this polyfunctional discursive strategy, probably because the inability of the state to manage similar projects in the country efficiently and transparently has provided the NO-TAV movement with extremely powerful arguments. Here, images of the partisans' resistance movement the untouched beauty of the valley, nature that is a home to those who protect and not violate it, can easily be matched by those of theft, appropriation of citizens' taxes, financial waste and bribes. These images were not invented, they had been already present in the media narratives, as well as in the ideological stances of local (mainly northern) political leagues.

In the other case studies, both the technical/environmental discourse and the ideological/identity based claims sooner or later became weak weapons against the modernity/efficiency paradigm underlying the EU enlargement project. It would be simplistic to think that this happened because of the different positions of these countries, as new member states of the EU and with less negotiating power than the western states. As an anthropologist, I am wary of those explanations that hail from with little care for the social and cultural forces coming from below. What, in my view, emerges from the four case studies in Central Eastern Europe, is an increased alienation of citizens from the political arena in which they could seek participation. This has been a slow process, with several fluctuations, but it has revealed that a genuine, generalized conviction that environmental risk can be tackled from below has weakened over time. Even the Czech case, so far successful, has proven that political issues are as important as environmental ones and that, in the end, the environmental/technical discourse is effective only among a very restricted circle of specialists.

In the several phases of the protests, the corruption discursive strategy has helped, to keep public interest alive, to strengthen the image of integrity of the civic organizations, to shift attention towards long-term goals, and to reveal the more complex local, national and transnational political dynamics. As in every human cognitive process, the communication and understanding of corruption language needs a pre-existing set of ideas and memory inputs. In all the countries under investigation people have, some more some less recently, developed their own cognitive maps of corruption. This explains why talking about corruption is still very effective, as a discourse, in societies where it is widespread. However, the other side of the coin is also to be considered. Excessive talk on corruption may render judgement more difficult by introducing some kind of cognitive disturbance in the way people assess and give meaning to murky practices. This may explain why, when there is a widespread and excessive reference to corruption, although easily communicable, these scandals tend *not* to leave permanent traces on the general public. Hence, using corruption as a discursive strategy in lieu, or in combination with environmental language can become a zero-sum strategy, as seen in the two Hungarian cases.

The new environmentalism

Scholars who have studied the transformation of environmental activism in recent years, although they take different perspectives, agree on one point: it is increasingly difficult to characterize green movements nowadays. Some approaches focused on how these movements shifted towards becoming main political actors, others saw a binary distinction between those movements that lost their ecological character to become increasingly institutionalized and the movements which have taken radical positions, and have been labelled as 'eco-terrorists'. Even among countries in western Europe, there are notable differences which do not pertain merely to the sphere of public participation, ecological awareness and civil action in general, but to more complex societal and political transformations (Rootes 2003). Furthermore, once the focus is placed on the global strategies of the interaction of these movements with larger transnational organizations, old sociological paradigms and models become of inadequate analytical validity. Even the approach that sees these movements as established political actors, that have gradually lost their unique 'monopoly' on the ecological discourse (Rootes 1999; Wapner 2002) to seek better participation in political decision-making and entrepreneurial goals, does not constitute a satisfactory alternative model of environmentalism.

I argue that the differences found between Western and Eastern European environmental movements, which is still an overlooked field of study, can provide some fresh answers to what appears to be a withering debate.

New environmentalism stems from several tensions in the economic, social and political spheres. One is the tension between the local nature of these movements, their ties with the social and ecological environments of the region in which they evolve, and the global arena in which they interact with transnational institutions, such as the EU and other environmental groups. The second tension has to do with the challenges facing the sovereignty (in policy making and development plans) of the state under the influences of neoliberal capitalism and global governance. The third concerns the above mentioned tendency of the movements to seek more direct political intervention and at the same time to have to deal with decreasing mobilization from below. The fourth is the need to maintain the appeal of the ecological discourse in a context of increasing politicization of their actions. The fifth, in the European case, is the sharp differences between Eastern and Western European concepts of mobilization, ecological awareness, institutionalization and political participation. All these tensions are, to different extents, present in new environmentalism.

New environmentalism has been inspired by the ideological, programmatic and policy objectives of the EU enlargement. The case studies in this volume are all examples of to what extent the project of a well-connected and cooperative EU can become stained by the emergence of a number of economic and political bottlenecks. These bottlenecks are not simply 'unintended consequences' or effects of NIMBY protests, as some analysts have hastily declared. They constitute the prices that each member state, and within them each regional government, has to pay for the realization of the idea of an efficiently enlarged European community. The gap between East and West, manifest from these case studies, is increasingly evident in the modalities in which the projects of infrastructural development are being planned, implemented and managed. However, the differences between East and West are not only in the culturally informed assessment of environmental hazard, as Douglas and Wildavsky postulated (1983). These differences can be interpreted from two perspectives: the top-down and the bottom-up approach. In the top-down approach, EU enlargement policies and EU-funded development projects, although built on the common notion of a well-connected Europe, still work along very different institutional and economic tracks. When local government institutions are plagued by widespread corruption, clientelistic practices, a high prevalence of personalized and informal strategies and the transposition of public and private interests, political bottlenecks can make the Enlargement project a highly costly one. Similarly, in the economic sphere, the aggressive intrusion of (mainly western European) corporate business investments have tended to preclude the positive results of environmental protests not only because of their strong influential power over local political decisions, but also due to the hard-to-die development rhetoric. In all case studies (including the Italian one), positive economic development and business investments have largely superseded the discourses of ecological sustainability, bringing about a waste of capital and resources at a local government level.

The ethnographic data of this book contribute mainly to build the second, the bottom-up approach. The new environmentalism benefits from a polyfunctional set of strategies devised by the different types of movements, both in their practices and in their discourses. This book demonstrates that the two fields (practices and discourses) cannot be looked at separately; they constitute a meaningful continuum that finds shape in the changing spatial and temporal conditions of the lives of these movements. Eastern European environmentalism is revitalized by the negative impacts of the EU enlargement policies. This stands alone as a demonstration that a genuinely local civil society can originate from globalizing and homogenizing trends. However, the novelty of the Eastern European environmentalism lies in the ways in which political discourses intermingle with environmental practices. The space to consolidation of corruption, lack of transparency and 'lower' quality of governance, being enlarged by the political and economic factors mentioned above, strongly influence the perception of the utility and harm of the development projects. As soon as these projects manifested their devastating potential, not only of an environmental but also of a political, economic and moral entity, the civic movements tried to inform the local public of the whole range of possible damage. The fact that, in the long-run, a discursive interest in ecological discourses was replaced by an interest in the transparency and quality of government is telling of the degree of involvement of local citizens in the protests.

New environmentalism is both ecological and political, the two fields cannot be disentangled otherwise the very meaning of the protest loses strength. Corruption in Eastern European countries, as well as in Italy, is a familiar discourse to local people. When environmental movements discover the benefits of using this discourse to communicate in a language that attracts people, their strategies change. This change, it can be argued, is influenced by political and economic pressures from above (the top-down approach). However, the choice to embrace the corruption arguments, when these have become manifested, cannot be explained as the mere attempt of juxtaposing contrasting sets of moral orders. Some of the environmental movements analysed have been able to use corruption in their discursive strategies efficiently. Some, however, have proved reluctant to do so, and others have attempted to do so, but have failed because of wrong timing or wrong communication strategies. This suggests that the point is not whether different sets of moralities could have been presented more or less convincingly to the public. Morality is a weak and transient argument.

The crucial issue is that corruption in state and local governments has provided legitimacy to the environmentalist discourses, helping them to remain closer to the people through the use of a common language. This tendency is unique in the Eastern European cases (and partially for Italy) for three reasons. First, the new civil society has assumed, as expected, different tones in these countries compared to Western Europe. This is due to the conditions under which civil society emerged during the last years of socialism: as an anti-political movement, and yet not definitively separate from the state, in symbiosis with which it often continued to exist. Second, corruption is present and widely exposed to the public by the media in these countries. This is not to argue that Eastern European countries are more corrupt than western European ones, as the Italian case eloquently proves. It infers that when generalized 'corruption talk' becomes a social norm, than this can be used as a powerful discursive tool to communicate the harm that may be caused by these environmentally, politically and socially intrusive projects. Third, Eastern European environmental movements are characterized by a high degree of dualism between formal and informal practices. This aspect could be seen as a liability rather than an asset. However, I believe that I have provided enough empirical evidence to show that by seeking a balance between formal and informal practices, the environmental movements have contrasted that excessive institutionalization and de-mobilization which has been lamented in their Western European counterparts. Corruption is very much part of this attempt to bridge formal and informal strategies, since discourses on corruption are built mostly informally (save for the Italian case in this book). When, as in the case of waste import, corruption becomes a formally communicated issue, the perceived effectiveness (by the environmental movements) of this communication decreases. Instead, as can be seen in the Czech case, using the language of corruption remains a fruitful way of transmitting to local inhabitants the risks, allegations and informal aspects of local politics.

Corruption is not only about discourses, it is a practice, as emerged from all the case studies. In this volume I have been concerned to show how the discursive use of corruption can become one of the 'hands' through which environmentalism operates, under particular conditions of global institutional transformation. Investigating the practices that underlie the emergence of corruption in the TEN-T transport projects as well as in the waste imports from Western to Eastern Europe, would have required a different methodological and theoretical angle that this book cannot provide. In the growing literature on corruption, ethnographic contributions are still relatively virgin territory. However, it was not in my intention to provide an ethnographic field research on corruption, I was not able to gain more information than what I presented on local practices of corruption.

I believe that in order to counterbalance the excessive recourse of this notion, that has recently become a magic formula that covers a whole range of political-economic practices and classifies them even uncritically, more attention is needed in the years to come to analyse the socio-cognitive processes through which corruption becomes a language. At least within the context of the EU enlargement eastward, local people willingly speak the language of corruption, which becomes a useful medium for conveying issues as different as legitimacy, morality, social needs, intimacy, secrecy, envy, identity, reputation, trust and fear. The true novelty of resorting to the language of corruption by locally rooted environmental movements is that this is an extremely risky strategy, mainly in the long-run. The failure cases (from the point of the environmental protest) presented in this book are revealing the danger of relying too much, too little, too early or too late, on this language. Corruption is a powerful social idiom as it can be communicated to render manifest widespread anomalies such as fragmentation of power, inequality and social injustice. However, because the environmental movements are trapped in the dilemma of being 'anti-political' (in the post-socialist characterization of civil society) and institutionalized political entities, they can be discredited, or made marginal through the same language of lack of transparency they have been using. Once this is understood, it becomes less useful to accept uncritically that widespread public exposition to corruption discourses is a good recipe to ensure transparency and democratic progress.

The final point is on the use of the idea of civil society. In this volume I have agreed on the problematic use of this notion, both on epistemic and on heuristic bases. I have been aware of the uneasiness of other social scientists, and among them notably anthropologists, to parallel civil society in Western with Eastern European social contexts. I have also accepted the stance that in order to deal with an alleged 're-vitalization' of civil society in Eastern Europe, attention needs to be paid to the historical trajectories underlying this phenomenon from the late 1980s onwards. I have continued to use the notion of civil society mainly because this was communicated to me by the interviewed activists. In all countries, civic movements were defined emically as 'civil society' by the actors themselves. I have never attempted to impose such a 'western-centred' notion on them.

After realizing that this was considered as a useful notion by local standards, I was stirred to reflect on this. On the one hand I thought that this expresses a tendency to seek confrontation with ideas of western European environmentalism. In several interviews I was invited to consider parallels between Eastern and Western European green movements, and I realized that the organizations with which I was dealing had a good degree of knowledge of some of their western counterparts. On the other hand, I was moved to conclude that civil society is to the local activist the junction point between local and global networks. They all share the same experience of applying for funding and of dealing with EU-funded projects. The notion of civil society may not be genuinely local, but it is surely imposed by the survival and political strategies of these movements, who increasingly seek transnational interaction. What can be inferred from the analysis of these case studies is that civil society in Eastern European contexts has been, strengthened by the EU enlargement process. This is a different kind of civil society compared to the one described by Gramsci, Tocqueville and Hegel. Some of the main differences are: the changing role of the state, the influence of the socialist experience, the global conditions of governance, the influence of neo-liberalism, changing perceptions of social justice, legitimacy and the public good. Nonetheless, it still makes sense to deal with civil society in the peculiar conditions of the post-socialist and EU enlargement experiences. This notion is undermined or exalted (according to the cases) by discourses on corruption and by the alternation of formal and informal practices. Hence, through its analytical use it is possible to test the validity of the idea that changing historical (and geographical) conditions permanently affect the relationship between state and society. This is true for Eastern Europe, but there is still scope in future years to dedicate more comparative attention with Western Europe too.

Bibliography

AAVV, (2008). 'A M0 multja and jövője'. Budapest: Adyliget Barátai Alapítvány.

Abéles, M. (2000). 'Virtual Europe'. In I. Bellier and T.M. Wilson (eds) *An Anthropology of the European Union. Building, Imagining and Experiencing theNew Europe.* Oxford: Berg, pp. 31–52.

Albania 1996. Industrial waste in Albania. http://www1.american.edu/ted/albania. htm.

Alvard, M.S. (1993). 'Testing the "ecologically noble savage" hypothesis: interspecific prey choice by Piro hunters in Amazonian Peru'. *Human Ecology* 21: 355–87.

Andvig, J. (2001) *Corruption: critical assessments of contemporary research.* Christian Michelsen Institute, Bergen, Norway.

Anheier, H.K., Priller, E., Zimmer, A. (2000). 'Civil society in transition: the East German sector after unification'. *East European Politics and Society* 15(1): 139–56.

Appadurai, A. (1996). *Modernity at Large: Cultural Dimensions of Globalization.* Minneapolis: University of Minnesota Press.

Atkinson, P. and Hammersley, M. (1987). *Ethnography. Principles in Practice.* London, Tavistock.

Badĕscu, G., Sum, P. and Uslaner, E.M. (2004). 'Civil society and democratic values in Romania and Moldova'. *East European Politics and Societies* 18: 316–41.

Banfield, E. (1958). *The Moral Basis of a Backward Society.* New York: Free Press.

Bardhan, P. *Corruption and Development: A Review of Issues*, Journal of Economic Literature, 35, September 1997, p. 1329.

Barrow, C. (2006). *Environmental Management for Sustainable Development.* New York: Routledge.

Bell, M.M. (2004). *An Invitation to Environmental Sociology.* (2nd ed.). Thousand Oaks, CA: Pine Forge.

Bellier, I. and Wilson, T. M. (eds) (2000). An *Anthropology of the European Union: Building, Imagining and Experiencing the New Europe.* Oxford: Berg Publishers.

Bennett, J.W. (1975). *The Ecological Transition: Cultural Anthropology and Human Adaptation.* New York: Pergamon.

—, (1993). *Human Ecology as Human Behavior: Essays in Environmental and Development Anthropology.* New Brunswick: Transaction Publishers.

Berkes, F. (1989). *Common Property Resources.* London: Belhaven Press.

Black, A. (2001). 'Concepts of civil society in pre-modern Europe'. In Kaviraj, S. and Khilnani, S. (eds) (2001). *Civil Society: History and Possibilities.* Cambridge: Cambridge University Press, 33–9.

Bobbio, L. (2007). 'L'alta velocità in Valle di Susa. Troppo decisionismo o troppo poco?'. In L. Briquet and A. Mastropaolo (eds) *Politica in Italia.* Bologna: Il Mulino, 209–28.

Brack, D. (2004). 'The growth and control of international environmental crime'. *Environmental Health Perspectives* 112: 80–81.

Brandt, L. (2007). 'Manipulation of public environmental discourse: issue expansion and contraction'. In L.K. Brandt (ed.) *Cultural Analysis and the Navigation of Complexity. Influences of Gerlach's Anthropology on Studies of Environmental Policy and Resource Management, Language and Discourse, Power and Belief, and Social Health.* Lanham: University Press of America, 39–54.

Bremeo, N. and Nord, P. (eds) (2000). *Civil Society before Democracy. Lessons from Nineteen Century Europe.* Lanham: Rowman and Littlefield.

Brosius, J.P. (1999), 'Analyses and intervention: anthropological engagement with environmentalism'. *Current Anthropology* 40(3): 277–309.

Brown, D.E. (1991). *Human Universals.* New York: McGraw-Hill.

Brunell, L. (2002). 'Cinderella seeks shelter. Will the state, church or civil society provide?' *East European Politics and Societies* 16(2): 465–93.

Brush, S. B. (1993). 'Indigenous knowledge of biological resources and intellectual property rights. The role of anthropology'. *American Anthropologist* 95(3): 653–71.

Bubandt, N. (2006). 'Sorcery, corruption and the dangers of democracy in Indonesia'. *Journal of the Royal Anthropological Institute* (New Series) 12: 413–31.

Buttel, F.H. (2000). 'Classical theory and contemporary environmental sociology: some reflections for the antecedent and prospects for reflexive modernization theory in the study of environment and society'. In G. Spargaaren, A.P.J. Mol and F.H. Buttel (eds) *Environment and Global Modernity.* London: Sage, 17–40.

Cancelli, C., Sergi, G. and Zucchetti, M. (eds) (2006). *Travolti dall'alta voracità.* Roma: Odradek.

Castelfranchi, Y. and Sturloni, G. 2006. 'Blind track'. *Journal of Science Communication* 5(1): 1–6.

Castro Leiva, L. and Pagden, A. (2001) 'Civil society and the fate of the modern republic of Latin America'. In Kaviraj, S. and Khilnani, S. (eds) (2001). *Civil Society: History and Possibilities.* Cambridge: Cambridge University Press, 179–203.

Cedolin, M. (2006). *TAV in Val di Susa. Un buio tunnel nella democrazia.* Casalecchio: Arianna Editrice.

Cellarius, B. and Staddon, C. (2002). 'Environmental nongovernmental organizations, civil society and democratization in Bulgaria'. *Eastern European Politics and Societies* 16(1): 182–222.

Charnley, S. and Durham, W.H. (2010). 'Anthropology and environmental policy. What counts'. *American Anthropologist* 112(3): 397–415.

Clifford, J. and Marcus, G.E. 1986 (eds). *Writing Cultures: The Poetics and Politics of Ethnography*. Berkeley, University of California Press.

Cohen, J.L. and Arato, A. (1994). *Civil Society and Political Theory*. New Baskerville: MIT Press.

Comaroff, J.L. and Comaroff J. (1999). *Civil Society and the Political Imagination in Africa: Critical Perspectives*. Chicago: Chicago University Press.

—, (eds.) (2001). *Millennial Capitalism and the Culture of Neoliberalism*. Durham: Duke University Press.

Comte, F. and Krämer, L. (eds) (2004). *Environmental Crime in Europe: Rules of Sanctions*. Gröningen: Europa Law Company.

Cotgrove, S. (1976). 'Environmentalism and utopia'. *Sociological Review* 24(1): 23–42.

Cowell, A. (1990). *The Decade of Destruction*. Sevenhoaks: Hodder and Stoughton.

Crumley, C.L., van Deventer, A.E., Fletcher, J. (eds) (2001). *New Directions in Anthropology and Environment: Intersections*. Walnut Creek: AltaMira Press.

Crush, J. (ed.) (1995). *Power of Development*. New York: Routledge.

Csizmadia, E. (ed.) (2005). *A magyar demokratikus ellenzék (1968–1988)* (The Hungarian democratic opposition). Budapest: T-Twins Kiadó.

Data availability on transboundary shipment of waste based on the European Waste List 2009. Copehnagen: European Topic Centre on Sustainable Consumption and Production.

Della Porta, D. and Vannucci, A. (1999): Corrupt Exchanges. Actors, Resources, and Mechanisms of Political Corruption. New York: de Gruyter

Della Porta, D. and Andretta, M. (2002). 'Changing forms of environmentalism in Italy: the protest campaign on the high speed railway system'. *Mobilization* 7: 59–77.

De Sardan, O. (1999). 'A moral economy of corruption in Africa?'. *The Journal of Modern African Studies* 37(1): 25–52.

Diani, M. and Donati, P. (1999). 'Organisational change in western European environmental groups: a framework for analysis'. In C. Rootes (ed.) *Environmental Movements*. London: Franck Kass, 13–43.

Dobson, A. (1990). *Green Political Thought*. London: Unwin Hyman.

Doig, Alan, and Robin Theobald (eds) (2000): Corruption and Democratisation. London, Portland, OR: Frank Cass.

Dorn, N,. Van Daele, S., and Vander Beken, T. (2007). 'Reducing vulnerabilities to crime of the European waste management industry: the research base and the prospects for policy'. *European Journal of Crime, Criminal Law and Criminal Justice* 15(1): 23–36.

Douglas, M. and Wildavsky, A. (1983). *Risk and Culture. An Essay on the Selection of Technological and Environmental Dangers*. Berkeley: University of California Press.

Dove, M. and Carpenter, C. (eds) (2007). *Environmental Anthropology: A Historical Reader*. Oxford: Blackwell.

Dryzek, J.S. (1997). *The Politics of the Earth: Environmental Discourses*. New York: Oxford University Press.

Dryzek, J.S., Downes, D., Hunold, C., Schlosberg, D., Hernes, H.K. (2003). *Green States and Social Movements: Environmentalism in the United States, United Kingdom, Germany and Norway*. Oxford: Oxford University Press.

Dunlap, W.E. and Catton, R.E. (1979), 'Environmental sociology'. *Annual Review of Sociology* V: 243–73.

Dunlap, R.E., McCright, A.M. (2008). 'Social movement identity: validating a measure of identification with the environmental movement'. *Social Science Quarterly* 89(5): 1045–65.

Enforcement Actions I, Learning by doing. Draft Final report IMPEL-TFS Enforcement Actions project, Enforcement of EU Waste Shipment Regulation 2008. IMPEL.

Escobar, A. (1991), 'Anthropology and the development encounter: the making and marketing of development anthropology'. *American Ethnologist* 18(4): 658–82.

European Environmental Agency 2009. 'Waste without borders in the EU? Transboundary shipment of waste'. EEA Report 1/2009.

European Commission Directorate General for Regional Policy Evaluation Unit, 2009.

Ex Post Evaluation of Cohesion Policy Programmes 2000–2006. Work Package 5A: Transport.

Falk, B. (2005). *The Dilemmas of Dissidence in East-Central Europe*. Budapest: Central European University Press.

Fisher, E. (ed.) (1995). *Towards Sustainable Development? Struggling over India's Narmada River*. New York: M.E. Sharpe.

Flyvbjerg, B. (1998). 'Habermas and Foucault: thinkers for civil society?' *The British Journal of Sociology* 49(2): 210–33.

Fukuyama, F. (1995). *Trust. The Social Virtues and the Creation of Prosperity*. New York: Free Press.

Gellner, E. (1994). *The Conditions of Liberty: Civil Society and its Rivals*. Allen Lane: Penguin Press.

Geoff, A. (2008). *The Slow Food Story: Politics and Pleasure*. London: Pluto Press.

Gerlach, L. (1980). 'Energy wars and social change'. In S. Abbott and K.J. van Wilingen (eds) *Predicting Sociocultural Change*. Athens: University of Georgia Press, 76–93.

—, (1987). 'Protest movements and the construction of risk'. In B. Johnson and V. Covello (eds) *The Social and Cultural Construction of Risk*. Dordrecht: Reidel, 103–45.

—, (1991). 'Global thinking, local acting: movements to save the planet'. *Evaluation Review* 15(1): 120–48.

Gibson, J.L. (2001). 'Social networks, civil society and the prospects for consolidating Russia's democratic transition'. *American Journal of Political Science* 45(1): 51–68.

Gledhill, J. (2004). 'Corruption as the mirror of the state in Latin America'. Pardo, I. (ed.), 2004. *Between Morality and the Law. Corruption, Anthropology and Comparative Society*. London: Ashgate, 155–80.

Goody, J. (2001). 'Civil society in an extra-European perspective'. In Kaviraj, S. and Khilnani, S. (eds) (2001). *Civil Society: History and Possibilities*. Cambridge: Cambridge University Press, 149–64.

Gramsci, A.S. (1968). *Lettere dal Carcere.* Torino: Einaudi.

Granovetter, M. (1973). 'The strength of weak ties'. *American Journal of Sociology* 78: 1360–80.

Greenhouse, C.G. (ed.) (2009). *Ethnographies of Neoliberalism.* Philadelphia: Pennsylvania University Press.

Gulyás, G. (ed) (2004). *Politikai Korrupció.* Budapest: Aula Kiadó.

Haenn, N. and Wilk, R. (eds) (2006). *The Environment in Anthropology. A Reader in Ecology, Culture and Sustainable Living.* New York: New York University Press.

Hall, J.A. (ed.) (1995). *Civil Society: Theory, History, Comparison.* Cambridge: Polity Press.

Hall, J.A. and Trentmann, F. (eds) (2005). *Civil Society: A Reader in History, Theory and Global Politics.* London: Palgrave Macmillan.

Haller, D. and Shore, C. (eds) (2005). *Corruption. Anthropological perspectives.* Londra: Pluto Press. Hann, C.M. (1980). *Tázlár: A Village in Hungary.* Cambridge: Cambridge University Press.

—, (1996) 'Political society and civil anthropology'. In C.M. Hann and E. Dunn (eds) *Civil Society. Challenging Western Models.* London: Routledge, 1–24.

—, (ed.) 2002. *Postsocialism. Ideas, Ideologies and Practices in Eurasia.* London and New York: Routledge.

Hann, C.M. and Dunn, E. (eds) (1996). *Civil Society. Challenging Western Models.* London: Routledge.

Hardesty, D.L. (1977). *Ecological Anthropology.* New York: John Wiley.

Hardin, G. (1968). 'The tragedy of the commons'. *Science* 162: 1243–48.

Hardt, M. (1995). 'The withering of civil society'. *Social Text* 45: 27–44.

Harrison, E. (2010). 'Unpacking the anti-corruption agenda: dilemmas for anthropologists'. *Oxford Development Studies* 34(1): 15–29.

Harvey, D. (1990). *The Condition of Postmodernity: an inquiry into the origins of cultural change.* Oxford: Blackwell.

Hasegawa, K. (2004). *Constructing Civil Society in Japan: Voices of Environmental Movements.* Melbourne: Trans Pacific Press.

Hasty, J. (2005). 'The pleasures of corruption. Desire and discipline in Ghanaian political culture'. *Cultural Anthropology* 20(2): 271–301.

Havel, V. (1978). 'The power of powerless'. In Wilson, P. (ed.) *Open Letters: Selected Writings 1965–1990.* New York: Alfred A. Knopf.

Headland, T.N. (1997). 'Revisionism in ecological anthropology'. *Current Anthropology* 38(4): 605–30.

Hearn, J. (2001). 'Taking liberties: contesting visions of the civil society project'. *Critique of Anthropology* 21(40): 339–60.

Heidenheimer, A.J., et al. (1989). *Political Corruption: A Handbook* (New Brunswick, NJ: Transaction Books.

Hoare, Q. and Smith, G.N. (eds) (1989). *Selections from the Prison Notebooks of Antonio Gramsci*. New York: International Publishers.

Holmes, D. (2000). *Integral Europe: Fast-capitalism, Multiculturalism, Neofascism*. Princeton: Princeton University Press.

Hedelman, M. and Haugerud, A. (eds.) (2005). *The Anthropology of Development and Globalization. From Classical Political Economy to Contemporary Neoliberalism*. Oxford: Blackwell.

Howard, M.M. (2003). *The Weakness of Civil Society in Post-communist Europe*. Cambridge: CUP.

Humphrey, C. and Sneath, D. (2004). 'Shanghaied by the bureaucracy. Bribery and post-Soviet officialdom in Russia and Mongolia'. Pardo, I. (ed.), 2004. *Between Morality and the Law. Corruption, Anthropology and Comparative Society*. London: Ashgate, 85–100.

Huntington, S.P. (1968). *Political Order in Changing Societies*. New Haven: Yale University Press.

Implementation of the priority projects progress report, May 2008. Brussels: TEN-T.

Imposimato, F., Pisauro, G. and Provvisionato, S. (1999). *Corruzione ad alta velocità. Viaggio nel governo invisibile*. Roma: Koinè.

Inglehart, R., (1977), *The Silent Revolution: Changing Values and Political Styles among Western Publics*. Princeton, N.J.: Princeton University Press.

James, P., Tayler, P. and Thompson, M. (1987). *Plural rationalities*. Warwick Papers in Management 9: University of Warwick.

Johnston, M. (2005a). *Civil Society and Corruption: Mobilizing for Reform*. Lanham, University Press.

—, (2005b). *Syndromes of Corruption: Wealth, Power, and Democracy*. Cambridge University Press.

Junghans, T. (2001). 'Marketing selves: constructing civil society and selfhood in post-socialist Hungary'. *Critique of Anthropology* 21(40): 383–400.

Kaldor, M. (1990). *The Imaginary War: Understanding East-West Conflict*. Oxford: Blackwell.

—, (2003). *Global Civil Society: An Answer to War*. Cambridge: Polity Press.

Kaneff, D. (2004). *Who Own the Past? The Politics of Time in a 'Model' Bulgarian Village*. Oxford: Berghahn.

Katz, S.N. (2002). 'Constitutionalism, contestation and civil society'. *Common Knowledge* 8(2): 287–303.

Kawata, J. 2006 (ed.) . *Comparing Political Corruption and Clientelism*. London, Ashgate.

Keane, J. (1998). *Civil Society: Old Images, New Visions*. Stanford: Stanford University Press.

—, (2003). *Global Civil Society?* Cambridge: CUP.

Kennedy, M. D. (1992). 'The intelligentsia in the constitution of civil societies and post-communist regimes in Hungary and Poland'. *Theory and Society* 21 (1): 29–76.

Kerby, A. (1991). *Narrative and the Self*. Bloomington, Indiana University Press.

Kondos, A. (1987). 'The question of "corruption" in Nepal', *Mankind* 17(1): 15–29.

Kopnina, H. (2011). *Environmental Anthropology Today: Cross-disciplinary Investigations*. New York: Routledge.

Kottak, C.P. (1999). 'The new ecological anthropology'. *American Anthropologist* 101(1): 23–35.

Kousis, M., Della Porta, D. and Jiménez, M. (2008). 'Southern European environmental movements in comparative perspective'. *American Behavioral Scientist* 51(11): 1627–47.

Kubik, J. (2005). 'How to study civil society: the state of the art and what to do next'. *East European Politics and Societies* 19(1): 105–20.

Kunmar, K. (1993). 'Civil society: an inquiry into the usefulness of an historical term'. *The British Journal of Sociology* 44(3): 375–95.

Kürti, L. (1990). 'People vs. the state. Political rituals in contemporary Hungary'. *Anthropology Today* 6(2): 5–8.

Ledeneva, L. (1998). *Russia's Economy of Favours: Blat, Networking and Informal Exchange*. Cambridge: Cambridge University Press.

Leff, N.H. (1964). 'Economic development through bureaucratic corruption'. *American Behavioral Scientist* 8(3): 8–14.

Lomnitz, L.(1995). 'Ritual, rumor and corruption in the constitution of polity in modern Mexico'. *Journal of Latin American Anthropology* 1(1): 20–47.

Lowe, P. and Rüdig, W. (1986). 'Political ecology and the social sciences. The state of the art'. *British Journal of Political Science* 16: 513–30.

Margaira, O. (2005). *O adesso o mai più*. Borgone Susa: Edizioni del Graffio.

Marincioni, F. and Appiotti, F. (2009). 'The Lyon-Turin high-speed rail: the public debate and perception of environmental risk in Susa Valley, Italy'. *Environmental Management* 43: 863–75.

Marsh, A. (1981). 'Environmental issues in contemporary European politics. In G.T. Goodman et al., *The European Transition from Oil: Societal Impacts and Constraints on Energy Policy*. London: Academic Press, 121–54.

Massari, M. and Monzini, P. (2004). 'Dirty businesses in Italy: a case study of illegal trafficking in hazardous waste'. *Global Crime* 6: 285–304.

Matsuda, K. (2004). *The Social Sciences in Modern Japan 1890–1990. The Marxian and Modernist Tradition*. Berkeley: University of California Press.

McCay, B.J. (1993). 'The making of an environmental doctrine: public trust and American shellfishermen'. In Milton, K. (ed.) *Environmentalism: The View from Anthropology*. London: Routledge, 83–94.

McCright, A.M. and Dunlap, R.E. (2008). 'Social movement identity and believe systems: an examination of beliefs about the environmental problem within the American public'. *Public Opinion Quarterly* 72(4): 651–76.

Meggers, B.J. (1954). 'Environmental limitations on the development of culture'. *American Anthropologist* 56(5): 801–24.

Mehta, D. and Ouellet, E. (eds.) (1995). *Environmental Sociology: Theory and Practice*. New York: Captus Press.

Melhuus, M., Mitchell, J.P. and Wulff, H. (eds) (2010). Ethnographic Practice in Present. European Association of Social Anthropologists Monograph Series 11. London, Berghahn.

Meloni, B. (ed.) (1997). *Famiglia meridionale senza familismo. Strategie economiche, reti di relazione e parentela*. Catanzaro: Meridiana.

Miller, R.A. (1974). 'Are familists amoral? A test of Banfield's amoral familism hypothesis in a south Italian village'. *American Ethnologist* 1(3): 515–35.

Milton, K. (ed.) (1993). *Environmentalism: The View from Anthropology*. London: Routledge.

—, (1996). *Environmentalism and Cultural Theory. Exploring the Role of Anthropology in the Environmental Discourse*. London and New York: Routledge.

Mitchell, R.C., (1984). 'Public opinion and environmental politics in the 1970s and 1980s'. In N.J. Vig and M.E. Kraft (eds), *Environmental Policy in the 1980s*. Washington D.C.: Congressional Quarterly Press.

Mol, A.P.J. (2000). 'Globalization and environment: between apocalypse-blindness and ecological modernization'. In G. Spargaaren, A.P.J. Mol and F.H. Buttel (eds) *Environment and Global Modernity*. London: Sage, 121–50.

Montinola, G.R, and Jackman, R.W. (2002) 'Sources of *corruption*: a cross-national study', *British Journal of Political Science* (32): 147–170.

Morán, E.M. (ed.) (1990). *The Ecosystem Approach in Anthropology. From Concept to Practice*. Michigan: University of Michigan Press.

—, (2006). *People and Nature. An Introduction to Human Ecological Relations*. Oxford: Blackwell.

Muraskin, W. 1974. 'Review: the moral basis of a backward sociologist. Edward Banfield, the Italians and the Italian-Americans'. *American Journal of Sociology* 79(6): 1484–96.

Murphy, R. (1997). *Sociology and Nature*. Boulder, CO.: Westview Press.

Nelissen, N.J., van der Straaten and L. Klinkers (eds) (1997). *Classics in Environmental Studies: An Overview of Classic Texts in Environmental Studies*. The Hague: International Books.

Norton, B.G. (1991). *Toward Unity Among Environmentalists*. Oxford: Oxford University Press.

Novotny, P. (2000). *Where We Live, Work and Play: The Environmental Justice Movement and the Struggle for a New Environmentalism*. Westport: Praeger.

Nuijten, M. and Anders, G. (2007). *Corruption and the Secret of Law: a Legal Anthropological Perspective*. Aldershot: Ashgate.

OECD (1995) *Corruption: Le cancer mondial.* Croissance, le monde en développement. OECD: Paris, France.

Organised environmental crime in a few candidate countries, 2003. Kassel: Betreuungsgesellschaft für Umweltfragen.

O'Riordan, T. (1981). *Environmentalism.* London: Pion Limited.

—, (1996). *The Politics of Climate Change. A European Perspective.* London: Routledge.

Orlove, B.S. (1980). 'Ecological anthropology'. *Annual Review of Anthropology* 9: 235–73.

Ostrom, E. (1990). *Governing the Commons.* New York: CUP.

Palmer, G. (2007). 'Movements of social transformation actually are just languages by another name. Toward a functional analysis of social movement language'. In L.K. Brandt (ed.) *Cultural Analysis and the Navigation of Complexity. Influences of Gerlach's Anthropology on Studies of Environmental Policy and Resource Management, Language and Discourse, Power and Belief, and Social Health.* Lanham: University Press of America, 21–38.

Pardo, I. (ed.) (2004). *Between Morality and the Law. Corruption, Anthropology and Comparative Society.* London: Ashgate.

—, (2004) 'Introduction: corruption, morality and the law'. In Pardo, I. (ed.) *Between Morality and the Law: Corruption, Anthropology and Comparative Society.* Aldershot: Ashgate, 1–18.

Parry, J. (2000). 'The crisis of corruption and the idea of India—a worm's eye view'. In I. Pardo (ed.) Morals of Legitimacy: Between Agency and System. Oxford: Bergahn Books, 27–56.

Peace, A. (1993). 'Environmental protest, bureaucratic closure: the politics of discourse in rural Ireland'. In Milton, K. (ed.) *Environmentalism: the View from Anthropology.* London: Routledge, 187–202.

Pepper, D. (1996). *Modern Environmentalism: An Introduction.* London: Routledge.

Peters, D. (2005). 'How diffferen spatial contexts result in different sustainability discourses – A discursive analysis of the Budapest Ring Road'. *European Spatial Research and Policy* 12(1): 69–88.

Petrova, V.P. (2007). 'Civil society in post-communist Eastern Europe and Eurasia: a cross-national analysis of micro- and macro- factors'. *World Development* 35(7): 1277–1305.

Pine, F. (2002). 'Retreat to the household? Gendered domains in postsocialist Poland'. In C.M. Hann (ed.) *Postsocialism. Ideas, Ideologies and Practices in Eurasia.* London and New York: Routledge, pp. 95–113.

Plamenova Ivancheva, M. (2007). *Civil society as a discursive frame. Understanding Vacláv Havel's Anatomy of Reticence as a case study.* Unpublished MA thesis, CEU Budapest.

POLWASTE 2010. Poland Waste Imports, http://www1.american.edu/TED/polwaste.htm.

Prato, G. (1993). 'Political decision-making: environmentalism, ethics and popular participation in Italy'. In Milton, K. (ed.) *Environmentalism: The View from Anthropology*. London: Routledge, 173–186.

—, (2004). 'The devil is not as wicked as people believe, neither is the Albanian. Corruption between moral discourses and national identity'. In Pardo, I. (ed.), 2004. *Between Morality and the Law. Corruption, Anthropology and Comparative Society*. London: Ashgate, 69–84.

Price, P. (1999). 'Cosmologies and Corruption in (South) India', *Forum for Development Studies* 2: 315–27.

Putnam, R. (1993). *Making Democracy Work. Civic Traditions in Modern Italy*. Princeton: Princeton University Press.

—, (2000). *Bowling Alone. The Collapse and Revival of American Community*. New York: Simon and Schuster.

Renwick, A. (2006). 'Anti-political or just anti-communist? Varieties of dissidence in East-Central Europe, and their implications for the development of political society'. *East European Politics and Societies* 20 (2): 286–318.

Ribeiro, G.L. (1994). *Transnational Capitalism and Hydropolitics in Argentina. The* Yacyretá *High Dam*. Gainesville, FL.: University of Florida Press.

Rivkin-Fish, M. (2005). 'Bribes, gifts and unofficial payments: re-thinking corruption in post-Soviet health care'. In D. Haller and C. Shore (eds) *Corruption. Anthropological Perspectives*. London: Pluto Press, 47–64.

Roberts, M.K. (2007).'Latin America's populist revival'. S*AIS Review* 27(1): 3–15.

Rootes, C. (1999). 'The transformation of environmental activism: activists, organizations and policy-making'. *Innovation* 12(2): 155–73.

—, (ed.) (2003). *Environmental Protest in Western Europe*. New York: Oxford University Press.

Rose-Ackerman, S. (1999). *Corruption and Government. Causes, Consequences, and Reform*. Cambridge, New York: Cambridge University Press

Rothstein, B. and Eek, D. (2009). 'Political corruption and social trust. An experimental approach'. *Rationality and Society* 21(1): 81–112.

Ruud, A.E. (2000). 'Corruption as everyday practice. The public-private divide in local Indian society'. *Forum for Development Studies* 2: 271–94.

—, (2001). 'Talking dirty about politics. A view from a Bengali village'. In C.J. Fuller and V. Benei (eds) *The Everyday State and Society in Modern India*. London: C.Hurst and Co., 115–36.

Salleh, A. (2010). 'From metabolic rift to "metabolic value": reflections on environmental sociology and the alternative globalization movement'. *Organization & Environment* 23(2): 205–19.

Sampson, S. 2010. 'Diagnostics. Indicators and transparency in the anti-corruption industry'. In S.A. Jansen, E. Schröter and N. Stehr (eds) *Transparenz. Multidisziplinäre Durchsichten durch Phänomene und Theorien des Undursichtigen*. Heidelberg; VS Verlag, 97–111.

Sasso, C. (2005). *No Tav. Cronache della Val di Susa*. Napoli: Intra Moenia.

Schmidt, G. (2010). *Baloldali Korrupciós Vállalat.* Budapest: Éghajlat Könyvkiadó.

Schnaiberg, A. (1980). *The Environment: from Surplus to Scarcity.* Oxford: Oxford University Press.

Schneider, J and Schneider, P. (2001). 'Civil society versus organized crime. local and global perspectives'. *Critique of Anthropology* 21 (40): 427–46.

Scott, J.C. (1972). Comparative Political Corruption. Englewood Cliffs, NJ: Prentice Hall.

Setianto, B.D. (2007). 'Somewhere in between. Conceptualizing civil society'. *The International Journal of Not-for-profit Law* 10(1): (http://www.icnl.org/knowledge/ijnl/vol10iss1/index.htm).

Sewanta, K. (2009). 'Local level perception of corruption: an anthropological inquiry'. *Dhaulagiri Journal of Sociology and Anthropology* 3: 163–74.

Sharma, A. and Gupta, A. 2006 (eds). *The Anthropology of the State: a Reader.* Maldern, Blackwell.

Shore, C. (2000). *Building Europe: The Cultural Politics of European Integration.* New York: Routledge.

—, (2005) 'Culture and corruption in the EU: reflections on fraud, nepotism and cronyism in the European Commission'. In D. Haller and C. Shore (eds) *Corruption. Anthropological Perspectives.* London: Pluto Press, 131–55.

Sillitoe, P. (1998). 'The development of indigenous knowledge: a new applied anthropology'. *Current Anthropology* 39(2): 232–52.

Silverman, S. (1968). 'Agricultural organization, social structure and values in Italy: amoral familism reconsidered'. *American Anthropologist* 70(1): 1–20.

Situ, Y. (1998). 'Public transgression of environmental law: a preliminary study'. *Deviant Behavior* 19: 137–55.

Skilling, G. and Wilson, P. (eds) (1991). *Civic Freedom in Central Europe: Voices from Czechoslovakia.* Basingstoke and London: Macmillan.

Smart, A. and Hsu C.L. (2007). 'Corruption or social capital? Tact and the performance of guanxi in market socialist China'. In Nuijten, M. and Anders, G. (eds) *Corruption and the Secret of Law: a Legal Anthropological Perspective.* Aldershot: Ashgate, 167–90.

Smith, M.J. (ed.) (1999). *Thinking through the Environment. A Reader.* London: Routledge.

Spargaaren, G. (2000). 'Ecological modernization theory and the changing discourse on the environment and modernity'. In G. Spargaaren, A.P.J. Mol and F.H. Buttel (eds) *Environment and Global Modernity.* London: Sage, 41–72.

Stepanenko, V. (2006). 'Civil society in post-Soviet Ukraine. Civic ethos in the frame of corrupted sociality?' *Eastern European Politics and Society* 20(4): 571–97.

Sun, Y.. (2004). *Corruption and Market in Contemporary China.* Cornell University Press.

Swain, N. (1992). *Hungary: The Rise and Fall of Feasible Socialism.* London: Verso.

Swanson, T.M. (ed.) (1996). *The Economics of Environmental Degradation. Tragedy for the Commons?* New York: Edward Elgar.

Szelényi, I. (1988). *Socialist Entrepreneurs: Embourgeoisement in Rural Hungary.* Cambridge: Polity Press. Szilágyi, L. (2007). '"Wasteful affairs" in Central Eastern Europe'. *Central and Eastern European Review* 3: 137–50.

Tarrow, S. (1996). 'Make social science work across space and time: a critical reflection on Robert Putnam's *Making Democracy Work'. American Political Science Review* 90(2): 389–97.

Tarrow, S. and Petrova, T. (2006). 'Transactional and participatory activism in the emerging European polity. The puzzle of East-Central Europe'. *Comparative Political Studies* 20(10): 1–21.

Thompson, M. and Tayler, P. (1986). *The Surprise Game: And Explanation of Constrained Relativism.* Warwick Papers in Management 1: Warwick University.

Thompson, M., Ellis, R. and Wildavsky, A. (1990). *Cultural Theory.* Boulder: Westview.

Tismăneanu, V. (1990). *In Search of Civil Society. Independent Peace Movements in the Soviet Bloc.* London: Routledge.

Torsello, D. (2003). *Trust, Property and Social Change in a Southern Slovakian Village.* Münster: Lit Verlag.

—, (2008) 'Trust, kinship and civil society in a Slovakian village'. *Sociologia – Slovak Review of Sociology* 40(6): 514–29.

—, (2010). 'Corruption and the economic crisis: empirical indications from Eastern Europe'. *Slovak Foreign Policy Affairs* 19 (2): 65–75

Townsend, P.K. (2009). *Environmental Anthropology. From Pigs to Politics.* Prospect Heights, IL.: Waveland.

Transboundary shipments of waste in the EU. Developments 1995–2005 and possible drivers, 2008. European Environmental Agency.

Vail, B. (2007). 'Illegal waste tran sport and the Czech Republic: an environmental sociological perspective'. *Czech Sociological Review* 43(6): 1195–1211.

Van der Heijden, A.H. (2006). 'Globalization, environmental movements and international political opportunità structures'. *Organization and Environment* 19(1): 28–45.

Varese, F. (2005). *The Russian Mafia Private Protection in a New Market Economy.* Oxford University Press.

Viesti, G. (2009). *Mezzogiorno a tradimento, Il nord, il sud e la politica che non c'è.* Roma: Laterza.

Vincent, J. (1978). 'Political anthropology: manipulative strategies'. *Annual Review of Anthropology* 7: 175–94.

Visvanhatan, S. (2008). 'The necessity of corruption'. http://www.india seminar. com/2008/590/590_shiv_visvanathan.htm, accessed 3–10–2010.

Wade, R. (1982). 'The system of administrative and political corruption: canal irrigation in South India', *The Journal of Development Studies,* 18(3): 287–327.

Wapner, P. (2002). 'Horizontal politics: transnational environmental activism and global cultural change'. *Global Environmental Politics* 2 (2): 37–62.

Wilk, R. and Haenn, N. (eds) (2005). *The Environment in Anthropology. A Reader in Ecology, Culture and Sustainable Living*. New York: New York University Press.

Woldring, H.E. (1998). 'State and civil society in the political philosophy of Alexis de Tocqueville'. *Voluntas* 9: 363–73.

World Bank Literature Survey on Corruption; 2000–2005, 28 March 2006, http:// www1.worldbank.org/publicsector/anticorrupt/ACLitSurvey.pdf   (accessed 1–10–2010).

Yang, M. (1994). *Gifts, Favors and Banquets: The Art of Social Relationships in China*. Ithaca: Cornell University Press.

—, (2002). 'The resilience of Guanxi and its new deployments: a critique of some new Guanxi scholarship'. *China Quarterly* 170: 459–76.

York, R. and Rosa, E. (2003). 'Key challenges to ecological modernization theory'. *Organization & Environment 16*(3), 273–88.

Zerilli, F. (2005). 'Corruption, property restitution and Romanianness'. In Haller, D, and Shore, C. (eds) *Corruption: Anthropological Perspectives*. London: Pluto, 83–102.

Zinn, D. (2001). *La raccomandazione: clientelismo vecchio e nuovo*. Roma: Donzelli.

Index